INTER-CORPORATE BUSINESS ENGINEERING:

STREAMLINING THE BUSINESS CYCLE
FROM END TO END

By

Gary G. Benesko, Ph.D.

RESEARCH TRIANGLE CONSULTANTS, INC.
CARY, NORTH CAROLINA

Inter-Corporate Business Engineering: Streamlining The Business Cycle From End To End is the third in a series on enabling technologies published by Research Triangle Consultants, Inc.

Editor: Joanne LeRose
Assistant Editor: Anthony Concia
Layout: Joanne LeRose
Printed and Published in the United States

Copyright: January, 1997

ISBN 1 - 883872 - 02 - 2
1. Inter-Corporate Business Engineering. 3. Title

DEDICATION

"To all those brave souls, past, present and future, who take up arms against the status quo, and by opposing, change it."

ACKNOWLEDGMENT

"I would like to acknowledge the contribution of Dr. David Byrd, who not only offered valuable suggestions in the writing of this book, but provided the inspiration for the second half of it."

ABOUT THE AUTHOR

Dr. Benesko is a recognized authority in the field of EDI and electronic commerce. He is the author of "Introducing EDI Into The Organization", "The EDI Control System", "Inter-Corporate Business Engineering", and several articles on EDI for Auerbach's "Information Systems Security" publication. He is known for his lectures on the subject of EDI and Electronic Commerce, and has addressed such audiences as the US Chamber of Commerce's "Committee of 100", the Government of the State of New York, and several EDI/Electronic Commerce conferences.

Dr. Benesko has almost thirty years of wide-ranging business experience in both public and private sectors, including Information Systems management, Manufacturing, Total Quality Management, Strategic Planning, and International Operations. As one of his many accomplishments, he served on a multi-national EDI initiative for the exchange of mail transport information among several Postal Administrations. This project was the first of its kind, and paved the way for the Computer-Aided Post in Europe (CAPE) project currently under way.

Dr. Benesko is Vice President, Electronic Commerce/Internet Services, with Research Triangle Consultants, Inc. (RTCI). RTCI is North America's largest independent ED/EDI consulting firm, specializing in systems integration and business process engineering for Electronic Commerce.

PREFACE

To use an old Hollywood cliché, this work has been years in the making. In the early 1980's, the author had occasion to become involved in the then-revolutionary concepts of Manufacturing Resource Planning (MRP II), as described by Oliver Wight (1984). This was a comprehensive set of integrated manufacturing disciplines and practices intended to coordinate and synchronize a company's manufacturing operation by instituting a consistent set of information, reliable production schedules, and common practices across the business. The two major shortcomings of MRP II were:

a) It concentrated solely on internal production efficiencies, and dealt very loosely with inputs to the production process such as the business plan, sales forecasts, new product engineering and marketing. These components were mentioned, but only in passing. They were not integrated into the whole, other than to acknowledge their presence.

b) It did not deal with the outside world (customers, suppliers) in any way. It was an internal system unto itself, and only spoke briefly about how a company's MRP II program would benefit the outside parties.

In the following years, new practices came into vogue, practices such as Just-In-Time Manufacturing (JIT), Total Quality Management (TQM), Distribution Resource Planning (DRP), and finally, Business Process Engineering (BPE). Each of these claimed ascendancy over the others and claimed to be the only truly comprehensive discipline. Each overlapped the others to some extent, demanded total commitment from top management. Within its own frame of reference, each was right, but none had the whole answer. Something more was needed. None of these disciplines, including BPE, really reached outside the company to include its major "trading partners" in its quest for operating efficiency. DRP and BPE came the closest, in that they acknowledged the existence of these outside parties and recognized the need to integrate their joint business practices in some way, but they stopped short of showing how to actually do it.

Between 1989 and 1991, the author had occasion to become involved in a multi-national consortium of Postal Authorities whose aim was to expedite the flow of mail between countries by exchanging pre-advice information about incoming mail volumes using Electronic Data Interchange (EDI). During this initiative, the author developed several new techniques to bring the participants together in a structured approach to synchronizing the participants' internal systems, and developing common business practices and operating procedures, leading to a successful implementation. These techniques have been refined and modified using the experiences gained on the project, as well as the constantly-evolving industry strategies in the field of electronic commerce. The result is discussed in this book as Inter-Corporate Business Engineering (ICBE). It is expected that these techniques will continue to evolve as models of commerce change. ICBE will enable companies to keep pace.

TABLE OF CONTENTS

LIST OF ABBREVIATIONS

APICS	American Production and Inventory Control Society
DRP	Distribution Requirements Planning
EC	Electronic Commerce
ECR	Efficient Consumer Response
EDI	Electronic Data Interchange
ERS	Evaluated Receipts Settlement
GUI	Graphical User Interface
ICBE	Inter-Corporate Business Engineering
JIT	Just-In-Time Manufacturing
LAN	Local Area Network
MRP II	Manufacturing Resource Planning
OOP	Object Oriented Programming
POS	Point of Sale equipment
QR	Quick Response
SLIP/PPP	Serial Line Interface Protocol/Point-to-point Protocol
TCP/IP	Transmission Control Protocol/Internet Protocol
TQM	Total Quality Management
URL	Uniform Resource Locator
VAN	Value-Added Network
VMI	Vendor-Managed Inventory
WAN	Wide Area Network

LIST OF TABLES

INTER-CORPORATE BUSINESS ENGINEERING:

A DEFINITION

Inter-Corporate Business Engineering (ICBE) is a multi-corporate business discipline that brings individual companies together in a joint crusade, acting as one to align their common business processes and streamline the overall operation, with the common goal of satisfying the customer's need for a product or service.

ICBE builds on the foundations established by successful disciplines such as Manufacturing Resource Planning II (MRP II), Just-In-Time Manufacturing (JIT), Distribution Resource Planning (DRP), Total Quality Management (TQM), and Business Process Engineering (BPE).

ICBE, however, expands these traditionally single-company disciplines outward to include all participants in the business cycle, and involves an entirely different set of organizational and implementation issues. To this end, MRP II, JIT, DRP, TQM, and BPE are discussed as they are currently applied internally within organizations, and these principles are then applied to the external conduct of business between multiple unrelated companies.

In this book, the basic characteristics of structured and unstructured electronic commerce are reviewed and discussed using a set of functional business models that employ EDI transactions supplemented by other electronic tools such as fax, E-mail, and imaging.

The traditional implementation approach of replacing paper-based transactions with electronic transactions is then analyzed. Traditional models are examined in light of the key business functions being automated using EDI, these being representative of today's structured inter-corporate electronic commerce environment.

New, non-traditional business models being implemented by leading-edge companies are reviewed and analyzed, along with the issues involved in moving away from the paper paradigm. This includes implementation examples of Quick Response (QR), Evaluated Receipts Settlement (ERS), and other cycle-compression strategies.

The concepts of ICBE are presented, and guidelines are created for: developing inter-corporate business teams; analyzing the Value System; identifying Response Gaps; designing business models to close the Gaps; and implementing the models simultaneously across multiple companies.

Finally, a comprehensive set of forms, checklists, charts, to-do lists, meeting agendas, and other planning tools are introduced to assist the reader in implementing ICBE.

Inter-CORPORATE BUSINESS ENGINEERING: STREAMLINING THE BUSINESS CYCLE FROM END TO END

GARY G. BENESKO

Abstract:

Inter-Corporate Business Engineering (ICBE) is a multi-corporate business discipline that brings individual companies together in a joint crusade, acting as one to align their common business processes and streamline the overall operation, with the common goal of satisfying the customer's need for a product or service. The concepts of ICBE are built on the foundations established by successful disciplines such as Manufacturing Resource Planning II (MRP II), Just-In-Time Manufacturing (JIT), Distribution Resource Planning (DRP), Total Quality Management (TQM), and Business Process Engineering (BPE).

ICBE expands these traditionally single-company disciplines outward to include all participants in the business cycle, and involves an entirely new set of organizational and implementation issues. To this end, MRP II, JIT, DRP, TQM, and BPE are reviewed as they are currently applied internally within organizations, and these concepts are then applied to the external conduct of business between multiple unrelated companies.

The traditional implementation approach of replacing paper-based transactions with electronic transactions is analyzed. Traditional models are examined in light of the key business functions being automated using EDI, these being representative of today's structured inter-corporate electronic commerce environment.

New, non-traditional business models being implemented by leading-edge companies are reviewed and analyzed, along with the issues involved in moving away from the paper paradigm. This includes implementation examples of Quick Response (QR), Evaluated Receipts Settlement (ERS), and other cycle-compression strategies.

Guidelines are created for: developing inter-corporate business teams; analyzing the Value System; identifying Response Gaps; designing business models to close the Gaps; and implementing the models simultaneously across multiple companies.

PART 1: THE THEORY

CHAPTER I INTRODUCTION

The Corporate Self: A Human Metaphor

Throughout the history of free-world commerce, companies have operated under the principle of corporate self-interest. The force that has guided the businessman through the centuries has been that of competition rather than cooperation.; activities that furthered the company's imperative to "live long and prosper," that returned cash to the investor's pockets quickly, and hastened the destruction of one's competitors to one's own advantage. This is neither good nor bad. It is merely the reality of conducting business in a world of individuals. It is a mindset that has prevailed since the dawn of time. It is the "corporate self."

It is much better to provide for the survival of the "self" than the "non-self." The basic human survival instinct dictates suspicion of and protection against the "non-self," which is just as concerned with its own "self" survival. As a result, the actions of any company or individual have always been based upon inward-directed self-interest, as opposed to outward-directed community interest. This is a normal expression of human instinct, and represents the stage of "corporate infancy" that corresponds to the stage of human infancy.

During the last few years, several new models of business practice have arisen that have truly attempted to move the business world towards "corporate maturity." These models are useful in helping companies grow through their adolescent stage by allowing them to improve their internal efficiencies and challenge their old ways of thinking.   They help companies develop control over the internal operation (the self) so that the company can operate effectively in the marketplace, and broaden the horizons beyond the corporate self to include the business community within which the company operates.

This literature describes some of the more well-known and successful models of business practice. These have provided the basis for the development of the concepts of Inter-Corporate Business Engineering.

Material Requirements Planning (MRP)

MRP, as originally described by Plossl (1983) and Wight (1984), concentrated on achieving a consistent set of unified data and information flows across all departments within a manufacturing organization. This advance knowledge of material requirements permitted a company to optimize production schedules within the plant, and to keep inventory to a minimum.

This was the advent of formal inventory management systems. Management's inventory policies could now be expressed in numerical terms instead of being a function of the experience and judgment of individuals on the shop floor ; (60 days supply for this part, a re-order point of 10 for that part, and so on). Inventory requirements could be accurately forecast. Orders could be placed using one or more mathematical models, granting the production manager a valuable tool for managing the flow of inventory through the production facilities.

A key concept was the accuracy and reliability of the product information that specified the component parts and subassemblies of a unit of inventory. To this end, the concept of a Bill of Material (BOM) was introduced (Wight 1984). It provided a structure for the product information for ease of ordering and ease of production. Each time a unit was ordered, its BOM was examined to see the component parts that had to be ordered or assembled to make it.

Manufacturing Resource Planning (MRP II)

MRP II, as described by Wight (1984) focuses on a wider range of activities and problems. MRP II goes beyond the material requirements and concentrates on all of the manufacturing resources required to produce an order, including machines and equipment that may be in use by other orders. MRP II is concerned with developing internal efficiencies of production and operation to lower costs, improve reliability of production schedules, and streamline the manufacturing process itself, rather than just manage inventory.

MRP II, like MRP before it, also concentrates on a consistent set of unified data that spans all departments in an organization, but broadens the scope of the data to include supplier information, accounting information, engineering information, and all other aspects of the information flows within the manufacturing process. This permits better coordination of the key activities of production than does inventory management by itself. The Master Production Schedule is the heart of the MRP II concept. It is what drives the operation. MRP II has been attempted by many companies across North America over the years, with only moderate success.

Some of the reasons for MRP II's relatively poor success rate in the field include: lack of top management commitment; the (in some cases) significant capital investment and training required; the existence of other corporate priorities; and the lack of support for MRP II outside the company, most notably the supplier base. Achieving internal efficiencies of operation is of limited value if the company is still held hostage to external factors such as long lead times or unreliable delivery from suppliers.

To this date, very few companies have achieved a full "Class A" MRP II implementation. Wight (1984) defines "Class A" to mean that a company has achieved a closed loop operation. All aspects of the business are run from the same set of numbers. The sales forecast feeds, along with customer orders, into the production plan. The production plan drives the procurement process, assists in inventory planning, and drives the daily production schedule; the production schedule feeds back into the production plan; and the actuals feed back into the business planning cycle. All operating departments are united by a single set of operating information and valid schedules.

Those companies who have achieved "Class A" status are usually the ones who have committed the full resources of the corporation. They have made it a way of corporate life. In return, those companies have generally achieved cost-competitiveness and a reputation for high quality (Black & Decker, Yamaha, Steelcase, AG&G, for examples).

By virtue of taking this path, the corporate child has now achieved the equivalent of an elementary school education. New knowledge has been gained. There is better "self" control, and the company is in a much stronger position. The status quo has been automated and perhaps improved upon. In order to reap the full benefits, however, the company must now look outward and exploit these newfound efficiencies by getting the right product to market at the right time at the right price. This requires taking the next of many steps toward maturity. Those who stop at MRP II and congratulate themselves are missing the whole point.

Just-In-Time Manufacturing (JIT)

JIT, as described by Goddard (1986), builds on the disciplinary foundations of MRP II. It introduces innovative manufacturing concepts such as more efficient assembly line layouts, reduced machine setup times, smaller lot sizes, flow operations, grouping of similar operations, team production (the Saturn car, for example), and other techniques that streamline the operation and maximize the flexibility of the manufacturing cycle. JIT has evolved from the Japanese techniques of manufacturing, most notably the Toyota production system.

JIT is a "pull" system of manufacturing, as opposed to the centuries-old "push" system based on incoming customer orders, or the wartime system of continuous production regardless of demand. JIT, however, concentrates on making only what is necessary and only when it is required, using the fewest possible resources and the least possible time.

Traditionally, the order was taken from the customer (and promises made for delivery) without regard for the capacity of the plant to actually produce the product. Product lead times became longer and longer as orders were "pushed" onto the shop floor. This caused scheduling problems, material shortages, increasing inventory, need for extra shifts, overtime, and high-cost special delivery methods such as courier services. Orders backed up as more demand was placed on the manufacturing resource, and general dissatisfaction was the norm.

By contrast, JIT sends replenishment signals back from the point of sale or sends order schedules in advance of anticipated demand. It calls for the exact amount of materials to arrive exactly when they will be needed to make the product, thereby "pulling" materials through the production system based on actual consumption or demand. In this way, JIT attempts to synchronize the production facilities of the company's suppliers to achieve "just in time" delivery, and to fine-tune the joint systems of delivery.

In theory, this results in lower inventories and carrying costs for the company, higher inventory turns, reduced obsolescence, and smaller, more frequent orders. The suppliers act upon more reliable advance orders. The result is an overall reduction in the inventories across the whole system. In practice, the burden of inventory has been simply displaced onto the supplier, who must comply with his customer's (GM, Ford, Chrysler, etc.) JIT system in order to keep the business.

This IS "just in time," but only for the customer. The supplier often has to carry more inventory and incur extremely high transportation and courier costs for "delivery on demand." This does not achieve the intended purposes of either inventory reduction or cost reduction. The cost of the extra supplier inventory and higher delivery costs inevitably appear in the cost of the material to the customer and in the cost of the end product to the consumer.

This is a case of a good idea poorly implemented. Even with these higher ideals and the broader perspective, the customer is still acting in its own self-interest at the expense of the supplier. Even in those cases where the supplier is considered a co-equal partner in the JIT system, the company is still acting in (enlightened) self-interest.

In these cases, the driving force behind the JIT effort is not to further the best interests of the participants. It is to improve the company's own internal efficiencies. Even though the partners are well treated and benefit from the exercise, the entire effort is still inward-directed and centered around the driving company. It is a good attempt to bring "self" and "non-self" together, but they remain separate and distinct entities without any other common purpose.

Distribution Resource Planning (DRP)

DRP (Martin 1990) takes the next logical step beyond MRP II. DRP is the first discipline to focus outward. It attempts to integrate the company's delivery operation with that of its partners in the distribution and supply chain.

DRP requires many of the same corporate disciplines and uses many of the same tools as MRP II. Scheduling is coordinated across several organizationally-separate entities. In addition, it requires that the supply and distribution partners use DRP and at least an embryonic form of MRP II, specifically an automated Master Production Schedule. DRP also requires a reliable means of communicating electronic DRP schedules, implying some level of standardization of systems and procedures between partners. To date, DRP is still in its infancy. It has not achieved widespread success, since the commercial world has not generally achieved the sophistication required to exploit its full potential.

In many cases, a company's own manufacturing divisions and warehouses are considered "non-self" by each other. They are set up by well-meaning management to be in competition, not to work together for the good of the company as a whole. This forces artificial conflict upon the operating divisions, supported by artificial measurements, to the detriment of the company as a whole. A division may "make its numbers," but it is usually at the expense of another division.

DRP forces management to scrutinize its policies in this regard, and to make the conceptual leap away from the "divide and conquer" mentality. That only works against the enemy, not your own company. The communication facility afforded by an integrated DRP system is one of the mechanisms that will help draw separate divisions into a single entity and allow them to operate as a single company.

Business Process Engineering (BPE)

BPE (Hammer and Champy 1993) attempts to achieve quantum improvements in the company's internal and external business processes by challenging the very conceptual basis of these processes. It institutes new industry "Best Practices" (McNair and Leibfried 1992) where warranted. It totally eliminates non-value-added overhead, up to and including re-inventing the entire business if necessary.

Unlike the more formal disciplines of MRP II and JIT, BPE does not necessarily proceed from a particular premise or business focus (although it can be directed to specific known problem areas). Rather, it addresses the entire business, using various tools and techniques to uncover the real problems in an organization and to develop innovative solutions to them. In its most ultimate form, it can involve a major corporate overhaul.

Given a specific focus such as employee job classification and career management, payroll or accounts payable, BPE can be used to procedurally align the various departments and divisions within a company. It discards or re-invents antiquated or ineffective processes, instituting Best Practices as appropriate.

BPE can be a major tool to redefine how companies do business together in a changing world. The explosive growth of electronic commerce in recent years has resulted in the quantum acceleration of standardized business communication. Standards have arisen that make it easier for company A's computer to send purchase orders or other business transactions directly to company B's computer without human intervention, streamlining the way in which business is conducted.

Electronic commerce facilitates the formation of virtual corporations, reduces the restrictions imposed by national borders, commonizes business processes, and demands that the boundaries of "self" be redefined. A mechanism is needed that allows all commercial partners to not only align their internal processes, but to do so in a manner consistent with the other members of this newly defined "self".

While the proponents of BPE correctly contend that it can be used for inter-company process engineering as well, the body of actual field experience is sparse. What has been accomplished to date consists primarily of operations-level coordination of common or overlapping processes driven by a dominant partner at arm's length (e.g. purchase orders and invoices), rather than direct collaboration of multiple companies toward a common purpose (e.g. reducing the cycle time and days of inventory within an entire commercial ecosystem such as the grocery industry).

As will be illustrated later, a number of commercial strategies have evolved with just such objectives in mind. However, they stop at the theory, leaving it to the individual companies to implement as best they can, often in a vacuum wherein the wheel gets re-invented may times over. There is no enabling mechanism to actually coordinate the activities, engineer the joint business processes of the participants and institute an ongoing program of closely coupled business operations.

The current BPE methodologies assume that a single corporation or at least a single authority is responsible for making decisions and coordinating activities. What is needed is a methodology that permits participation by different corporate entities at the same decision-making level, while still retaining the disciplines and formality of BPE.

Total Quality Management (TQM)

TQM (Berry 1991) is a continuous process that focuses on customer satisfaction, consistent measurements, fact-based management, continuous process improvement, reduction of non-value-added overhead, and meeting the real requirements of the marketplace. TQM stresses continuous, incremental improvement, and redefines the concept of "customer" to include both internal and external customers. By its nature, TQM engenders incremental rather than quantum improvements. It should be used as the vehicle for fine-tuning rather than major overhaul. Once the radical changes have been implemented through BPE, TQM disciplines should then take over and manage the continuous improvement of the new processes.

Inter-Corporate Business Engineering (ICBE)

ICBE, as outlined in this book, takes the much-needed next step. It introduces new concepts, tools and mechanisms to permit multiple companies to enter a win-win arrangement that will break the old boundaries of "self" and help streamline the conduct of commerce.

As an infant human slowly becomes aware of the existence of others, and of their political and social significance to him or her, the world of commerce is also realizing that "self" is not the only one in the sandbox. There are other companies out there, and the rules are changing. Cooperation and synergy are valued more than competition and rivalry, and the "self"ish attitudes are disappearing.

Electronic Commerce (EC)

Recent advances in technology have resulted in the phenomenon of Electronic Commerce (EC) (Cadaret 1992). Briefly stated, EC replaces the traditional paper artifacts in the business cycle (purchase orders, invoices, etc.) with standardized electronic transactions or messages, and manages their flow through the computer systems of the participants. This has resulted in dramatic improvements in the flow of information between companies, and has substantially reduced the errors and redundancies inherent in paper-based commerce.

With paper-based commerce, for example, company A prints out (or types) a purchase order, puts it in an envelope, and sends it through the mail (or faxes it) to company B, who re-types the purchase order into its computer system. This process can involve many manual steps, each introducing a potential for error or delay. It can take several days from end to end.

With EC, company A's computer system produces a purchase order that is converted by the computer directly to an Electronic Data Interchange (EDI) standard purchase order format. It is sent through the network to company B, whose computer converts the EDI standard directly into its own purchase order format and processes it without human intervention. This usually takes minutes or hours as opposed to days, and cuts the cost from many dollars to a few cents. For example, General Motors has publicly quoted a reduction in the cost of issuing a purchase order to participating suppliers from $57.00 to $0.16 (EDS 1990). A multitude of other companies have experienced cost savings of the same order of magnitude.

Not only is EC gaining momentum in the business community, it has now reached what is being described as "critical mass." As of this writing, the EDI Council of Canada (Wood 1993) estimates that over 50,000 companies in North America alone are now doing business electronically using EDI and other EC tools (this figure does not include those companies using only fax and electronic mail, which are unstructured messages). The growth rate for EDI utilization is around 45% annually, and is relatively constant (Wood 1993).

EC, since it uses standardized tools such as EDI, demands a degree of standardization in business practice as well as in the content of the business transactions themselves. Companies are finding that in addition to the immediate cost savings being experienced as a result of replacing paper, there are quantum improvements to be had by simultaneously re-engineering the processes they are automating, or by adopting industry Best Practices.

Conversely, as companies re-engineer their internal business processes as a result of other corporate activities such as TQM or JIT, they find that they are drawn directly to the benefits of EC as the natural mechanism to support these new processes. In this way, EC is in the unique position of being both the catalyst/driver for BPE activities, and the end result of those activities within a given company.

EC is the enabling factor (and the requirement) in modern inter-company strategies such as Quick Response (QR) (AIM Quick Response Conference Proceedings 1993), Efficient Consumer Response (ECR) (Salmon 1993), Evaluated Receipts Settlement (ERS) (Schaap 1991), and others to be discussed later. EC is the operational cornerstone of these strategies, using EDI transactions to standardize data content and accelerate the flow of business information between companies.

By standardizing the information, pressure is exerted on all participants to standardize the business processes that use that information. By accelerating the flow, pressure is exerted to develop systems and procedures capable of coping with the greater speed, higher transaction volumes and reduced manual intervention resulting from EC.

Due to this, EC will usually be the primary driver for an ICBE initiative. In fact, most companies will recognize the real need for ICBE only when they begin implementing formal EC strategic programs with other companies. It is within this contextual framework where ICBE is most effective. Individual companies may still realize significant improvements by pursuing internal BPE efforts (and should achieve internal efficiency before undertaking any outward-directed strategy). The real quantum improvements in cycle time reduction and cost reduction across the entire business cycle cannot be realized without EC.

CHAPTER II

BUSINESS PROCESS RE-ENGINEERING: THE BEGINNINGS

Initially referred to as Business Process Re-Engineering, the "re" is gradually being dropped in favor of the more politically correct and positive-sounding "engineering." In the early days of office automation, integrated computer applications, MRP II, shop floor automation and computerized manufacturing, the focus was on automating the status quo. It was felt that if a company could do the same things faster, it would also be doing them better. This was seldom the case. As manual systems were automated, it became evident that they never really worked in the first place. There were always inefficient and sometimes conflicting policies and procedures. It required human ingenuity to find a convoluted work-around that somehow made a cumbersome system work in spite of itself.

MRP II addressed the inefficiencies of the old-style shop floor manufacturing environment, but did nothing for the supporting functions such as accounting, marketing, human resources, data processing, or any of the other functions of the organization. MRP II began to change some mindsets, however, specifically in the realization that there were really two systems in force--the "formal" system and the "informal" or "shadow" system. Finally, managers were made to face the fact that the way they thought things were being done often bore no resemblance at all to what was really happening.

MRP II also began to work on uniting previously warring factions within the organization. Historically, Sales blamed Production; Production blamed Sales, Purchasing and Engineering. Engineering blamed Marketing and Accounting; and everybody blamed Data Processing. Everyone had the excuse that no one else except them was doing their job. Thus it was everyone else's fault that schedules weren't being met and customers went elsewhere. MRP II looked at the entire manufacturing operation as an integrated whole. A whole that could be controlled and scheduled, with reliable information linking all of the segments of the operation together to develop efficiencies of operation that would result in the ability to meet schedules reliably. This was the first major step in BPE.

Even with these innovations, real progress was slow in coming. Few companies had the confidence to make the investment in time and money to achieve MRP II's full potential. The supporting systems and processes were still not integrated and often lagged far behind in their ability to cope. Finally, MRP II did not really address radical change, rather it automated and improved on the status quo. The informal system was still in force.

JIT introduced radical change to the operating environment. JIT thinking demanded that the processes themselves be re-invented, not only in the manufacturing area, but in the delivery of services as well. Managers and employees alike were constantly being challenged to find a way to produce single lots rather than lots of 500. They needed to find ways to reduce machine setup time from hours to minutes and then to seconds; and to rearrange the plant so that production bottlenecks could be eliminated and material could flow through in an assembly-line fashion. To accomplish these things, new machines had to be invented, new production methods designed, and entirely new thinking had to prevail. This was the next major step in the journey.

About the same time as JIT was coming into prominence, office automation began to come into its own. In the mid-to-late 1980's, software vendors began to package the various spreadsheets, word processing, telecommunications, and data base software into "office automation" systems. These systems enjoyed limited success because, while they got everyone using the same tools, they did not address the underlying problems of inefficient and cumbersome office procedures that were not linked to the actual operation.

The next breakthrough came with the joint technologies of document imaging, optical character recognition, electronic forms, and document management software. Now the tedious task of data entry was eliminated, along with the attendant errors. Now documents could be converted directly to electronic form, manipulated and filed without handling and loss of information. Orders could be scanned in, employee performance reviews could be filled in electronically, invoices could be generated and faxed to the recipient, and so on. This resulted in significant gains in the reliability of information and the speed of processing it. Jobs changed, and with them, employees' skill sets changed from paper handlers to information managers.

This led to the concept of "workflow management." Now companies began to think of information processing as a series of parallel functions. Freed from the physical paper artifact traveling between workstations, information was now on the system, available to all. There was no practical reason for the sequential processing of an insurance claim, for instance, if there were several things that could be done by different people at the same time.

Workflow management systems not only handled documents, they handled them intelligently. Commonly-used documents were kept in a central electronic file, with controlled accessibility to those needing to work with the contents of those documents. Programmed routing mechanisms electronically "moved" copies of these documents between people and monitored the response, prompting individuals to complete tasks within a certain time. Electronic signatures provided the necessary authorizations for continued processing or for completion of the task.

This inevitably resulted in the total redesign of some of the tasks that people had done the same way for years. It begged the question, "Why do we do it this way, in fact, why do we do this at all?." This was the beginning of BPE. BPE attempted to create a clean slate and design the processes from the ground up. It eliminated the inefficiencies that had evolved due to misunderstanding, inability, lack of technology tools, or lack of authority for individuals to act on their own.

As profound as this change was, it still limited itself to an inward-directed approach to doing business. It was the internal processes that were being redesigned, not the processes between the company and its business partners. This is a perfectly valid approach (taken unknowingly, in most cases), since the inter-corporate problems cannot be addressed until the company has its own house in order. The real benefits are to be gained from reducing the time and cost of doing business between the participants in the business cycle.

TQM, DRP, JIT, and BPE all strive to achieve some degree of inter-company coordination. They do so from an essentially parochial, inward-directed manner, proceeding from the perspective of the business unit's own "Value Chain." Porter (1985) defines the Value Chain as the set of co-ordinated, interdependent activities that create value to consumers of its product or service, or provide input to their individual Value Chains. These activities are, in summary:

- Marketing/design/sales (recognizing the need, designing the solution and getting the orders).
- Inbound logistics and supply (obtaining the material).
- Production and operations (making the product).
- Outbound logistics (getting it to the customer).
- Service and support (external service and internal support for operations).

Porter (1985) said that "Linkages" must exist between these activities to provide coordination and cost-effective operation. He further states that, as well as developing Linkages between the activities within a business unit, Linkages should also be developed between that Value Chain and the Value Chains of the other participants in the overall Value System (such as suppliers and channels).

ICBE takes that concept one step further, maintaining that Linkages are usually external interfaces. Therefore they can only be marginally effective in contributing to overall smoothness of operation or in achieving a truly synergistic benefit to the participants. While these Linkages may add incremental or even significant value in many situations, they serve primarily as an external mechanism to pass synchronization signals between individual participants. Linkages do not address duplication of effort or underlying inefficiencies of operation across the total Value System. Therefore, they do not bring fundamental, quantum improvements to the business cycle. These Linkages are shown in **Figure 1** on page 12.

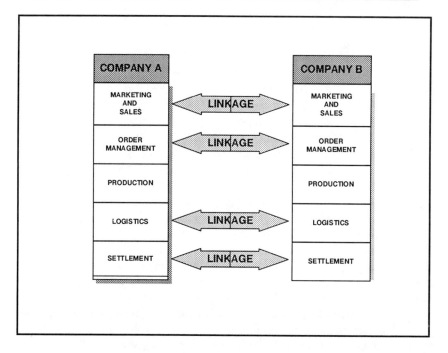

Fig. 1. The Value Chain and its Linkages

To attain true synergy, it is necessary for all participants to step up to a higher level and strive to integrate and optimize each of the individual Value Chains within the entire Value System.   ICBE is the mechanism that brings the participants together in a formal, structured   fashion to realize quantum improvements in the business cycle.

CHAPTER III

SHORTCOMINGS OF THE INWARD-DIRECTED APPROACH

Improper Focus

Looking inward lures the company into adopting the fallacy that everything is under its own control and that all problems can be solved if given enough time and money. In an inward-focused model, managers and BPE facilitators alike live in the closed universe of the company processes. If they do investigate industry Best Practices, it is through the spectacles of the company's version of those practices.

The very concepts of BPE are themselves affected and defined by what is best for or achievable by the company. There is little regard for how other participants in the business cycle are affected by the changes that are being made. The tendency is to focus on reducing waste within the company (since that is within the direct control of management), not on reducing the time and costs of the overall business cycle itself.

It is the overall business cycle that is the determining factor in a company's success in the marketplace, not how efficient the company is at doing its own job within that cycle. An inward-directed approach almost ensures that the grand view will be overlooked in favor of the "easy" solutions offered by internal BPE.

Diminishing Returns

Blackburn (1991, p. 30) maintains that 95% of the value-delivery chain occurs outside of the manufacturing plant. This consists of the processes of marketing, new product development, product engineering, order management, transportation and logistics, invoicing and collection. Even if we adopt a more conservative figure and grant that internal processes can account for as much as 20% of the business cycle, we are still left with the bulk of the cycle time (80%) outside the control of the company.

If a company spends significant amounts of time, effort and money reducing its internal business processes, it is still looking at only 20% of the total problem. Even if the internal processes can be thoroughly optimized and all non-value-added activities can be eliminated, it is difficult in real practice to reduce the "in-house" time by more than 50%. If we put actual numbers to the problem, it might look like the scenario outlined in **Table 1** on the next page.

13

Table 1
Business Cycle Reductions

Time for complete business cycle (conception to consumption)	60 days
Time for internal production processes (60 days * 20%)	12 days
BPE reduction of internal processes (12 days * 50%)	6 days
New business cycle time (60 days-6 days)	54 days

Total savings (6 days) = 10 percent of total cycle time

If the company now uses the TQM practice of continuous improvement to reduce the in-house time by another 50%, another 3 days will be shaved off the cycle time, reducing it to 51 days. With each iteration, more and more time effort and money will need to be expended in order to erode away increasingly smaller amounts of time. The effort will eventually become insupportable. The concepts of BPE will come under serious questioning and criticism by management, and may be at risk of cancellation.

It is not uncommon for a company to spend hundreds of thousands of dollars to re-engineer several of their internal business processes, and end up not seeing the anticipated improvements in time-to-market or customer satisfaction. It may, however, see dramatic staff cuts, remarkable cost reductions, higher quality, and an increase in the output in goods and services related to the investment in plant and equipment. These in themselves are important for the company's well-being, but are not (or should not be) the central reasons for undertaking BPE.

BPE, if used in an inward-directed manner, focuses naturally on the problems that are immediately visible to management. This approach ignores the other 80% of the business cycle that adds not only time, but significant cost to the delivery of the end product to the customer. This 80% can be and often is the determining factor in getting the right product on the shelf at the right price, and thereby securing the customer's business away from the competition. It is this 80% that must be addressed if the business cycle is to be reduced in any meaningful way or if there is to be any real benefits to be realized from the effort.

Fragmentation Of Effort

Since efforts are directed inward, little if any attention is paid to the other participants in the cycle. Given the awareness level enjoyed by BPE, it is conceivable, even likely, that they are engaged in similar initiatives aimed at improving their own internal efficiencies (Value Chains). These efforts may or (likely) may not coincide with what the company is doing, and may in fact be at cross purposes.

Every company is trying to do what is in its own best interests. That can result in multiple re-inventions of the same wheel. At best, this can cause unnecessary costs across the Value System (hereinafter called the "System") as a whole. At worst it can cause outright conflict of priorities between companies engaged in the same business cycle. There is no common purpose, just individuals acting alone.

This fragmentation of effort raises the costs and the time associated with moving goods and services through the System to the consumer. The final processes do not mesh smoothly together from company to company to achieve lower inventories and faster throughput for the System. They may, in fact, slow things down while everyone is individually trying to come to grips with their own re-engineered systems.

Even while re-engineering with the best of intentions, a company may misunderstand the significance of certain aspects of industry best practices unless those practices are looked at in the context of the company's interaction with the other participants in the System. The company may proceed from false assumptions about how the overall System works. It may inadvertently enshrine the status quo because it does not see how its practices affect the other participants in the System. Bad practices or "self-ish" practices may arise because the company is looking only at its own bottom line, and not that of the entire System.

If all of the participants in the System were to proceed in this manner, the potential benefits of BPE could be significantly diminished or even negated, leaving some or all of the participants worse off than before they started. Significant costs would have been incurred without the expected paybacks. Once again BPE itself would be held up to criticism, not the implementation of it.

A common initiative resulting from BPE is the introduction of a "paperless" environment to handle some of the more common business transactions such as purchase orders and invoices. These represent not only the most common transactions that companies engage in, but also the most voluminous and paper-intensive. In addition, the manual processes that accompany these transactions have been traditionally cumbersome and subject to stringent management and controls.

BPE seeks to re-engineer these processes and eliminate paper. While this does reduce costs and speed up the processing of orders and invoices by eliminating the paper and the excessive manual handling of it, it does so only for the company engaging in the re-engineering. These companies are sometimes referred to as "Hubs."

The other companies with which it deals (called "Spokes") still must process orders and invoices, and now must submit these electronically through EDI. This can impose hardship on a Spoke company who is not set up to use EDI, since it must usually purchase software and hardware to accommodate the new requirement, and must subscribe to the services of a Value-Added Network (VAN) to deliver the electronic transactions. This being done, the Spoke has not changed the way it does its own business. It must accommodate its old methods, systems and procedures to adapt them to this new requirement. This is never a simple task. It can send the Spoke off into an unplanned BPE exercise of its own, thereby raising its costs and possibly its response or delivery time. Obviously, that benefits no one and can compromise the overall System.

False Economy

It is a common practice to consider the walls of the company as the "self", and to operate solely in the interests of that "self". This automatically relegates other participants in the System to the status of competitors to be negotiated with. Sometimes they are taken advantage of in an adversarial fashion, especially where prices or terms are considered. It is considered to be good form to get the lowest prices, the best delivery or payment terms, and the most concessions from the other parties to the deal (even if they lose).

The measurement here is short-term unit profitability or margin for the company. It is not improved time to market, increased market share, customer satisfaction, lowered total cost of sales or any of the longer term goals that a company should strive to attain. While this elicits praise from those who manage the quarterly financial statements, it does nothing for the real problems facing the business.

Often, real costs are ignored or simply not understood. Managers fail to take into account the total costs across the System, such as advertising and promotion, transportation and logistics, cost of materials, and other costs they are paying without realizing it. There is no free lunch. By gaining service concessions or low prices from their "adversaries" in the System, the real costs are just being hidden and passed on to the company anyway, either in the form of lower quality, higher delivery costs, or artificially high prices.

These hidden costs are usually accounted for in the overhead (General and Administrative) cost categories and are allocated across the rest of the company. This further disguises the real problem and causes the company to undertake a BPE initiative to try to correct the excessive overhead. It would seem to make more sense to try to bring these "adversaries" into the "self" and streamline the entire System from beginning to end. Then, all participants would profit but the total costs and time are reduced permanently. Everyone has a stake in making the venture a success.

Other not-so-obvious costs might include a drop in employee morale and productivity (of those employees that escape the inevitable layoffs). BPE is becoming increasingly synonymous in the public mind with downsizing and layoffs. While a company can make significant short-term cost reductions by going paperless and laying off 20-50% of its staff, it can have a long term impact on the company's image as an employer or as a concerned corporate citizen. Also, it can compromise its ability to attract and keep the best people.

There are always legitimate reasons to be found for implementing cost reductions. The wartime mentality that still prevails in North American industry dictates that costs be cut from the ranks of indirect labor. In many cases, however, it may be argued that labor is not the most significant of the contributors to cost. The 80% of the business cycle is the major contributor. This 80% may involve System-related factors such as:

1. long supplier lead times;
2. artificially high material prices;
3. customer order changes;
4. product re-engineering;
5. inventory inaccuracies;
6. supplier over shipment or short shipment;
7. outdated production technology;
8. poor management systems;
9. high-cost special delivery services to meet deadlines;
10. delays in collection of accounts receivable;
11. excessive banking charges and inventory carrying charges;
12. and a host of other contributors that have nothing to do with the number of people working in the company's accounts receivable department.

A company that looks only inward does not always see the full scope of the problem, and sometimes makes "tough" choices that did not need to be made at all.

CHAPTER IV
INTER-CORPORATE BUSINESS ENGINEERING: ICBE

A New Paradigm: ICBE

Inter-Corporate Business Engineering (ICBE) is a multi-corporate business discipline that brings individual companies together in a joint crusade. They act as one to align their common business processes and streamline the overall operation within the Value System of which they are a part. They have a common goal of satisfying the customer's need for a product or service.

In his 1985 Harvard Business Review article, "From Competitive Advantage to Corporate Strategy", Michael Porter identified the concept of individual companies' Value Chains. He refers to the overall "Value System" that consists of all of the companies involved in a given business cycle. Briefly, Porter defines the individual company's Value Chain as the set of co-ordinated, interdependent activities that create value to consumers of its product or service, or provide input to the individual Value Chains of other companies. These Value Chain activities are, in summary:

- Marketing/design/sales (recognizing the need, designing the solution and getting the orders).
- Inbound logistics and supply (obtaining the material).
- Production and operations (making the product).
- Outbound logistics (getting it to the customer).
- Service and support (external service and internal support for operations).

Porter said that "linkages" must exist between these internal activities to provide coordination and cost-effective operation. He further stated that, as well as developing linkages between the activities within a business unit, inter-company linkages should be developed between that Value Chain and the Value Chains of the other participants in the overall Value System (such as suppliers and channels).

ICBE takes that concept one step further. It maintains that such inter-company linkages are usually nothing more than "interfaces" between dissimilar, duplicative, or conflicting processes. Therefore they can have only a marginal effect on the overall smoothness of operation or in achieving a truly synergistic benefit to the participants.

The very act of implementing these linkages may dramatically reduce costs or add significant value in many situations. They still serve primarily as an external mechanism to pass synchronization signals between individual participants, and do not cut to the heart of the processes at each end of the linkage.

Linkages do not address duplication of effort or underlying inefficiencies of operation across the total Value System. They do not bring fundamental, quantum improvements to the business cycle as a whole. An example of inter-company linkage is shown in **Figure 2.**

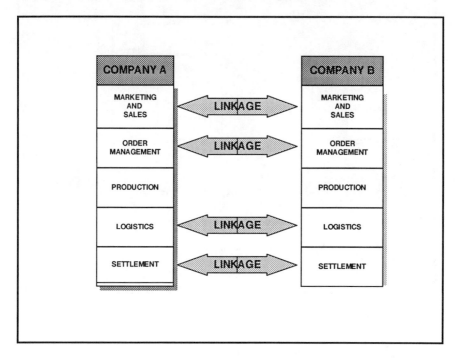

Fig. 2. Inter-Company Linkages

To attain true synergy, it is necessary for all participants to step up to a higher level. They must strive to optimize each of the individual Value Chains within the entire Value System, and to integrate them with each other where they intersect. ICBE is the mechanism that brings the participants together in a formal, structured fashion to realize quantum improvements in the business cycle.

ICBE concentrates on the Value System itself, observing from a position "outside" the System instead of from within one of the member companies looking outward. ICBE looks at the Value System as a single "multi-departmental" organization with a single management team that is focused upon eliminating waste and streamlining the entire business cycle from end to end. This demands new thinking and new approaches, some of which may appear radical, heretical, and even irrational to traditional managers steeped in centuries of adversarial business tradition.

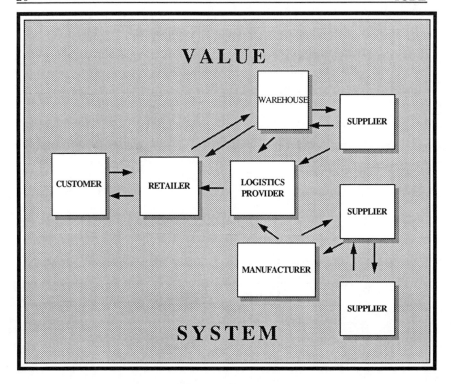

Fig. 3. The Value System

A New Mindset: The Expanded Self

ICBE builds upon existing industry experience. It draws on the underlying concepts of successful disciplines such as Manufacturing Resource Planning II (MRP II), Just-In-Time Manufacturing (JIT), Distribution Resource Planning (DRP), Total Quality Management (TQM), and Business Process Engineering (BPE).   ICBE, however, expands these traditionally single-company disciplines outward to include all participants in the business cycle. It involves an entirely new set of organizational and implementation issues.

Indeed, these companies can no longer be just "participants", a passive, third-party role at best. They must now become fully-constituted "Members" of a common Value System with all rights, privileges and responsibilities of that membership. They are now "self," just as surely as if they all belonged to the same fraternal organization or to a single company's "expanded business unit."

This terminology and thinking is central to the philosophy of ICBE. Under ICBE, the adversarial model of commerce is abandoned in favor of a completely cooperative model. All Members are co-equal and none enjoy advantage at the expense of others. This is a radical concept to business people accustomed to speaking in terms of "targets," "penetration," "barriers," "competition," and a host of other hostile and warlike metaphors that have set the business paradigm for thousands of years. Yet it is perhaps no more radical than some of the other paradigm changes over the last few years, such as total quality, electronic commerce or re-engineering the corporation. It is, in fact, the logical and natural extension of those changes.

A New Mandate: Joint Responsibility

The ICBE Manifesto

The Members of the Value System must jointly and severally subscribe to the following credo. They must utilize their best efforts to make it a corporate culture within and between their organizations.

"All Members are jointly responsible for the product that gets to the customer. We all share the responsibility for giving the customer the right product of the right quality at the right price at the right time, and we all share in the proceeds, each in a manner befitting our contribution."

This may seem to be rather naive. It is hard to believe that individual companies who are accustomed to the traditional competitive environment would subscribe to such a philosophy since it strikes directly at their individual profits. Or, if they do, they would only pay lip service to it and continue to do "business as usual." That is very likely to be true of all companies in the initial stages of implementing ICBE. Some companies will abandon the effort because they simply cannot make the conceptual leap or see the broad picture.

Those that do make the leap and accord ICBE an honest effort will find that things work much better and faster this way. It really is easier and less costly to do things cooperatively. Profits and market share will tend to increase as the Members gain experience with the new order of things. There will be disagreements and operating snags along the way, and for the first while it will not appear to be generating results consistent with the effort. Those that make it work, however, will be able to streamline the System to the point where dramatic payback has been achieved, and outside competition has been reduced, eliminated, or assimilated.

Over time, this may give rise to new kinds of strategic relationships as the outside competition realizes that it can no longer compete, and seeks to join the System itself. It should be noted that any given company may have several different Value Systems, each involving a different business unit. ICBE offers the capability to selectively streamline these Systems across the corporate structure, focusing resources where they will be most effective and generate the highest payback.

Joint responsibility implies a limited Member set. A company that currently deals with hundreds or thousands of suppliers should really be looking at reducing this to a more manageable level. It should select a few key strategic partners to become Members.

One of the main reasons for having so many suppliers in the first place is usually that they are largely unknown entities, assumed to be generally unreliable in terms of either quality, delivery, or longevity. Normal prudence demands that there be alternatives whenever possible. Another reason is the negotiating power that a company can bring to bear if there are a number of other suppliers that are competing for its business. A third reason often quoted is the "hostage" argument, wherein a single-source supplier can set the terms, conditions and prices, and the company is held hostage to the supplier's pricing strategy and its ability to deliver.

The TQM process, among other things, seeks to reduce the number of suppliers, selecting only the more stable and reliable ones that have met certain requirements for quality and on-time delivery. TQM objectively assesses these suppliers and maintains the ongoing relationships based on fact and objective measurement. It is not based on any of the imprecise "soft" methods that have been used traditionally such as personal connections, historical relationships, or "special arrangements." The suppliers that are selected through these techniques are now known entities and most of the uncertainty in dealing with them has been reduced or eliminated.

TQM therefore provides a valuable set of tools to be used in conjunction with ICBE, from the outset through ongoing continuous improvement of the inter-corporate processes themselves. ICBE does not replace or invalidate any of the corporate initiatives such as TQM, JIT or BPE itself. It merely augments the efforts internally and expands these disciplines outward along inter-corporate lines.

A New Concept: Closing the Response Gap

Because companies differ greatly in internal efficiency and production capacity, they respond to external demand slower or faster than others, resulting in wide variability in the overall process across the Value System. To compound the problem, it is very rare for any two unrelated companies to employ the same, or even mutually compatible, internal systems and procedures in the course of doing business. This process incompatibility further slows the speed at which companies can respond to each other's demands for products and services. It creates a series of time delays where no value is being added to the System, only cost.

This is analogous to the internal situation in an MRP II implementation. In MRP II terminology, this type of delay is referred to as "wait time", "queue time", or "move time". It represents the time that material is moving between work stations or is sitting at a work station waiting for processing for one reason or another. One of the goals of MRP II and JIT is to reduce or eliminate these delays, and move the material from one work station to the next and through the processing steps as fast as possible. This is so that value may be added and the total dollar amount of inventory in the system is reduced.

This time delay is analogous to that experienced as a demand from one participant waits for satisfaction by another participant in the System. When applied to time delays at the inter-organizational level, it is herein identified as the "Response Gap." One of the major goals of ICBE is to close the Response Gap. Therefore, value may be added sooner and the total dollar value of goods or pending services in the System is reduced. **Figure 4** below illustrates the concept of the Response Gap.

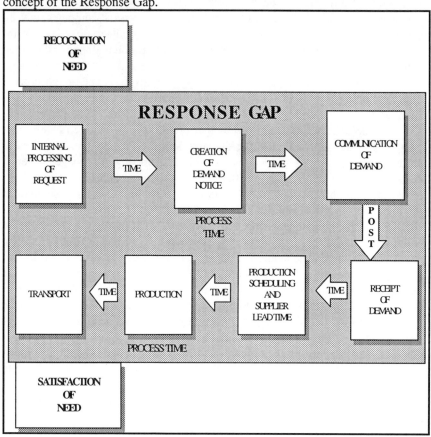

Fig. 4. The Response Gap

The Response Gap is defined as that period of time between the realization of a need, and the satisfaction of that need, <u>including</u> the hands-on "process time" taken to communicate the demand and produce the product. The Response Gap involves both the initiator and the respondent. Therefore it has two elements; demand-side activities and supply-side activities. These activities incur varying degrees of delay in their execution. This is where ICBE is applied with the goal of reducing both the "Demand Lag" and "Supply Lag" to zero, thereby making the Response Gap exactly equal to Process Time.

The Demand Lag is defined as that period of time between recognizing the need for a product or service and communicating the demand to the appropriate respondent, less the process time taken to construct the demand. For example, company A, during production, runs out of widgets. The foreman creates a shortage slip and sends it to the parts cage. The inventory manager enters a suggested order into the computer at the end of the day (day 1). The next day, the purchasing officer negotiates with his list of suppliers, and selects company B. He creates a purchase order on the computer (day 2), which is printed off overnight and sent to the mail room (day 3) for distribution. The purchase order goes out in the afternoon mail and is delivered 2 days later (day 5) to the supplier. The elapsed time is 5 days from realization of the need until the demand is received by company B. The actual process time for company A to create the purchase order is less than an hour. The Demand Lag is therefore (5 days * 24 hrs. -1), or 119 hours.

The Supply Lag is defined as that period of time between receipt of a demand and the satisfaction of the demand, less the Process Time required to produce the product or service. For example, company A's widget order is delivered to company B on day 5 after the realization of the need. Company B's clock starts ticking. On its "day 1," company B receives the purchase order in the mail room, sorts it and delivers it to the data entry staff. On day 2, it is entered into the computer system and processed. If it passes the credit checks and other criteria, it is logged into the production system as a firm order. On day 3, the production schedule is released and the order takes its place in line with others, according to its priority. With this type of order, company B has determined that it must in turn order other parts from other suppliers, and it quotes a lead time of 14 days. When the order is received into production on day 3, the parts are ordered and production is suspended pending receipt. On day 10, the parts arrive and production resumes. On day 11, the widget order is complete and is sent to the shipping dock. On day 12, the product is shipped and arrives at company A's dock on day 14. Actual shop floor Process Time to produce the widgets was 1 day. Therefore the Supply Lag is 13 days.

In company A's MRP II terms, this is known as "supplier lead time". It is factored into its scheduling calculations to determine when to place the order to company B in order to meet its own production and delivery commitments. MRP II simply takes the stated 14 days for granted and works with that number, but is unaware that 13 of those days (or some portion thereof) is an unnecessary delay--a Supply Lag.

Taken together, these form the Response Gap. In this example, the Response Gap is 19 days, including total delays of 18 days. During this time, the work-in-process inventory is tied up in the system, and total costs are increased due to unnecessary administrative costs and delays. Company A must carry his inventory another 18 days, lowering his inventory turns, raising his costs, and causing delays in other production.

Response Gaps are the loci of unnecessary time delays and/or additional cost. There are Response Gaps in every System, occurring at the Linkages where formal business communication or exchange of goods and services takes place between two or more Members. Response Gaps may occur because of the inefficiencies of supporting a number of different internal processes across the System, or because of the existence of non-value-added external or Linkage processes.

Just as TQM and BPE seek to reduce non-value-added overhead and reduce process variability in internal company-wide processes, ICBE seeks to identify the external System-wide Response Gaps and reduce or eliminate them through the use of joint workflow analysis and other techniques.

Where TQM and DRP seek to develop interfaces to make the external processes between companies more efficient, ICBE seeks to optimize both external processes and internal processes across the entire Value System. These are referred to in this book as "common processes" that focus on the external activities between companies (such as transportation), and "reciprocal processes" that focus on the internal activities that complement each other (such as billing and accounts payable).

Common Processes and Reciprocal Processes

ICBE brings participants together as Members in a closed community with a common focus. In the cooperative ICBE model, participants are not considered as a series of individual companies or islands of commerce, but as Members of an integrated System. As such, they each must follow certain common activities and processes in pursuing their joint efforts. They must endeavor to bring their existing business processes as closely into line with each other as possible.

In the traditional world of commerce, every company performs much the same internal tasks as it goes about its day-to-day business.

1. marketing,
2. design,
3. engineering,
4. order management,
5. production,
5. accounting
6. data processing,
7. human resource management,
8. and other functions that support the day-to-day operation of the organization.

These internal tasks are tailored (or have evolved) to satisfy the specific needs and personality of the organization. In general they tend to accomplish the same ends in every company.

Normally, these internal tasks are performed in near-complete isolation from outside participants except for the areas where their communications and business processes overlap, such as:

- The production and exchange of paper artifacts (price catalogs, purchase orders, engineering and product documentation, invoices, payments, and other business documents).
- Human-to-human communication (telephone, fax, electronic mail).
- Process linkage (design, procurement, scheduling, shipping, receiving, and accounting).

These are the "linkages" that Porter referred to as key elements in a company's Value Chain. For ease of analysis, these inter-corporate linkages may be subdivided into external "common processes" that may be combined or shared between participants, and internal "reciprocal processes" that augment or complement each other.

Common Processes

Common processes are those that surround or support the linkages, and can help close the Response Gap if jointly managed or coordinated by the participants in the Value System. These are:

- Sales analysis
- Order management
- Production scheduling
- Logistics

Common processes are characterized by the fact that they employ signals to activate processes throughout the Value System. The sales analysis process feeds the forecasting systems of the Members. Order management signals Member A's placement of a demand for goods or services on Member B, and sends a signal to Member B's own order management process or production scheduling process. Production scheduling sends signals up and down the System that indicate the time of availability of the product or service. The logistics process sends signals up and down the System that indicate the time of delivery of the goods or services requested.

In the traditional model, no process was activated without the proper signal, such as a paper purchase order or a planning schedule, resulting in unnecessary delays due to the lack of visibility and coordination. In the ICBE model, these processes are shared among all Members, accelerating the processes themselves through elimination of redundancy and closing the Response Gap through coordination of activities.

This sharing of common processes spans a continuum. Beginning from the low end, Members will share a standardized set of agreed-upon signals and special priorities that will accelerate their response to demand from other Members for particular goods or services. At the high end of this continuum, Members will share common procedures, computer systems, human resources, sources of supply, transportation resources, even plant and equipment that will optimize their entire Value System.

Reciprocal Processes

Each process or activity in an individual Member's Value Chain has a "reciprocal" process or activity in another Member's Value Chain. For example, company A's purchasing system has company B's order entry system as its reciprocal. Company B's billing/accounts receivable system has company A's accounts payable system as its reciprocal, and so on. To ensure a smooth business flow and thereby further close the Response Gap, these reciprocal processes must be aligned or re-engineered to operate together as one.

This also spans a continuum. At the low end, the alignment may take the form of standardized documents that flow between designated individuals in each of the companies, such as purchase orders, acknowledgments and invoices. accompanied by the appropriate prioritization procedures. At the high end, it may involve partial or complete sharing of computer systems, the use of common software packages supported by common procedures, or the use of an outside agency to perform the reciprocal functions on behalf of the participants.

Electronic Commerce: the Cornerstone of Business Operations

The business cycle cannot be optimized in any Value System without the use of EC tools such as EDI, fax, electronic mail, or other means of moving large volumes of transactions quickly and reliably in a format recognizable to all. Therefore, ICBE seeks to maximize the use of EC tools and integrate their use across the entire System.

This book emphasizes EC as the operational cornerstone of business, both domestic and global, and ICBE as the key to achieve the full potential and benefits across the Value System. It is a symbiotic circle: ICBE cannot achieve its full potential without EC, and EC cannot achieve its full potential without ICBE.

CHAPTER V

STRUCTURED VS. UNSTRUCTURED COMMERCE

Structured Commerce

Structured commerce is the traditional company-to-company model. The primary focus is the purchase, sale and movement of goods and services. Structured commerce follows well-defined protocols of business behavior, established over the centuries to protect the interests of the parties involved. It is characterized by a limited set of stable business relationships and a high volume of traditional business transactions, usually supported by paper or electronic artifacts.

Structured commerce is usually of a predictable nature. The initiating event (such as a purchase order) directly drives a standard sequence of process steps or resource requirements. Its conduct generates statistical information that can be used to forecast the demand for a particular item or resource with varying degrees of certainty. Structured commerce usually involves high volumes of well-established and rigidly controlled "transaction sets."

Some examples of structured commerce include:
1. Purchase and Sale of Goods
2. Manufacturing Orders to a Plant or Warehouse
3. Procurement
4. Joint Product Design and Development
5. Credit Reporting and Authorization
6. Funds Transfer
7. Import/ Export/ Customs and Excise
8. Government and Other Institutions

Purchase and Sale of Goods

Purchase orders result in purchase order acknowledgments, internal production orders, picking and packing orders, warehouse and transportation orders, invoices and payments. Promotional announcements and price changes may be received at any time, and may result in purchase orders or shipping orders.

Manufacturing Orders to a Plant or Warehouse

These, along with the "purchase and sale of goods" transactions, are the least rigid of the structured transaction sets. There is a wide variation in business practice across the various industries. Transactions that are mandatory in one industry, such as purchase order acknowledgments, are optional in another.

Procurement

In both the government and the private sector, a request for quotation (RFQ) results in the exchange of transactions such as quotations, price catalogs, discount structures, price negotiations, and contract awards.

Joint Product Design and Development

Technical specifications, quality assurance and control data, computer assisted design (CAD) designs, and other product-related images, data and information are exchanged between customers, manufacturers and end suppliers during the design of a product, such as an aircraft part. This is known as "Concurrent Engineering" (Kilmer 1992), and is becoming more widespread as technology progresses.

Credit Reporting and Authorization

A "request for credit authorization" or "request for credit report" transaction is generated at the point of sale or service. It is responded to with either an authorization number or a credit report. This is a very simple example of structured commerce, but is very common and involves a high volume of transactions every day.

Funds Transfer.

A very rigidly structured set of commercial transactions is the ATM (automated teller machine) where a request for funds at the point of service results in a request to the data base to establish the available balance, and an electronic funds transfer (EFT) between the financial institutions involved. This is the most tightly regulated example of structured commerce (those transactions involving the transfer of value) and are therefore the most highly structured and controlled.

Import/Export/Customs and Excise

This is another highly structured set of commercial transactions, reasonably well standardized around the world. There is a well-defined set of transactions that are necessary to effect the importation and exportation of goods, their arrival and acceptance at the point of entry, and the domestic and international transportation. This is an area that is becoming increasingly electronic in nature as paper is being rapidly replaced by electronic transactions.

Government and Other Institutions

Government and institutional transactions are perhaps the most structured of all, whether internally between government departments and agencies or externally with the public. Doing business with these entities requires rigid adherence to the forms and procedures, and proper observance of sequence and protocol.

It is ironic that this very structure and form has in fact resulted in a form of BPE, as companies in both the private and public sector are forced to comply with government procedures and forms in order to conduct business. This has resulted in internal changes for these companies to enable them to cope more effectively with that mode of doing business. That does not imply any degree of efficiency. It simply implies the existence of a standard mode of business conduct that results in large-scale organizational and procedural change.

Unstructured Commerce

Unstructured commerce, by contrast, focuses more on the ad hoc exchange of information or requests for services. It is characterized by random demand from an ever-changing assortment of companies or individuals exchanging low volumes of unrelated transactions or requests on an intermittent or one-time basis, usually but not always involving supporting artifacts such as paper forms.

Unstructured commerce does not follow a particular business protocol, such as purchase order/acknowledgment/shipping notice/invoice, but is often driven by external events or unfolding situational conditions at the time of the transaction. One transaction can often lead to one or more others, in a decision-tree manner.

An example of unstructured commerce would be a hospital emergency room, where activity is initiated by an external event (that being the arrival of a patient). The doctor's diagnosis determines the materials, information, facilities, and services that are needed to treat the problem. This results in a generally unpredictable demand for medical supplies, hospital bed space, admissions information, insurance entitlement, medical history, laboratory and diagnostic testing, referrals, medical library resources, and other resources or materials that are not directly predictable from the initiating event (the arrival of the patient).

Another example is an on-line service such as CompuServe, where individuals can dial in, access retail price catalogs, select goods, and purchase them. The same individual can, in the same session, browse through other services, or can access information resources where the results of one transaction determine the criteria for the next. In this case, the demand is situational, being determined by the unfolding needs and desires of the individual, by the cost of the services, and by the time available.

Summary

Both structured and unstructured commerce lend themselves to "electronification" very easily. The greatest opportunities for overall Value System improvements exist within the structured model, as we will see in the following sections. Structured commerce, since it is the prevalent mode of business conduct and since it involves multiple companies executing complex processes, is where ICBE is best concentrated.

ICBE may also be applied to unstructured commercial models, but only indirectly, and through the exercise of broad influence. Since unstructured EC consists of a widely variable trading partner base exchanging random transactions, it is not possible to bring them into the kind of cooperative, interactive forum that the structured model offers. It is still desirable, however, to institute some level of standards and controls over the system. This is so that everyone is operating on more or less common ground and that the overall trading environment does not get out of control.

With unstructured EC, ICBE may be effectively applied only at the "macro" level. It can be led by a cooperative governing body such as the Internet Engineering Task Force (IETF), who defines standards for using the Internet, or by a major stakeholder/hub/service provider such as CompuServe, who is responsible for the overall operation of a commercial system or service. These are called the "owners" of the commercial system, and they set the rules and standards for its use.

The owners can use ICBE techniques to establish external "Best Practice" business standards and operating guidelines that, when followed, will tend to close the Response Gap between the participants. Adherence to these externally-oriented Best Practices will furthermore exert broad influence on each of the participants to adopt internal Best Practices to support them. This will thereby increase their internal efficiency of operation.

Examples include:
1. Payment at Point of Sale
2. Code of Practice
3. Transaction Protocol Structuring

Payment at Point of Sale

This involves the institution of procedures for connecting to the service or network that will automatically verify the credit position of the buyer (for purchase and sale of goods systems). It will set the expectation in the customer's mind that he will be direct-billed to a credit card for goods or services obtained during the session.

This will eliminate the entire cycle of purchase order, invoice and check-based payment, resulting in the timely delivery of value to the seller, closing the financial Response Gap. This requires the seller's internal systems to handle electronic orders and payments, and to communicate these transactions in a standard manner. This is the "broad influence" principle at work. It achieves alignment of business practice by modifying the behavior of the participants in a common manner at a Response Gap.

Code of Practice

This would require subscribers to conduct business according to a common "Code of Practice", (Wright 1994). It lays out the terms and conditions governing purchase and sale, and the requirements and regulations for exchanging other types of transactions.

This code of practice may be implemented in several ways:

1. as an automated part of the subscriber's initial sign-up to the service, such as with CompuServe;

2. as a separate unilateral written agreement that comes with the license to use the system, much like the software licensing agreements distributed in the box with off-the-shelf software;

3. or it may be displayed each time the user accesses the system, as a reminder of his obligations, like at the beginning of a Lotus or WordPerfect session. It may be stipulated at that time that proceeding to use the system constitutes agreement with these terms and conditions, and that the user is bound by the results.

This unifies the general approach of all parties, binds them to performance, and further inculcates these practices in companies or individuals where there was no standard before, or where the standard terms and conditions printed on their business forms were seldom adhered to in actual practice.

Transaction Protocol Structuring

This would require imposing a nominal structure on various groups of transactions (such as purchase and sale of goods) by prompting for the necessary information to complete a transaction and correcting erroneous entries as necessary, and by issuing other transactions such as a purchase order acknowledgment in response. By doing this, the information contained in the system as a whole is rendered into a semblance of order and standardization. The underlying business procedures at both ends of the transactions are at least partially brought into synchronization.

CHAPTER VI

BASIC ELECTRONIC BUSINESS MODELS

This chapter deals with the concept and practice of using pictorial business models to plan both the implementation of an electronic commerce environment, and the application of ICBE to the Value System involved in that environment. Pictorial business models are not a new concept. Some of the specific models used herein do not originate with this book. "Box-and-arrow" models are widely used in articles, presentations, courses and planning materials to depict the form and structure of electronic business communications. That tradition is continued here for ease of recognition (Shaw 1993).

A pictorial model is a useful and unambiguous tool for defining the mechanics of a given business process or set of processes, and forms the basis for clear understanding and informed process design between the parties involved. Properly designed and tested business models may be used as a set of high-level guidelines for EC implementation. They can serve to focus attention on problem areas in the Value Chain or identify Response Gaps in the Value System. For this reason, they are one of the primary tools used in ICBE.

The Electronic Commerce Toolset

Before beginning a discussion of the various business models that direct electronic commerce activities, it may be useful to provide an overview of the tools that are used in these activities. Briefly, these tools are:

1. Facsimile Transmission (FAX)
2. Electronic Mail (E-mail)
3. Electronic Data Interchange (EDI)
4. Global Directory Services (X.500)
5. Imaging Technology
6. Document Management Systems
7. Workflow Management Systems
8. Business Process Engineering (BPE)
9. EC Utility Applications

Facsimile Transmission (FAX)

Facsimile transmission, or FAX, is especially effective for sending low volumes of information such as flyers or price lists to a few recipients on a casual or time-critical basis but the trnsmission costs are prohibitive for wide distribution. Many of the newer software packages have the capability to send a single document to a preset distribution list, to send and receive faxes directly to and from computer files, and to perform basic character recognition on incoming faxes.

This is normally useful only for human-to-human communication, however, and then primarily to facilitate human decisions. It does not provide electronic data that is directly usable by computer applications without a significant degree of manipulation and a correspondingly high potential for error.

Electronic Mail (E-mail)

E-mail is also known more generically as interpersonal messaging, or IPM. This is also effective for human-to-human communication, and to a large extent, for some of the simpler application-to-application communication between different computer systems. Most E-mail packages on the market today have the capability to "attach" files that are readable by common PC utility programs such as word processing packages, graphics packages, and databases. The main text of the E-mail message may then be used to describe the contents and disposition of the attached file.

If the parties at both ends are using the same software package such as Microsoft Word (TM), Microsoft Powerpoint (TM), or Microsoft Works (TM) database, they can successfully communicate data to each other in machine-readable form. If not, then some kind of additional manipulation must be performed to render the data machine-readable by the recipient. This can then be brought directly into the application package at the other end for human viewing, or it can be manipulated by a PC-based utility program to provide input to a valid application, either on the PC or on another host computer.

This is useful once again for relatively low volumes of information, such as price list updates and promotion announcements. The major disadvantage of doing this for large volumes of information is the time required for transmission (even for compressed files). The cost to the consumer is usually much lower than for FAX. E-mail is a store-and-forward mechanism, and normally does not use direct-dial long distance lines. It employs local gateways or 1-800 numbers to the mail server. CompuServe, America Online, Prodigy, and the Internet are some examples of public E-mail services.

Another disadvantage is the degree of standardization and coordination necessary between the two parties in order to make this mechanism work smoothly for business documentation. For multiple parties the standardization is often difficult to achieve, since each party constructs his database with different conventions.

For example, the supplier has a different means of encoding items such as "case lots", or positions the part number in a different place than the recipient wants it to be. Without an objective set of standards, few parties will want to change their own systems. This will ultimately result in each party maintaining tables in their software that will convert between all versions of the standards, requiring extensive maintenance for everyone involved in the arrangement.

This is essentially the same problem that is faced when one company sends another company disks or tapes containing trade-specific information. Even if the two companies agree on standards for the software at each end of the link, and for the representation of information between them, it is a self-limiting proposition. It is valid only for that set of business partners, and does not permit universal automation. Others wishing to become part of such an arrangement must either cope with the de facto standard that have been set by the early adopters, or must enforce their own standard.

Electronic Data Interchange (EDI)

EDI is the major mechanism for moving large volumes of standardized business transactions between companies on a worldwide basis. As of this writing, there are in excess of 500 business documents with a defined EDI standard (DISA 1994), and over 50,000 companies in North America alone are using EDI to transact some portion of their daily business (Wood 1993).

EDI offers advantages in reliability and security for transferring high volumes of sensitive information. It provides a standard set of formats and conventions for the exchange of business documents between any number of companies. EDI is not self-limiting in the way that E-mail, FAX or imaging are. The basic standards are already defined and adopted by the majority of businesses. The other technologies require the re-invention and re-adoption of the standard between the initiator and each company involved in the business arrangement.

Global Directory Services (X.500)

It has been recommended by the X.500 Working Group that the X.500 Global Directory structure can be used for storing reference data about its users, such as their EC/EDI capabilities, their systems configuration, and other information including graphic images.

It has been suggested that such a facility could be useful for storing price catalogs for online access by other X.500 users, eliminating the necessity to send them to each party that wishes to view the catalog. Once again, the issue is standardization and utilization. However, a global facility such as the X.500 Directory is in a position to exercise strong leadership in this area.

Imaging Technology

Imaging technology is a useful tool in the exchange of graphical or pictorial information such as logos, diagrams, CAD drawings, technical specifications, medical images, video, and other non-textual information necessary to support a business function.

Imaging can be misused by those attracted to the technology for its own sake. It is generally inappropriate to use imaging technology to interpret business documents such as purchase orders, invoices, or other documents that have a high degree of variability at their source.

For example, if a company has three or four hundred customers sending in purchase orders, each on their own company-specific form, it is inadvisable to scan them in and try to interpret the data on them in order to avoid the exercise of manual data entry. The expense of the equipment and the overhead involved in maintaining all the different form configurations can be prohibitive and can inhibit the pursuit of a more elegant long-term solution.

Imaging technology is best employed where the document itself is the product, such as a photograph, a technical drawing or a medical image, not where the information contained in the document is the product, such as a purchase order or invoice. In the latter case, EDI is usually the more appropriate tool.

An exception to this rule may be found in the processing of individual income tax returns or other highly structured mass-distributed document. In general, the public is not equipped to submit its tax returns via electronic means, except through an agent such as H&R Block. In this case, image scanning and optical character recognition (OCR) technology has been used to great effect to lower the cost of processing the (usually handwritten) tax returns. In the world of corporate taxation, however, governments are actively encouraging or mandating the use of EDI to submit income tax and sales tax returns.

Document Management Systems

Document management systems can be successfully employed in the management of large volumes of documents such as in a tax records system or in a driver's license registration system. Various types of documents and images can be collated and stored under a number of different indexing arrangements. It allows access by any number of different search criteria, such as name, social security number, street, city, or even keywords within the documents themselves.

Document management systems permit the sequential processing of "files" or "dossiers". They can almost exactly simulate existing manual methods of processing these artifacts, including "sticky notes" or annotations such as signatures or voice-overs.

While these systems are useful in automating the status quo, they usually maintain the paper paradigm and enshrine the concept of sequential processing of a physical artifact over time. There are certainly situations where this is the best way of preserving the integrity of an operation such as in the processing of passports or citizenship papers. However, the industry in general is moving away form sequential handling of paper.

Workflow Management Systems

Workflow Management is, at present, an area that has not been widely exploited by software vendors. At the low end of the continuum, it can consist of a simple forms management and routing capability based around a word processing package such as Microsoft Word (TM) or WordPerfect (TM). At the high end, it can consist of advanced workgroup computing facilities such as shared documents, version control, electronic signatures, task lists, automated routing and timed responses, and other automated intelligence facilities designed to accelerate the flow of internal business operations.

While this can result in some short-term benefits for the company, there is also a trap in the assumption that the current workflow is indeed efficient, correct and worth the effort of automating.   In most cases, this assumption is not true.   Often, the workflow system has evolved over many years and many people. It sometimes reflects poor organization, inefficiency, and poor business practice.   These workflows should not be automated as is. Rather they should be re-engineered along current industry Best Practices prior to automating them.

While a properly implemented workflow system can be used to automate common or overlapping processes between companies and thus provide a low level of inter-corporate business engineering, it is still primarily an inward-directed, tactical approach rather than a strategic one. If improperly implemented, this can have the effect of locking the processes of the participating companies together in ways that may prove limiting in the future endeavors of all companies involved.

Business Process Engineering (BPE)

Rather than looking at BPE as a stand-alone discipline existing in isolation, BPE should be considered an integral part of the toolkit for shaping and customizing the technological components of electronic commerce systems. EC programs such as Document management, workflow management, EDI and others that are undertaken without a strong BPE influence are not as likely to achieve optimum benefit, since they target symptoms rather than causes.

The normal tendency is to focus on the existing paper-based processes and to try to automate or streamline them, in other words, to concentrate on the tasks instead of the processes. BPE questions the basic assumptions underlying the performance of the tasks. It attempts to redefine or re-invent the overall processes and the supporting work systems instead of casting the status quo in electronic concrete. There is another, more subtle trap.   When the above tendency is identified, the reaction is usually to swing to the other polar extreme and concentrate on the new technologies themselves, such as EDI, and to redesign existing processes to exploit the new technology.

As Dr. Walton (1994) observes, EDI is a task-oriented technology in that it focuses on replacing paper artifacts such as purchase orders and invoices (the tasks) rather than on streamlining or eliminating the processes (procurement and settlement) of which purchase orders and invoices are components.

This is an attractive trap, and easy to fall into. Upon examining the literature surrounding EDI and electronic commerce, it becomes apparent that there is a wide variety of "transaction sets" that are available and ready for use with minimal effort. The temptation is to pick one, such as purchase orders, customize it and proceed with an implementation in the belief that one is now conducting electronic commerce through the use of EDI. However, these transaction sets are in fact separate and discrete "tasks" in the business cycle that have been developed independently by majority need, without an overall cohesive strategy.

Therefore, concentrating on "getting purchase orders up on EDI" automatically orients the company to the task instead of the process. It reinforces the view that purchase orders are central to the conduct of business, when this may not be true at all. BPE challenges that concept and focuses on the core processes themselves with the intent to eliminate everything that does not add value such as adversarial or self-defensive documentation, purchase orders included.

EC Utility Applications

There are a number of computer systems tools that may be acquired or developed whose function it is to coordinate and support the technologies of EC. Among these are such facilities and utilities as:

A. System Agents
B. Mappers and Translators
C. Message Delivery Systems
D. Automatic Identification

System agents. A system agent is a software program that runs on the computer and manages the flow of transactions in and out of the applications. A system agent will not only route inbound and outbound transactions between the outside world and the computer applications, but will also route data communication between different applications residing on the computer itself. An example of a system agent would be an E-mail system that has programmatic "hooks" into the different applications on the computer, and knows the special operating characteristics of each. This system frames requests between applications and presents them in the proper format to each of the recipients. For example, it collects inbound EDI purchase orders and submits them to an overnight batch run of the order entry system.

Mappers and translators. The mapper/translator class of utility program sits between the system agent and the outside world. It is used to manage the EDI messaging environment and translate application data into EDI format for transmission, or to translate inbound EDI messages into data for input to the applications. The basic translator moves EDI transaction data to and from a specifically formatted file called a flat (fixed length ASCII text) file. It usually requires that there be some additional programming work to intercede between the flat file format and the "native" file formats of the applications involved.

The mapper class of utility is an extension of the translator functions, and provides the final bridge between the EDI translation function and each of the applications' data structures. The more feature-rich mappers provide a general-purpose mapping facility with the ability to map "any-to-any" even between applications residing on the same computer. It performs many of the functions of a system agent.

It is advisable for any company implementing EDI to install one of the many commercially-available translators or mappers. At the time of this writing, there were over 70 vendors of this software (EDI World 1994 EDI Software Directory). These are usually well-proven in the field with several thousand users. They provide functions and capabilities that the company's programmers would have to build on their system at a much higher cost.

Mappers can be useful for other aspects of EC, including mapping to and from E-mail or character-recognized fax messages using existing applications data files. This can significantly reduce programming time and cost. It can provide greater operational flexibility as the company migrates from older applications to newer ones. Some of the more sophisticated mappers are capable of mapping information between existing applications, whether or not those applications are in any way related to EDI. These tools are useful beyond the parameters of EC. They can assist in the actual integration of EDI data with the applications that use it or produce it.

Message delivery mechanisms. This class of utility is responsible for the end-to-end transport and control of messages. Properly implemented delivery mechanisms are essential to the success of EC systems. In the EC world, delivery mechanisms are usually regarded as public utilities in the sense that the telephone companies or the electric companies are (they are usually ignored, taken for granted or assumed to be in place). If the delivery mechanism is not designed into the EC environment at the beginning, control and/or continuity may be sacrificed in the ongoing operation of the EC system.

As an example, X.400/435 is the set of CCITT recommendations that specifies the architecture and communications protocols for the development of a worldwide store-and-forward messaging system. X.400 defines how varying types of related messages may be carried in the same transmission, such as E-mail, images, video, data files, and EDI messages. This creates a single control structure. All related messages destined for the same recipient are carried together, controlled in the same way, and delivered to the same destination at the same time.

This means that a buyer can send a technical drawing, an EDI-based request for quote, and an E-mail message describing both of them, all in the same transmission "envelope". This is delivered intact at the other end as a complete "package" instead of as a set of unrelated transmissions spread out over time. The recipient's workflow management system then takes over, coordinating the different types of messages and launching the applications necessary for the user to view and respond to them.

Another example is the use of the X.500 Global Directory to maintain a distributed database containing information about the population of EC trading partners, including their technological capabilities, system configurations, and other information up to and including price catalogs (O'Mahony and Weldon 1993). This can have the effect of reducing the network traffic flow by having a "centrally" available repository of information that any X.500-capable user can access. It can also facilitate the conduct of unstructured electronic commerce by reducing (but not eliminating) the need for complex agreements between parties and by publishing the parties' specific usage of each of the EDI transaction standards.

Information such as transactions supported, version, segment and data element usage details, and special field-level codification may be stored in a user's entry in the X.500 directory. It allows automated or semi-automated mapping between parties' different transactions sets without extensive negotiation and system set-up.

Automatic Identification. These technologies support EC by providing a standardized, machine-readable mechanism for identifying the physical items being transferred as a result of other EC activities such as purchase orders or invoices. They provide a means to relate the item to its initiating transaction and to track it through all stages of movement from source to destination. These technologies consist primarily of barcoding and radio frequency (RF) identification devices, and are used to supplement EC strategies such as "Quick Response," "Efficient Consumer Response," "Just-In-Time Manufacturing," and other "purchase and sale of goods" strategies.

An example of their use would be where an EDI purchase order results in a shipping order. The picking ticket is printed in the warehouse, along with the customer's bar code labels for the merchandise (contained in the EDI purchase order). The bar code labels are affixed to the case lots, and the pallets are affixed with "license plate" bar codes for tracking purposes.

At the shipping dock, the bar codes are scanned in and enter the system, updating the computer files. As they are loaded into the truck, the RF tag affixed to the truck is scanned. A manifest is generated for the driver, and a shipping notice is generated for the customer. Upon arrival at the customer's dock, the truck is scanned, the pallet is scanned, and, optionally, each case is scanned. This generates a reconciliation report for the AP department and an automated payment authorization to the bank.

There are many examples other than those described above. This discussion has outlined the more common tools and some of their applications in an EC environment. These will be discussed in more detail throughout the book as the various business models are explored in light of their relation to the principles and practices of ICBE.

THE BUSINESS MODELS

In this book, business models are used as multi-purpose planning tools:

1.   as a visual aid for helping the practitioner customize an EC strategy;
2.   as a road map for sequencing or grouping the EC functions
3.   and as a mechanism to identify Response Gaps in the EC environment, so that ICBE may be properly focused.

In this way the business model provides planning continuity and a built-in validity check on the application of ICBE. There are two basic types of models:

1. the outward-directed, "Macro" models at the inter-company level, that describe the business processes, hand-offs and relationships among Value System Members;

2. and the supporting inward-directed "Micro" models at the intra-company level, that describe the internal process flow and systems environment required to support the major business functions outlined in the macro models.

Macro Models

Macro models consist of two levels of detail:
1. "Level Zero"
2. "Level One"

Level One

Level One is the working level, and models the EC relationship between two companies. Level One is customized by mutual agreement and becomes the basis for electronic trading between those companies. In these models, implementation proceeds from the top down. The topmost step is the entry point into the process, building the foundations for the next steps.

Level Zero

The Level Zero model is simply the high-level design of the overall alue System. The summarization of all of the Level One diagrams for that System expanded to highlight the Linkages and the Response Gaps.

Level Zero can be used either as the initial design for a multi-company EC implementation, or it can be used to consolidate existing EC relationships into a strategic approach. In either case, it is the starting point (and focal point) for ICBE. In this book, the Level Zero Model is also referred to as the "Big Board", since it is used as a conference-room tool for ICBE planning sessions.

Level Zero Models tend to be highly specific to the Value System under consideration and the particular conditions of commerce. Only the broadest examples will be presented here for illustration purposes. The real definition is put to them in actual ICBE situations, where an "Alpha Team" consisting of the Members' executive and operations staff uses the model to design the logic and mechanics of the Inter-Corporate Business Processes from the ground up.

The intent of the Level Zero is, as stated earlier, to serve as a diagrammatic summary of the entire Value System, highlighting all of the Linkages and their Response Gaps, and the relationships between the Members. These relationships may be stated in any way that is convenient to the parties and relevant to the exercise. They may include diagrams depicting the flow of information or documents between companies, and/or the timings and the dependencies of operation across the Value Chain.

The next three illustrations depict various samples and techniques for representing a Level Zero business model. They use mythical companies and hypothetical information flows and relationships. These are for purposes of illustration only, and should not be considered to represent actual situations or relationships that may exist in the real world.

Figure 5 represents generic information flows between Members in a hypothetical health care Value System. These generic flows are then reduced to a lower level of detail through appropriate analysis techniques. **Figure 6** represents an attempt to "map" these detailed information flows to an EDI transaction environment. **Figure 7** represents a hypothetical chain of dependencies between Member organizations in a sample Value System.

Computer systems people may find similarities between these Business Models and Data Flow Diagrams (DFD's) that are commonly used in Systems Analysis work. That is a valid observation, since we are analyzing a large, multi-corporate system. The relationships involve the flow of information between corporate entities. The detailed DFD's will come into play as we progress further into the details of Levels Two, Three and Four, where actual data modeling will be done.

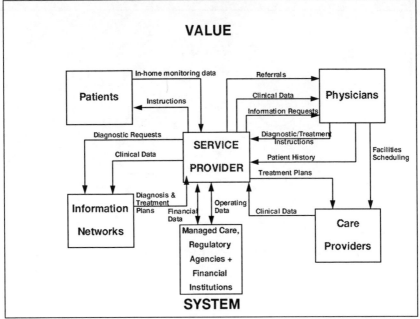

Fig. 5. Level Zero information flows in a hypothetical Value System

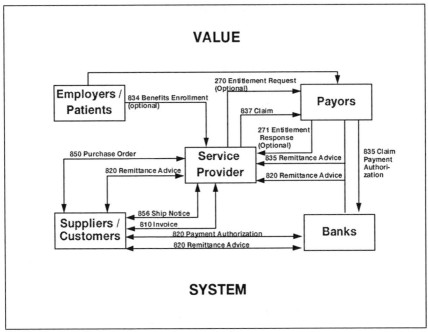

Fig. 6. Level Zero EDI-related information flows

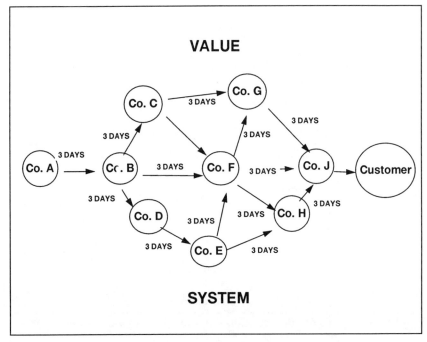

Fig. 7. Level Zero inter-corporate time dependencies

Level One

Unlike Level Zero Models, the Level One models are more traditional in that they represent standard business processes that everyone follows in much the same way. The following Business Model diagrams are intended as examples only. It is the task of the practitioners to customize these models according to the needs of the particular business process being implemented. The models cover the basic "Value Chain" elements including those situations involving the disciplines of procurement, order management, logistics management and settlement/finance.

In addition to providing a tool for design of business processes, the Level One model also provides a tool for the analysis of existing processes. During an ICBE exercise, the Level One model is used to document the existing inter-corporate business processes. It provides a worksheet for understanding the times and dependencies of activity between the companies. Then it depicts "Best Practices" against which the existing processes are mapped and improved.

In summary, Level One diagrams are used to visually describe existing processes, planned processes, and the migration path to be taken to achieve the "Best Practices" model. They provide easy-to-understand reference points for strategic planning and worksheets for tactical planning. Examples will be shown in later chapters.

Business Model 1: Electronic Procurement

Figure 8 below is a generic business model that depicts the transaction flows in a procurement situation.

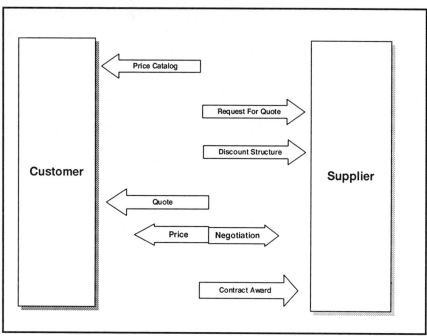

Fig. 8. Electronic Procurement Business Model

In the procurement business model, there are six main functions that may be automated or augmented through electronic means. These are:

1. Price Catalogs
2. X.500 Global Directory
3. Request for Quote
4. Discount Structure
5. Price Negotiations
6. Quotation
7. Contract Award

Price Catalogs

The first step in the procurement process is to get the price catalog, promotion announcements, and other advertising material into the hands of the customers in a timely manner. This may be done on a scheduled distribution basis or on demand for specific items by the customer. Traditionally, this has been accomplished by sending a standard hard-copy catalog, promotion flyers or a price list, often including color photographs or technical specifications. Electronically, this could be distributed through means such as:

>A. FAX and/or E-Mail
>
>B. EDI

Fax and/or E-mail Selected customers could be sent periodic fax or E-mail messages outlining new promotions or price changes. E-mail messages may also be used to provide information about accompanying EDI transactions. Images may be "attached" to the E-mail message as well.

EDI The issue of format standardization can be addressed through using EDI to automate the exchange of price catalog information between applications. This normally consists of data that is used by the application, not human-readable information for buying decisions. In addition, it is usually used for specific products only, as opposed to an entire catalog.

EDI may also be used to automate the exchange of promotional announcements and price changes, if the parties have an agreement in place to accept this medium for such exchange. Once again, the data content is standardized to the extent that the information is laid out in a certain sequence and placement within the EDI message. The problem is still one of standardization of coding and utilization of the data fields.

Before continuing, it would be useful to provide a short discussion of EDI for the benefit of those readers who are unfamiliar with it. EDI has been around in one form or another for more than twenty-five years. It began in the 1960's with the transportation industry, who was seeking to streamline paperwork and cut costs by standardizing key transportation documents and exchanging them electronically. Waybills, manifests and schedules could now arrive at the destination before the carrier. They could be processed while the goods were still in transit. Costs came down, and a high level of information standardization resulted. This was the beginning of formal Electronic Data Interchange, otherwise known as EDI.

In 1978, the American National Standards Institute (ANSI) examined the progress of the transportation industry. It created an Accredited Standards Committee (ASC) called X12 to look at expanding industry-specific standards to accommodate the general needs of North American commerce ("X" denotes computer standards, and "12" is the sequence number of the committee). X12 was chartered to be the North American body responsible for the development and approval of standards for EDI, and remains so to this day. It has to date approved, or has in the approval process, well over 200 separate business transactions, mostly centered around US domestic commerce.

At the same time, EDI standards also began to emerge in Europe. In 1986, the UN authorized Working Party 4 to be responsible for the development of EDI standards. Out of this was born the EDIFACT standard (EDI For Administration, Commerce and Transport), which has now evolved from a strictly European focus into a global standard for EDI. To date, there are almost 200 EDIFACT transactions, mostly centered around international transport, customs and trade.

It is widely stated in the computing industry that more than 70% of data that is input to computer applications comes from another computer. This data, already in electronic form at the source, is converted to paper, sent by manual means, and re-converted at the other end into electronic form by re-keying or scanning. EDI provides a reliable mechanism for keeping the data in machine-readable form, communicating it quickly, and standardizing its presentation between dissimilar applications residing on dissimilar technology platforms.

EDI should not be confused with file transfers. It deals with individually traceable transactions, each encoded in a publicly accepted format, not a collection of records in a file. Transferring sets of files among multiple companies with different file management systems is a difficult and labor-intensive exercise. It becomes more complex each time a new "trading partner" is added.

EDI provides a common bridge, enabling any company to communicate business information with any other company by simply adopting the public standard and installing a relatively inexpensive EDI translator software package. A translator provides a drop-in "front end" to the applications by encapsulating application-generated flat-file data into an EDI-compliant transaction. It manages its transmission to the proper trading partner. The Translator also receives inbound EDI transactions and converts them to a flat-file format for input to the application. This effectively insulates the applications and makes it possible (but not necessarily advisable) to install EDI without making any changes whatever to the applications.

These packages can range anywhere from $500 to $3,500 for a PC, $10,000 to $40,000 for a Unix platform, and around $75,000 to $100,000 and up for a mainframe. It is not necessary for all trading partners to use the same translator. The standards tables are what determine the way in which the data is encapsulated and decapsulated. These standards tables are identical from one translator to another.

The EDI messages that are relevant to the procurement process are described in **Table 2** on page 48. For this and all other EDI tables in this paper, both X12 transactions and EDIFACT messages have been given, along with the transaction number for X12 and the six-character message identifier for EDIFACT.

Table 2
Procurement EDI Transactions

X12		EDIFACT	
832	Price/Sales Catalog	PRICAT	Price/Sales Catalog
879	Price Change	PRODEX	Product Exchange
888	Item Maintenance		
889	Promotion Announcement		
893	Item Information Request		

Sources: Data Interchange Standards Association, X12 Standards List,
EDIFACT Standards List, (EDI Council of Canada 1994)

X.500 global directory.

The X.500 Global Directory, once in place and operating, can serve as a repository for price catalogs and associated information. Access to this information can be public or restricted, depending on the sensitivity assigned by the owner. When updated by the owner, the new information is "replicated" across the distributed database network, keeping all copies current.

Request for quote (RFQ)

The RFQ is normally distributed to qualified suppliers electronically via Fax, E-Mail with attached images (drawings, etc.) or EDI. The specific EDI transactions are described in **Table 3** below.

TABLE 3: RFQ EDI TRANSACTIONS			
X12		**EDIFACT**	
840	Request for Quote	REQUOTE	Request for quote
841	Technical Specifications	CONDRA	Drawing Administration
871	Component Parts Content	CONDRO	Drawing Organization
896	Product Dimension Maintenance	CONITT	Invitation to Tender
243	Request for Product Source Information		
244	Product Source Information		
502	Solicitation Mailing List		

Sources: Data Interchange Standards Association, X12 Standards List,
EDIFACT Standards List, (EDI Council of Canada 1994)

In US government procurement, it is customary to post certain RFQ's on one or more of the public electronic bulletin boards maintained for that purpose.

Discount structure

"Discount structures" detail how a chain store's various outlets participate in discounts from the supplier, as well as specifying volume price breaks. This can be accomplished through the use of fax, E-mail, or EDI. The specific EDI transactions involved are described in **Table 4** below.

Table 4
Discount Structure EDI Transactions

X12		EDIFACT	
816	Organizational Relationships	INFENT	Enterprise Information
882	Direct Store Delivery Summary		
885	Store Characteristics		
155	Credit Report		
251	Pricing Support		
503	Pricing History		

Sources: Data Interchange Standards Association, X12 Standards List, EDIFACT Standards List, (EDI Council of Canada 1994)

Quotation

The quotation process may be handled electronically via FAX, E-mail, or EDI. The specific EDI transactions are the X12 "843 Quotation" or the EDIFACT "QUOTES."

Price negotiation

Negotiations regarding prices and terms/conditions may also be accomplished through fax, E-mail, or EDI transactions. This is an iterative process, and can involve several items of correspondence before agreement is reached. Sometimes, the EDI Discount Structure messages form part of the negotiation process. The EDI messages involved in negotiation are the X12 "845 Price Authorization" and the EDIFACT "PRICE" and "AUTHOR" messages.

Contract award.

The contract award may be made via FAX, E-mail, or EDI, setting out the contract number, the contract abstract, the goods and services to be contracted for, specific terms and conditions, the award notification itself, and other pertinent information such as additional clauses and provisions, contract pricing, and support requirements for the contract. In the government awards process, this can also be posted on a public electronic bulletin board much like the RFQ. The currently available EDI transactions are described in **Table 5** below.

Table 5
Contracting EDI Transactions

	X12	**EDIFACT**	
836	Contract Award	CONEST	Establishment of
504	Contract Clauses and Provisions		Contract
505	Procurement Support		
506	Procurement Notice		
805	Contract Pricing Proposal		
561	Contract Abstract		

**Sources: Data Interchange Standards Association, <u>X12 Standards List</u>,
<u>EDIFACT Standards List</u>, (EDI Council of Canada 1994)**

Business Model 2: Order Management

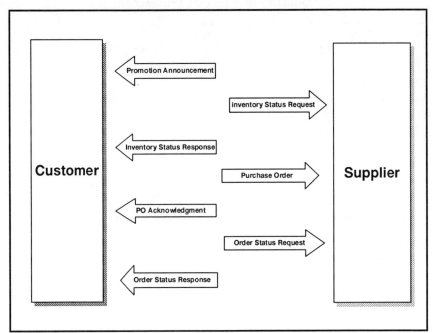

Fig. 9. Order Management Business Model

Order management consists not only of the day-to-day transactions that facilitate the purchase and sale of goods, but also those transactions that communicate sales and inventory information between the seller and the buyer, as well as those transactions that communicate the status of the order in the supplier's manufacturing process. They are:

1. Promotion Announcement
2. Inventory Status Request
3. Inventory Status Response
4. Purchase Order
5. Purchase Order Acknowledgment
6. Order Status Request/ Response

Promotion announcement

This is a periodic message sent out to the buyers at need. It can be via fax, E-mail, or EDI with accompanying images such as coupons, bar coded sticker information, images and other advertising material for the merchant's local market. The EDI messages are described in **Table 6** on the next page..

Table 6
Product/Promotion EDI Transactions

	X12	EDIFACT	
878	Product Authorization	PRICAT	Price Catalog
879	Price Change		
889	Promotion Announcement		
887	Coupon Notification		
888	Item Maintenance		
893	Item Information Request		

Sources: Data Interchange Standards Association, X12 Standards List, EDIFACT Standards List, (EDI Council of Canada 1994)

Inventory status request

The buyer sends a message inquiring into the availability and delivery dates for the product in question. The EDI transactions are described in **Table 7** following.

Table 7
Inventory Inquiry EDI Transactions

	X12	EDIFACT	
846	Inventory Inquiry/Advice	CONWQD	Work Item Quantity
893	Item Information Request	DELFDR	Delivery Schedule
830	Planning Schedule With Release	IFTSAI	Schedule & Availability

Sources: Data Interchange Standards Association, X12 Standards List, EDIFACT Standards List, (EDI Council of Canada 1994)

Inventory status response

The supplier responds back with the availability and projected delivery schedules for the inventory items requested. The EDI messages are described in **Table 8** on the next page.

Table 8
Inventory Status EDI Transactions

	X12	EDIFACT	
846	Inventory Inquiry/Advice	CONWQD	Work Item Quantity
		DELFDR	Delivery Schedule
		IFTSAI	Schedule & Availability
		INVRPT	Inventory Report

Sources: Data Interchange Standards Association, <u>X12 Standards List</u>,
<u>EDIFACT Standards List</u>, (EDI Council of Canada 1994)

Purchase order

The buyer places an order electronically via fax, E-mail or EDI. The order can be explicit, for a stated number of items at a stated price, or it can be an indirect order based on a predetermined sales forecast. It can be actual sales data at the point of sale, or usage data at the point of consumption.

In the latter case, there is usually a strategic arrangement between the buyer and seller that forecast. Actual usage information will serve as a signal for the automatic replenishment, such as in a Quick Response partnership, Efficient Consumer Response partnership, or a Vendor Managed Inventory relationship. The EDI transactions are described in **Table 9** below.

Table 9
Purchase and Sale of Goods EDI Transactions

	X12	EDIFACT	
850	Purchase Order	ORDERS	Purchase Order
830	Planning Schedule With Release	SLSFCT	Sales Forecast
875	Grocery PO	SLSRPT	Sales Data Report
867	Product Transfer and Resale		
852	Product Activity Data		

Sources: Data Interchange Standards Association, <u>X12 Standards List</u>,
<u>EDIFACT Standards List</u>, (EDI Council of Canada, 1994)

Purchase order acknowledgment/change

The supplier may optionally acknowledge the purchase order, thereby formalizing the offer/acceptance protocols necessary for contract formation. At this stage, the buyer and seller may also make iterative adjustments to the purchase order based on changes in need and availability of the product or service. As with all other messages, this may be accomplished through either fax, E-mail or EDI. The transactions are described in **Table 10** below.

Table 10
Purchase Order Change/Acknowledgment EDI Transactions

	X12		EDIFACT
855	PO Acknowledgment	ORDRSP	PO Response
860	Buyer's PO Change	ORDCHG	PO Change
866	Seller's PO Change		
876	Grocery PO Change		

Sources: Data Interchange Standards Association, <u>X12 Standards List</u>, <u>EDIFACT Standards List</u>, (EDI Council of Canada 1994)

Order status request/response

The buyer may make periodic status requests regarding his order, using the normal EC mechanisms above. The supplier responds with the information using a "mirror" version of the same transaction. The EDI messages are the X12 869 "order status inquiry" from the buyer and the 870 "order status report" from the supplier. There is no specific EDIFACT message for these functions, but many companies may use a version of the "ORDERS" message to accomplish the same effect.

Business Model 3: Logistics Management

Once the order has been produced and is on the supplier's dock waiting to be shipped, the process of logistics management comes into play to move the product between the supplier and the buyer via the most economical and fastest route. **Figure 10,** on the next page, illustrates a simple model involving only three participants: the customer, the supplier, and the carrier. Actual situations may involve several carriers, but the logic is the same.

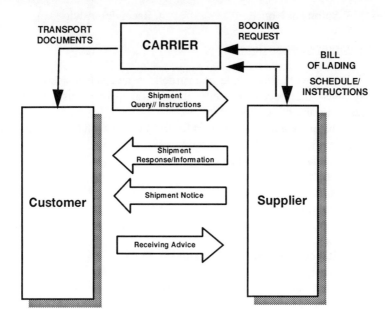

Fig. 10. Logistics Management Business Model

Logistics Management involves those activities necessary to transport and track the items moving between buyer and seller. The EDI industry began in this area, as transport companies began to standardize and automate their shipping documentation as early as 1968.

The Transportation Data Coordinating Committee (TDCC) became the EDI Association of America (EDIA), and was responsible for developing the majority of the early EDI standards. To date, there are more than 100 X12 messages specific to U.S. national transportation and logistics, and more than 75 EDIFACT messages specific to international movement of goods (DISA 1994). These EDI messages cover all aspects of air, rail, surface and ocean transport, as well as hazardous materials, customs and excise, booking , stowage, and container disposition.

In a domestic environment, where ICBE is most likely to be applied, there are four main functions to be performed between the buyer and seller. These are:

    1. Shipment Query/Instructions   2. Shipment Response/Information

   3. Shipment Notice   4. Receiving Advice

Shipment query/instructions

   These are the multitude of instructions and status queries that pass between buyer, transporter and seller during transit of goods. They include messages and transactions involving:

   1. bayplan and stowage plans for trucks, trains, and ocean vessels;
   2. returned goods notification;
   3. damage and loss claims;
   4. shipment tracers;
   5. special handling orders;
   6. returned merchandise notifications;
   7. container and truck assignments and reassignments;
   8. delivery and pick-up orders;
   9. direct store delivery summaries;
   10. route guides;
   11. and container packing and disposition information, among others.
They are described in **Table 11** following.

Table 11
Shipment Query/Instructions EDI Transactions

X12		EDIFACT	
853	Routing & Carrier Instruction	COEDOR	Container Disposition
882	Direct Store Delivery Summary		Order
920	Loss or Damage Claim	COMAOR	Container Special
925	Claim Tracer		Handling Order
926	Claim Status & Tracer Reply	COPINF	Container Pick-up
180	Returned Merchandise		Information
	Notification	COSTOR	Container Stuffing
213	Motor Carrier Shipment Status		Order
	Inquiry	IFTMIN	Instruction Message
217	Motor Carrier Loading and	GENRAL	General Instructions
	Route Guide		
304	Shipping Instruction		
317	Delivery/Pickup Order		
527	Material Due-In		
536	Logistics Reassignment		
869	Order Status Inquiry		

  Sources: Data Interchange Standards Association, <u>X12 Standards List</u>,
    <u>EDIFACT Standards List</u>, (EDI Council of Canada 1994)

Shipment response/information

This consists of information supporting the movement of goods and the securing of transport services, including:
1. responses to the above queries;
2. information about shipments;
3. scheduling and booking information and confirmations;
4. instructions between buyer, transporter and seller and between transporters relating to the routing and handling of goods;
5. tracking information;
6. load information;
7. and rate information.

These differ from the instruction and special handling transactions and messages identified above in that they are more related to the core "paperwork" business of the transportation industry. They deal with the documentation aspects of freight booking, waybills, manifests, insurance, cargo and rate information. They are described in **Table 12** on pages 58 and 59.

Shipment notice

These are the messages concerning the actual shipment as it travels between seller, transport provider and buyer. These messages are primarily intended to:
1. assist the buyer and seller in tracking the order or orders contained in the shipment; 2. to aid the buyer in reconciling the quantities ordered vs. shipped vs. received;   3. to provide input to in-transit and terminal dock scheduling operations;   4. and to provide a basis for invoicing. Some of these messages serve more than one purpose, and are therefore listed under different functions. These messages usually are traded between transport providers via EDI, but can be sent to buyers and sellers via fax or E-mail if necessary. They are described in **Table 13** on page 59..

Receiving advice

These messages are sent from the buyer to the seller to confirm the arrival, receipt, and receipt status of an order or orders, including acceptance certification, non conforming or damaged goods, returns, claims, and other disputes involving delivery.

In EC strategies such as Evaluated Receipts Settlement (ERS), the receiving advice serves to entirely eliminate the invoicing process by automatically triggering payment (manual or electronic) for the goods received, according to the specific agreement that has been negotiated with the supplier. They are described in **Table 14** on page 60.

Table 12
Shipment Response/Information EDI Transactions

	X12		EDIFACT	
846	Inventory Advice	COACOR	Cont. Acceptance Order	
104	Air Shipment Information			
125	Railcar Load Details	COEDOR	Cont. Disposition	
128	Dealer Information	COHAOR	Cont. Special Handling	
129	Vehicle Carrier Rate Update		Order	
161	Train Sheet	COITOR	Inland Transp. Order	
180	Return Merchandise Notification	COPINF	Cont. Pickup Info.	
204	Motor Carrier Shipment Info	COREOR	Cont. Release Order	
214	Transport Carrier Shipment Status	COSTOR	Cont. Stuffing Order	
218	Motor Carrier Tariff Info	DELFOR	Delivery Schedule	
319	Terminal Information	DELJIT	JIT Delivery Schedule	
362	Cargo Insurance Shipment Advice	GATEAC	Gate & Intermodal Ramp Activities	
400	Shipper's Railcar Order			
404	Rail Carrier Shipment Info	HANMOV	Cargo Handling	
414	Rail Carhire Settlements	IFTCCA	Fwd'ing/Transp.Shipm	
417	Rail Carrier Waybill Interchange		ent Charge Calculation	
418	Rail Advance Interchange			
419	Advance Car Disposition	IFTMBC	Booking Confirmation	
420	Car Handling Information	IFTMBG	Firm Booking	
422	ETA & Car Scheduling	IFTMBP	Provisional Booking	
423	Rail Industrial Switch List	IFTRIN	Rate Information	
425	Rail Waybill Request	IFTWAI	Schedule & Availability	
426	Rail Revenue Waybill			
427	Rail Waybill Response	IFTSTA	Int'l Multimodal Status	
431	Rail Station Master File			
433	Railroad Reciprocal Switch File	IFTSTQ	Int'l Multimodal Status Request	
435	Commodity Code Master			
440	Shipment Weights	ITRGRP	In Transit Groupage	
451	Railroad Event Report			
452	Railroad Problem Log Inquiry/ Advice			
453	Service Commitment Advice			
455	Railroad Parameter Trace Registration			
466	Rail Rate Inquiry			

X12		EDIFACT
490	Rate Group Definition	
492	Miscellaneous Rates	
494	Scale Rate Table	
622	Intermodal Ramp Activity	
940	Warehouse Shipping Order	
943	Warehouse Stock Transfer Shipment Advice	
944	Warehouse Stock Transfer Receipt Advice	
945	Warehouse Shipping Advice	
412	Trailer/Container Repair Billing	

Sources: Data Interchange Standards Association, <u>X12 Standards List,</u> <u>EDIFACT Standards List,</u> (EDI Council of Canada 1994)

Table 13
Shipment Notice EDI Transactions

X12			EDIFACT
180	Return Merchandise Notification	BAPLIE	Bayplan/Stowage
204	Motor Carrier Shipment Info	CODECO	Container Departure
210	Motor Freight Details & Invoice	COLADV	Documentary Collection
325	Consolidation of Goods in Container	COPARN	Cont. Pre-Arrival Notice
326	Consignment Summary List	COPINO	Container Pickup Notice
410	Rail Freight Details & Invoice	COPRDP	Container Predeparture
536	Logistics Reassignment	COPINO	Container Pickup Notice
848	Material Safety Data Sheeet	COSHLA	Short-Landed Advice
856	Advance Ship Notice/Manifest	DESADV	Dispatch Advice
857	Billing & Shipment Notice	IFTDGN	Dangerous Goods Advice
859	Freight Invoice	IFTIAC	Dangerous Cargo List
		QUALTY	Quality Data
		SAFHAZ	Safety Hazard Data Sheet

Sources: Data Interchange Standards Association, <u>X12 Standards List,</u> <u>EDIFACT Standards List,</u> (EDI Council of Canada 1994)

Table 14
Receiving and Adjustment EDI Transactions

EDI		EDIFACT	
180	Return Merchandise Notification	COARCE	Container Arrival Confirmation
362	Cargo Insurance Shipment Advice	COMDIS	Commercial Dispute
527	Material Due-In & Receipt	CONQVA	Quantity Valuation
842	Nonconformance Report	COREOR	Container Release Order
847	Material Claim	ICNOMO	Insurance Claim
854	Delivery Discrepancy Info	IFTMAN	Arrival Notice
861	Receiving Advice/Acceptance Certificate	QALITY	Quality Data
863	Report of Test Results	RECADV	Receiving Advice
867	Product Transfer/Resale Report		
894/5	Delivery/Return		
920/4	Loss or Damage Claim		
925/6	Claim Tracer/Status Response		

**Sources: Data Interchange Standards Association, X12 Standards List,
EDIFACT Standards List, (EDI Council of Canada 1994)**

Business Model 4: Electronic Settlement

Once the goods or services have been delivered and accepted, settlement must occur. Traditionally, this was accomplished with paper invoices, credits, adjustments for returned goods, and payment via paper checks.

The electronic model operates in much the same way, except for the time delays involved in the movement of paper. Removal of this time delay has caused concern on the part of financial managers who fear the loss of the "float" if payments are made electronically, causing some companies to be reluctant to implement electronic settlements. They want to invoice electronically, but they don't want to pay quickly. **Figure 11** on the next page shows a simple scenario for electronic settlement.

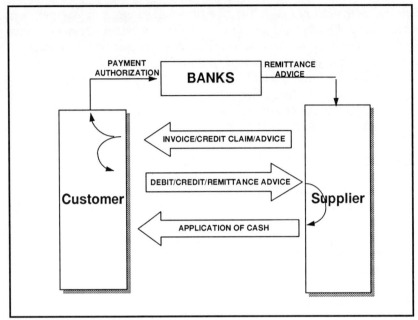

Fig. 11. Electronic Settlement Business Model

The loss of the "float" is largely illusory, and is ceasing to be a concern as managers become more informed in electronic commerce. In many cases, the cost of maintaining the float either negates or exceeds the value derived from it, particularly in times of declining or stable interest rates and escalating labor rates.

The impression in the minds of financial managers is that electronic settlement is "immediate". Therefore, it places a drain on cash reserves. This is a false impression. Electronic settlement can be made "float neutral" in that payment can be scheduled by mutual agreement to take place in 3 days, 10 days, or whenever convention dictates, just as if the mail had been used. This maintains the relative positions of both parties to the transaction, but does not offer the advantage to either.

The savings comes into play as the cost of cutting and reconciling manual checks is reduced or eliminated, and cash requirements can be planned with greater accuracy. Payments are "cashed" exactly on the due date, making the task of reconciling easier, and reducing the need to incur short term debt. As an incentive, many suppliers offer additional discounts for immediate electronic payment, thereby saving time effort and cost at both ends and creating a win-win situation.

In financial EC, the actual transfer of value between bank accounts is considered to be a separate issue, and it remains the exclusive province of the banks. In practice, the operative EC transactions are those that demand or authorize the transfer of value. They create debit and credit transactions, and instruct financial institutions to take action. They provide notification of such action, and verify the application of cash receipts and/or error conditions to specific items. The general areas are as follows:

1. Invoice/Credit Claim/Advice
2. Debit/Credit/Remittance Advice
3. Application of Cash
4. Miscellaneous Information

Invoice/credit claim/advice

Invoices, statements, claims, or demands for payment are submitted, modified by credits between the parties. Depending on the agreement between the parties, invoices may be eliminated in favor of "Evaluated Receipts Settlement" (ERS) or "Paid On Production" (POP) arrangements. Payment is remitted automatically either on receipt of goods or on production of the end product of which the material is a part.

Debit/credit/remittance advice

These transactions include:

A. credit payment (buyer-initiated, where the buyer instructs the bank to transfer funds to the account of the seller),
B. debit payment (seller-initiated, where the seller instructs the bank to transfer funds from the account of the buyer)
C. and remittance advice, where the parties notify each other that a payment has been made.

Application of cash

This is a transaction passing from the seller to the buyer indicating the invoice items that the payment has been applied to. The specific EDI transaction that is used for this purpose (X12 824 "Application Advice") is also used to send back specific information related to error conditions or improper submissions electronically so that corrections can be made and "pegged" to the original submission.

Miscellaneous information

These are the "indirect" transactions that establish conditions for payment or merchandise credit, such as notification of a retail sale or transfer/resale of a product on consignment.

These indirect transactions can provide a trigger for payment, rather than result directly in a payment. Other miscellaneous transactions include peripheral charges such as freight invoices for special delivery that may or may not be included in a retail agreement. The EDI transactions that deal with the entire spectrum of financial and settlement activities are described in **Table 15** below.

Table 15
Financial EDI Transactions

	X12		EDIFACT
170	Revenue Receipts Statement	BANSTA	Banking Status
180	Return Merchandise Notification	BOPBNK	Bank Transactions
410	Rail Freight Invoice	BOPINF	Bal. of Payment
810	Invoice		From Customer
811	Consolidated Service Invoice	CONPVA	Payment Valuation
812	Debit/Credit Adjustment	CREADV	Credit Advice
820	Payment Order/Remittance Advice	CREEXT	Extended Credit Adv
823	Lockbox	CREMUL	Multiple Credit Adv
824	Application Advice	CURRAC	Current Account
826	Tax Information Reporting	DEBADV	Debit Advice
828	Debit Authorization	DEBMUL	Multiple Debit Adv
829	Payment Cancellation Request	DIRDEB	Direct Debit
844	Product Transfer Account		
	Adjustment	DOCADV	Documentary Credit
857	Shipment and Billing Notice	DOC***	Other Documentary
859	Freight Invoice		Credit transactions
880	Grocery Products Invoice	FINCAN	Financial Cancell'n
887	Coupon Notification	INVOIC	Invoice
895	Delivery/Return Adjustment	PAYORD	Payment Authoriz'n
852	Product Activity Data	PAYEXT	Extended Payment
		PAYMUL	Multiple Payment

Sources: Data Interchange Standards Association, <u>X12 Standards List</u>,
<u>EDIFACT Standards List</u>, (EDI Council of Canada 1994)

Micro Models

Micro models are the inward-directed models for conducting electronic commerce within the company. They are intended to address the internal process and applications environment once the Macro model is established. The Micro models give company-specific operating definition to a Macro model by utilizing a combination of manual procedures and supporting technologies such as:
1. FAX,
2. E-mail,
3. imaging,
4. bar coding,
5. document management,
6. workflow management,
7. computer applications
8. and EDI

All are systems working in concert to support the particular version of the Macro model being implemented. Micro models are the next step in the ICBE process. They provide the direction for classical BPE disciplines in the same way that the Macro models provide the direction for ICBE.

Micro models, while they represent the company-specific implementation of the Macro model, should not be developed in isolation. Rather they should be engineered in conjunction with the other Members as an integral part of the overall Value System. Different Members, while they may do things differently internally, can nevertheless benefit from the synergy of designing their reciprocal processes together to mesh efficiently.

Like the Macro model, the Micro model consists of a series of levels, beginning with Level Two. Level Two depicts the process and system flow from the perspective of the company's entire Value Chain. It highlights the points of external Value System interface and the hand-offs. Level Three depicts the process and system flow for each of the elements of the Value Chain, such as procurement and order management.

Once these have been defined, the detailed technology plan may be put in place to support the model. This is a very detailed and complex exercise, and beyond the scope of this book. The Micro models are presented here as tools for the development of guidelines, not as definitive answers to technological problems, or as suggested technical architectures.

The following example, in **Figure 12**, illustrates the concept of a Level Two Micro model. It is not intended to be generically accurate, merely to show the type of visual representation that may be useful in analyzing the high-level activities of the core processes within a company's Value Chain.

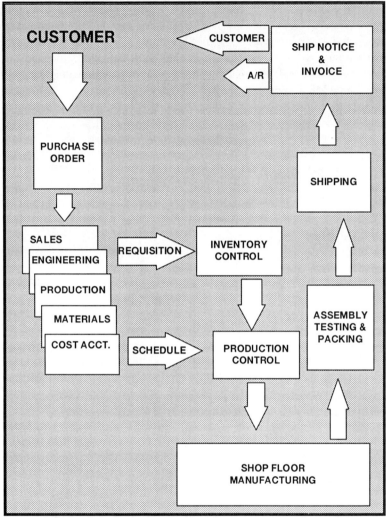

Fig. 12. Level Two Process Model for Order Management

This model illustrates a mythical company's order management process. It is initiated by an incoming purchase order, which is routed to various internal departments for approval, scheduling and pricing. A material requisition is cut for the inventory control department, and a production schedule is created for the manufacturing and assembly of the product. The product is made, assembled, tested, packed and shipped. An Invoice is cut with a copy to the accounts receivable department and a copy to the customer.

This is nothing more or less than a high-level documentation of the process, which may be of value by itself if it has not been produced before.

Each of the elements of the model, such as Engineering or Inventory Management, may be broken down into a Level Three model, detailing the flow of processes and information through that function. There may be a further breakdown into a Level Four, which details the specific manual procedures or computer systems involved. As an example, we will use the Inventory function for a Level Three Micro model, as shown in **Figure 13** below:

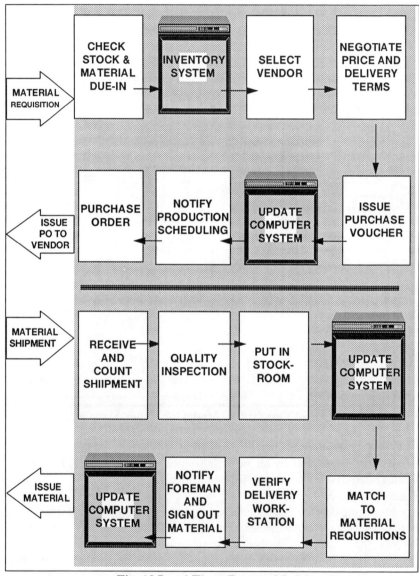

Fig. 13 Level Three Process Model

Each box on this model can break down further into a Level Four model, giving a high degree of detailed insight into the procedures and systems involved.

CHAPTER VII

TRADITIONAL APPROACHES TO ELECTRONIC COMMERCE

EDI has provided both a forum and a physical mechanism for industries to standardize the content of the information that flows between them, and the method of transferring that information. The structure of EDI offers a measure of security and control not afforded by paper. The value-added services that have grown around EDI, such as EDI value added networks (VAN's), offer even greater levels of security, integrity and continuity.

This makes EDI a highly desirable mechanism for relieving the burden of paperwork that is responsible for slowing down the processes of doing business between companies. Now that critical mass has been reached and there is a body of experience surrounding the use of EDI in daily commerce, more and more companies are adopting it as a new way of doing business. Some companies, are using electronic commerce in a truly strategic manner. However, the vast majority of implementations in North America have been of a tactical nature. These will be discussed in this chapter.

As electronic commerce and EDI are still in their infancy, and the adversarial mode of commerce still prevails, there has arisen a general inward-directed, corporate-self bias toward implementing it. EDI tends to be thought of as a solution rather than a tool. It is used primarily for tactical rather than strategic purposes (even though it is widely proclaimed as a strategic initiative).

Systems analysts looking to solve electronic commerce problems find that there are a number of readily available EDI transaction sets that, when strung together, can electronify the existing processes quite well, with a few minor modifications in systems and processes. This results in lower costs and earlier evidence of success, thereby elevating the company's confidence in the solution. This type of implementation, if properly done, can actually result in dramatic cost savings. It can give the appearance of resounding success, causing the company to rest on this success and fail to follow throughout the advantage it has gained.

The trap is that the paper-document-replacement, task-oriented nature of EDI leads naturally to the automation of documents and tasks within an individual company. It does not reinvent the processes of which these documents and tasks form a part, or institute new models of inter-enterprise commerce.

It has already been seen that the implementation of EDI to date has been driven primarily by inward-directed considerations. Even though multiple companies may be involved, it is usually one company driving the implementation of EDI with their own cost savings as the major objective.

A common practice among management, at least in North America, is to view electronic commerce as a one-time exercise of replacing existing paper documents with a few EDI transactions such as purchase orders and invoices, since they usually involve the highest volume of transactions and represent the most dramatic payback. However, to gain full advantage of the costs and effort incurred in even a basic EDI implementation, other EC tools such as E-mail and imaging need to be considered so as to provide a comprehensive EC environment capable of sustaining all aspects of the conduct of commerce, human as well as computer.

Typically, EC is seen by management as a purely technical problem to be handled by MIS, perhaps with the assistance of the operating departments and perhaps not. With this type of mandate, the EDI implementation automatically takes on a technological perspective, and usually achieves the expected result. It automates the status quo.

If BPE is involved at all in these implementations, it is usually as an afterthought. It is a post-implementation "discovery" that internal processes need to change to handle the new way of doing business. This discovery is usually made by MIS, who in good conscience tries to program around the situation or to persuade departmental staff to institute new procedures to compensate for the unanticipated changes in the business process. At best, this results in failure to exploit the full potential of electronic commerce. It leaves money on the table. At worst, it results in complete chaos and a backlash against EDI, with the affected departmental staff giving only faint and grudging compliance because they have been given no choice.

A traditional EDI implementation model for the manufacturing or retail sector would resemble the example in **Figure 14** on the next page. That is not to say that all EDI transactions would be implemented, only that this would be the model after which a specific company's implementation would be patterned.

For the sake of simplicity, third parties such as transport providers and banks have not been shown. This model represents the EDI-based information exchange between two typical companies, using the most commonly implemented transactions. In practice, the majority of EDI implementations in

For example, some companies and government departments have settled on the procurement process to lower the existing complexities and costs involved. In this case, the "supplier" side can consist of hundreds or thousands of respondents. The resulting reduction in paperwork can result in a savings of millions of dollars in time and materials for the procurement agency involved. This alone is a valid reason for proceeding, even if no other use of EDI is planned. Extending into the order management segment of the model would yield even greater savings, with only an incremental increase in costs. North America have followed this model to some degree.

Many companies in the manufacturing and retail sector have implemented all or a portion of the order management segment of the model. They reasoning that the cost of issuing large volumes of purchase orders is unnecessarily high, and that significant savings can be gained by reducing this cost. In addition, it permits them to automate their inventory management and production systems, yielding a large payback for a small outlay.

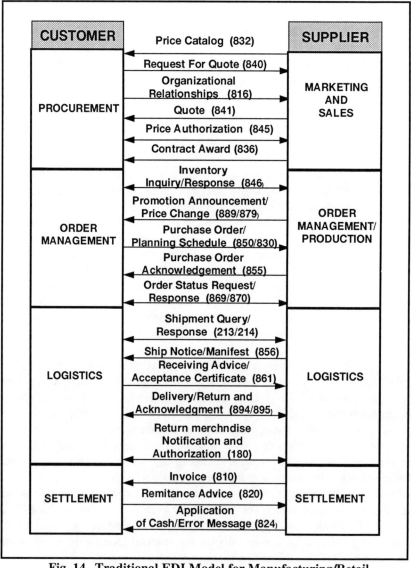

Fig. 14. Traditional EDI Model for Manufacturing/Retail

This seems to signify that the manufacturing and retail sectors have identified the procurement and order management activities as one of their (perceived) core processes underlying inter-corporate commerce. It is the most visible, time-consuming and prone to errors and delays. For this perception to change, the order management process must first become automated to the degree that it ceases to become a visible problem. Once this happens, the real core processes will become visible and it will be possible to make true progress in ICBE.

The transportation industry in general has led the way in implementing the logistics segment of the model. It utilizes EDI to automate the scheduling and paperwork involved with moving freight. The remainder of the business community has been slow to exploit the potential of streamlining the logistics function, and has not proceeded much beyond the exchange of advance ship notice and receiving advice transactions. There is a great potential for a company to plug into its transport providers, warehouses and other channels of distribution to close the Response Gap in the movement of merchandise between the seller and the buyer.

Once again, the choice of EDI transactions and the sequence of implementation is indicative of the perception the transportation industry has of its own core processes. Once the paperwork has been automated or eliminated, the real core processes will become visible, such as load planning, scheduling and resource management.

There are other EC models now coming into prominence, such as the health care model. To date, however, it has centered around the insurance and payment functions, particularly in North America where the health care insurance system is complex and cost reduction is the watchword. The implementation of health care EC in Europe has tended to center around the core business of health care itself, such as patient records, referrals, laboratory results, prescriptions, hospital admissions, and so on.

There is a tremendous potential in North America for these types of implementations. A typical North American model is shown in **Figure 15** on page 72.

Even though the claims and settlement model is now coming into its own, health care EC implementations have so far been primarily in the procurement and order management area. It has been called "health care EDI", but it is merely "EDI in the health care industry". In this case, since it does not address the unique core business of health care itself, it is indistinguishable form a manufacturing, retail, or grocery company performing the same functions.

The following examples are typical of larger organizations that have undertaken EDI. While it is not an exhaustive study, it will serve to illustrate the goals that have driven the efforts, and the results that have been achieved. The use to which EC has been put in actual practice is a good barometer of the current management thinking about EC. It can tell us a great deal about how to extend that thinking beyond corporate boundaries. There is very little information available from the smaller companies who have met with limited or no success, since they do not tend to publicize such information.

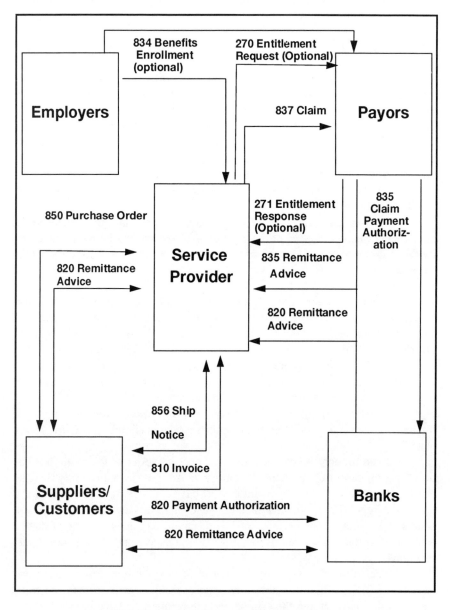

Fig. 15. Health Care Claims Processing

Example 1: General Motors (Golden 1990)

GM has been actively involved in EDI for financial transactions since 1982, when it began collecting wholesale vehicle receipts from the banks that financed the dealers.   In 1984, the Buick Division began the process of 'electronifying' its invoices with dealers and banks. At the same time, GM acquired EDS and began to investigate other uses for EDI.   The Saturn program was chosen as a pilot for several EDI initiatives, among them cash management in the accounts payable area.

The focus was on reducing administrative time in administration functions. GM reasoned that managing the float did not add value to their product, and that productivity increases were the key to improving their profitability. Benefits to the suppliers were also considered as a bonus because cost reductions at their end would ultimately be reflected in the prices GM had to pay. GM decided to share the float savings with its suppliers by adjusting electronic payment terms to reduce the normal float time. The company reasoned that in spite of some loss in float benefit to GM, the overall benefits were greater due to a higher level of predictability of cash flow and the ability to reduce costs through the electronic application of remittance data to their accounts receivable.

The operational flow is similar to the paper check process. GM sends an 820 payment authorization transaction to its banks authorizing transfer of funds to the supplier on a given date.   The participating banks include Chase Manhattan, Citibank, First Chicago, Manufacturers-Detroit, National Bank of Detroit and Pittsburgh National. The original design of the system allowed the remittance portion of the EDI message to be sent either with the payment to the supplier's bank, or printed off by GM's bank and sent by mail if the supplier's bank was not EDI-ready.

In practice, the electronic remittance delivery option has not met initial expectations. Many of the suppliers' banks are not EDI-ready, and therefore a large proportion of the remittances must be sent via paper. This detracts from the benefits of electronic remittance. GM has instituted several options and incentives to their suppliers and their banks to become EDI-ready. Of the estimated 15,000 eligible suppliers, 5,300 have agreed to receive payments electronically, and 21,000 payments are made this way each month. For the first quarter of 1990, when the article was written, GM's electronic payments had averaged $1.3 billion monthly.

In addition, EDI purchase orders, material releases, and advance ship notices have been implemented between GM and its suppliers. GM is also using an ERS approach with about 90% of its suppliers.   Payments are triggered by receipt of material, not by supplier invoices.

GM is using advanced electronic commerce techniques between its Saturn Division and the Saturn suppliers and dealers. The entire EDI procurement model, order management model, and settlement model have been integrated with production planning, resulting in an almost paperless environment.   The only paper in the entire system is the "Manufacturer's Statement of Origin", which is required for title purposes.

GM is a leader in the traditional implementation of EDI to support electronic commerce and to reduce costs, both direct and indirect. This is an excellent start, and has produced some real benefits for GM, its dealers, and its suppliers. It is, however, still classical commerce at work. There has been no significant re-engineering of processes (except for ERS), only the automation of paper-based documentation. The initiatives have been undertaken from an inward-directed perspective for the purpose of improving GM's productivity and reducing costs, not for the purpose of making the System work better, or for streamlining the supply chain.

Example 2: Sears (Dailey and Douglas 1990)

Sears is another leader in both traditional and non-traditional use of EDI and electronic commerce systems. Some of the more traditional examples are:

      1. Sears' Inventory Replenishment Systems
      2. Sears' Source Availability System (SAS)

Sears' inventory replenishment systems

Systems such as the Source-Filled Customer Orders system (SFCO), have been designed around EDI transaction sets for ease of communication with the largest possible population of suppliers. This Sears Catalog system sends the customer's order directly to the source of supply, who ships directly to the customer's home, eliminating the store entirely, and offering a much wider range of merchandise than any retailer could stock.

Time-consuming forms have been eliminated, and large numbers of small orders can be filled without the usual delay inherent in a paper-based ordering system. On a single day, one supplier of video tapes received 12,000 purchase orders from SFCO. As of 1990, the SFCO orders accounted for over 25% of catalog items. The transaction flow is as follows:

      1. Telephone operators take an order from the customer and enter it into the computer.
      2.The SFCO system sends an 850 purchase order to the supplier.
      3.The supplier ships the order to the customer via courier and sends and 856 advance ship notice to Sears, who then charges the customer.
      4. If the order is canceled, Sears sends a 860 purchase order change notice to the supplier.
      5. If the supplier cannot fill the order, he sends an 870 order status report to Sears, who notifies the customer.

6. Sears keeps track of the order by sending the supplier an 869 order status inquiry.

7. The supplier bills Sears through an 810 invoice, which Sears matches with the purchase order and advance ship notice.

Figure 16 below depicts this flow.

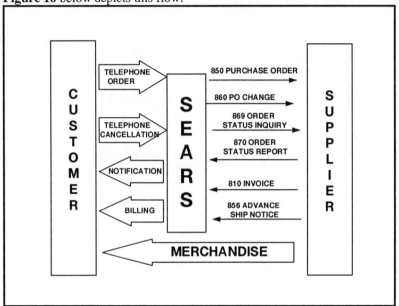

Fig. 16. Sears Source-Filled Customer Orders (Dailey and Douglas 1991)

Using SFCO, Sears has reduced its overhead costs in order processing staff from 120 to 15 people, handling about 200,000 source-filled purchase orders per month. While this is a conventional use of EDI, it has resulted in an unconventional offering, and a significant strategic advantage for Sears in the consumer marketplace.

Sears' Source Availability System (SAS)

This is an on-line, EDI-based system that permits a high level of customer service without the need to carry inventory at the store level. Suppliers are required to periodically submit and maintain inventory availability data on the Sears system using 846 inventory advice transactions.

When a customer buys an appliance or a piece of furniture on the showroom floor, the sales associate can commit to delivery with up-to-date information available right at the cash register. An EDI 850 purchase order is sent to the supplier, who ships the merchandise to a Sears cross-docking facility. 870 order status reports are sent by the supplier so that Sears can keep the customer apprised of any changes in the status of his order. The supplier also sends an 856 advance ship notice and 810 invoice to Sears, so Sears can bill the customer. Thirty source suppliers participated in SAS in 1990, with another 20 targeted at that time. **Figure 17** below illustrates the concepts.

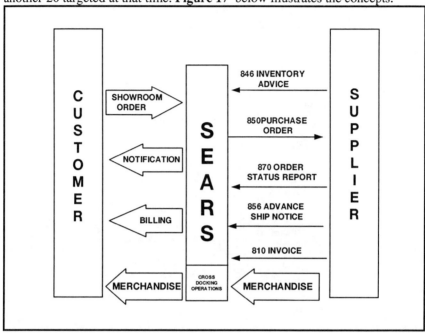

Fig. 17. Sears Source Availability System (Dailey and Douglas 1991)

Once again, the use of conventional EDI has leveraged the vast resources of the supplier base. It has reduced Sears' own reliance on inventory, and has allowed the suppliers to have access to orders sooner and more reliably.

Example 3: Baxter Health Care (Foerster 1991)

In 1976, Baxter introduced ASAP 1 (Analytical Systems and Automated Purchasing), providing small hospitals or single departments with an automated order entry capability using a touch-tone phone. The system was later enhanced to include the ability to accept orders from a teleprinter/teletype device. It allowed the customer to use the printback as an order confirmation and as a receiving document.

ASAP 3, implemented in 1981, allowed customers to order using their own internal item numbers and to build electronic files on Baxter's mainframe computer for repetitive ordering. This reduced ordering time for the customer and improved accuracy. Customers could also specify their own internal format for receiving order confirmations, receiving documents, inventory lists and requisition forms. They could inquire on-line into the status of active orders, back orders, price lists and expected delivery dates.

This allowed the customers to reduce their own inventory and obsolete items, and allowed Baxter to reduce its back orders due to a greater degree of predictability in customers' ordering patterns. Baxter's clerical and administrative load diminished due to a smaller number of purchase orders (with a greater number of line items), which reduced order processing and accounts payable efforts.

ASAP SCAN was introduced in 1982, permitting barcode ordering and tracking. In 1983, ASAP Link permitted computer-to-computer interfacing using a high-speed telephone hookup and a Baxter-proprietary ordering format. Confirmations were returned the same way. By 1984, 43% of Baxter's sales (4,000 customers) were through ASAP.

In 1985, as ASAP usage continued to expand, Baxter converted their proprietary ordering formats to X12 standards and introduced ASAP MICRO, the PC version. In 1986, ASAP ADVANTAGE linked ASAP order entry and materials management. It provided a bridge for customers to migrate to a materials management system along with ASAP MICRO. Also in 1986, Baxter introduced ASAP Interchange, with an electronic invoicing and electronic funds transfer capability. This was seen to close the loop on the customer procurement cycle and provide completely paperless purchasing.

In 1987, Baxter teamed with GEIS (General Electric Information Systems, an EDI VAN) to offer ASAP EXPRESS, an all-vendor system. Customers could use ASAP to send orders to suppliers other than Baxter, such as medical/surgical, laboratory and pharmacy. Today, over 1700 customers are using ASAP EXPRESS.

Baxter is one of the leaders in the health care industry. Their innovative use of technology has profited themselves, their customers and suppliers and has reduced costs across the board. In fact, ASAP has been customer-driven right from the beginning. The thrust here, however, has simply been in the replacement of the paper artifact. It creates a passive "paperless purchasing environment" accepting orders from customers rather than actively participating in or anticipating the supply or replenishment decisions themselves.

If any process re-engineering has been involved, it has been at the departmental level within Baxter. It has not included either the customers or the suppliers in any organized manner. Given Baxter's visible trend toward greater and greater electronic functionality. It is to be expected that they have future electronic commerce plans that involve their customers and suppliers.

Example 4: Ciba-Geigy (Buffkin 1991)

As part of its internal quality process, the Ciba-Geigy plant in McIntosh, Alabama identified the need to improve paperwork flow and internal/external communications in the purchasing department. Annually, there are about 50,000 purchase orders with about 200,000 line items and expenditures of about $400 million. A strategic plan was developed around the use of existing X12 EDI transaction sets, sequenced as described in **Table 16.**

Table 16
Ciba-Geigy EDI Implementation

850	Purchase Order (send)	August, 1988
810	Invoice (receive)	January 1989
860	PO Changes (send)	June 1990
855	PO Acknowledgments (receive)	no date specified
863	Certificate of Analysis (receive)	no date specified
848	Material Safety Data Sheets (receive)	no date specified

Source: (Buffkin 1991)

There were two reasons for not pairing the purchase order changes with the purchase order. The first was that the TQM process had identified improvements that substantially reduced the number of purchase order changes. The second was that the accounting and MIS groups were working in parallel on improvements in the manual processes of invoicing, and a number of trading partners had inquired about automating the invoices via EDI.

This is an excellent example of BPE working in conjunction with an electronic commerce activity, both being driven by a TQM process within the organization. An important issue in this implementation was the cooperation of the various departmental teams within Ciba-Geigy itself. The accounting, purchasing and MIS departments worked and communicated together in a way that was calculated to "make it happen".

The implementation of the 850 purchase order began in August, 1988 and was operational by October 1990 with 65 partners, accounting for almost 40% of the orders. The 810 invoice became operational in January 1989, but, as of this writing, signing up partners has been delayed due to ongoing changes in accounting that would impact the 810, and due to the desire to build a larger base of 850 purchase order trading partners.   The 855 purchase order acknowledgment may be pushed back or removed entirely.

While this has resulted in gains for Ciba-Geigy and has advanced the state of EDI in the state of Alabama, it was nevertheless undertaken from a traditional mindset position. The company's internal processes were the driver for the initiative. The implementation itself was technologically-driven; that is to say, the EDI strategy was determined by existing transaction sets, not by the business need or a vision of the future.

The strategy, while it was modified by other activities in the TQM area, was still a task-oriented, document-centric approach to a problem that may have benefited more from a more innovative solution. This points out the need for senior management to become more aware and involved in the EC implementation, rather than to let it become driven by technological considerations.

Example 5: Digital Equipment Corporation (Ericsson 1992)

This article was written to describe a major BPE initiative that Digital Equipment Corporation (otherwise known as DEC) undertook, using EDI as the enabling technology. The initiative arose from a strategic planning effort in 1989, where the planners resolved to restructure DEC's acquisition process, particularly in the area of non-manufacturing goods and services.

This involves two closely related strategies:

1. Centralizing the purchasing expertise into "Acquisition Business Centers" (ABC's).
2. Enabling the end users to execute their own orders using EDI.

The ABC's source the suppliers and negotiate contracts, and work with them to lower costs and improve material flows. The end users select and order goods from an online electronic catalog that employs video-text. The order is sent directly to the supplier via EDI without intervention by a DEC purchasing agent and without the standard paperwork. The supplier drop-ships the order directly to the end user and sends an EDI invoice to DEC, who pays by EFT. DEC plans to eventually eliminate the invoice and pay automatically upon verified receipt of the product.

This is an innovative use of EDI to conduct EC for internal purposes, in an area that is not traditionally automated. The savings in time, administrative overhead and expense are significant. At the same time, values of employee empowerment are being inculcated in the organization. **Figure 18** on the next page provides an illustration of the X12 EDI transaction flows.

DEC began a pilot with a major office supplier in August 1990. Benefits included:

- High productivity gains for end users, purchasing and accounts payable.
- Immediate $900,000 savings from freed stockroom and warehouse space.
- Reductions in office supplies spending.
- Improved service and turn-around for end users.

- More accurate orders for the supplier.
- Elimination of order and delivery "spikes."
- Faster payment from DEC to the supplier.

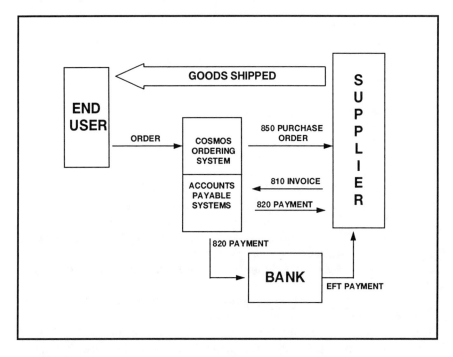

Fig. 18. DEC End User Acquisition

Based on the success of the pilot, DEC has expanded the office supplies systems to all its sites in the US. They are expanding the pilot system to include as many non-manufacturing goods and service suppliers as possible.

DEC's objective, rather than automating an existing process, was "to attain a world-class acquisition process and the attendant benefits". This is an entirely different perspective on the problem and shifts the focus away from the tasks and documents towards the process itself. Once again, while it has benefits for the suppliers, and reduces costs all around, it is more of an experimental application of BPE and EC than it is a strategic use.

SUMMARY

Most of the traditional implementations of EC have been task-oriented and document-centered out of necessity. Even though many astute managers in every industry have realized the value and potential of EC, there has not been either the incentive or the resources to undertake the necessary re-engineering effort because of short-term pressures in the business arena. This is a transition phase, however, it represents a major milestone in the growth from corporate adolescence toward maturity. As time passes, the body of knowledge and experience grows, critical mass is achieved, and corporate mindsets change, EC will come to the forefront as a truly strategic tool.

As companies work together in concert for the first time, they will discover that EC is not only an excellent vehicle for streamlining the exchange of key documents and business transactions, but is also the springboard to discovering innovative solutions to long-standing operational problems. As EDI and its supporting technologies are implemented at each of the Trading Partners, the Linkages become more formalized and standardized. Once this is accomplished and all parties are speaking the same language, new ways of working together can be devised that will make maximum use of the technological advances.

Core processes, or at least the company's perception of their core processes, will change. The paradigm will move away from the "common" processes underlying inter-corporate commerce and focus on reengineering the real core processes for the company, those that drive its business and make it a unique contributor.

CHAPTER VIII

NON-TRADITIONAL ELECTRONIC COMMERCE MODELS

With the rapid spread of EDI over the last few years, industry groups have begun to realize its tremendous potential, and have developed major commercial strategies to exploit that potential. These strategies are aimed primarily at reducing the total cycle time and the dollar value of goods and services in the System. They are the first genuine attempts to look outward beyond the confines of the company's walls and to coordinate all participants' activities and resources to their mutual advantage. These are complete, self-contained operational systems that strive to streamline one aspect of the business. Some of the more common examples are:
1. Sears (Dailey and Douglas, 1990)
2. Paid On Production/Evaluated Receipts Settlement (Schaap, 1991)
3. Domestic Health Care (WEDI report, 1992, 1993)
4. Blue Cross/Blue shield Implementation (O'Roark, 1993)
5. International Business Exchange (Jalinous, 1994)
6. Shared- Resource/Workgroup Computing (DeJean and DeJean, 1991)

Sears (Dailey and Douglas 1990)

In addition to the more traditional uses of EDI for electronic commerce as discussed in the previous chapter, Sears has instituted some non-traditional approaches to electronic commerce. Briefly, these are:
A. Retail Logistics/ Quick Response (QR)
B. Financial EDI at Sears

Retail Logistics/Quick Response (QR)

The QR model, as practiced in the Retail and Grocery industries, is an automated replenishment system that feeds retail point-of-sale data to the supplier on a periodic basis. This serves as a signal to the supplier to restock the items that have been sold, plus or minus seasonal variations. The purchase order as such is completely eliminated. The supplier has the advantage of smaller, manageable, more frequent orders that are not subject to the normal fluctuations of cancellation or change. This also gives the supplier timely usage and demographic information so that he may adjust his forecasts and production schedules as required. **Figure 19** on page 83 provides a pictorial representation of a typical Quick Response EDI transaction system.

In 1989, Sears introduced the Apparel Merchandising System (SAMS). It allows the logistics group access to all aspects of merchandising including expediting, truck routing and store delivery. SAMS allows Buyers to

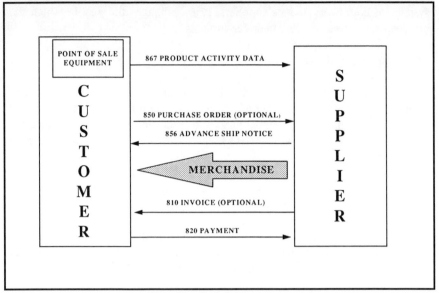

Fig. 19. Quick Response

forecast needs down to the store level, using sales data from the store cash registers, and to automatically order merchandise from suppliers using EDI transactions.

In 1989, Sears used SAMS to implement a QR strategy with Fruit of The Loom. As a result, Sears reduced its average inventory by 6%, improved turns by 16% and improved sales by 28%. Sears also has a system called "Replenishment Information Management" (RIM) for non-fashion apparel items such as socks, shorts, jeans and shoes. Sears and Levi Strauss exchange EDI purchase orders and invoices weekly.

QR enables Sears to pass on sales information electronically to various internal business units and to suppliers at whatever level of detail is required. In return, the suppliers must commit to EDI purchase orders, and 72 hour shipments. While this does not conform to the classical model of QR, it nonetheless is a good example of an automated replenishment system in action. Purchasing activity is driven by actual consumption at the point of sale, rather than an after-the-fact, order-point-driven inventory control system.

Future enhancements could easily include the ability (and authority) for the supplier to generate a replenishment order based on the 867 product activity data transaction. Sears would pay automatically (via EDI) upon receipt of the goods, using the 856 advance ship notice to reconcile to. Once the basics are in place such as they are here, refinements are easily made.

Sears has effectively changed its mindset to focus on its real core business of merchandise management and sales, allowing the suppliers to focus on their core business, the movement of merchandise into the stores. The ordering process has been eliminated in this scenario, changing the internal systems of both Sears and its suppliers. It also changes the way in which the sales representatives operate their departments.

Financial EDI at Sears

Sears helped develop the first format that allowed remittance information and payment instructions to move through the banking system and into the trading partners' systems. Sears is a leader in the National Automated Clearing House Association (NACHA), and participates actively in the design of standards.

Since not all banks are capable of handling full financial EDI where remittance and payment information accompany payment, Sears formed a network of eight cash management banks to handle its EDI payments using the "X12 820 payment authorization and remittance advice" transaction. These banks in turn are able to customize the payment format and the detail distribution according to the needs of the receiver. In 1990, over 200 vendors were receiving over 1,000 payments each month.

Once again, Sears managed to determine that accounts payable was not a core process, and focused on the transfer of value. While this is not in itself a core process to Sears, it demonstrates the ability to look beyond the documents and the current processes that support those documents, and come to grips with the real issue. In this case it is the transfer of value to the supplier. Again and again, leaders in the industry such as Sears are demonstrating the growth from corporate adolescence toward corporate maturity. By its example, it will pull its suppliers and customers along.

Paid On Production/Evaluated Receipts Settlement (Schaap 1991)

Another of the unconventional strategies surrounding EC is the Paid On Production model used (primarily) by the automotive industry. In 1985, GM implemented ERS with selected suppliers. This is a process by which payment for goods or services is based upon shipping and receiving records, not on invoices. This eliminates the reconciliation of the shipping documents with the purchase order, the receiving report, and the invoice, all of which may be different. This has been a major cause of delayed payments to suppliers, and unnecessary effort on the part of accounts payable staff over the years. ERS is the most elegant solution.

Under ERS, a company does not pay for what it said it wanted, or what the supplier said it shipped. It pays only for what was actually shipped, and actually received, whether or not the supplier was able to ship all the items that were requested, or whether a shipment is due to arrive after the invoice is received.

ERS, by paying against actual receipts, eliminates at least two sources of error. It reduces the information to electronic form where it can be matched and manipulated by computer systems, instead of humans with several conflicting pieces of paper to contend with.

A company wishing to implement ERS or any similar strategy should exercise caution in not only the business controls that are put around such a strategy, but the implications in terms of the timing of asset recognition and revenue recognition. Under ERS, revenue may have to be recognized at the point of receipt rather than at the point of shipment. **Figure 20** illustrates:

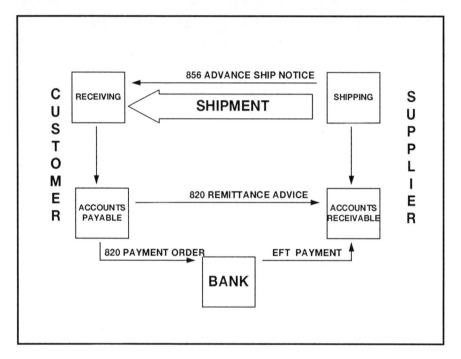

Fig. 20. Evaluated Receipts Settlement (Source: Schaap 1991, published by The EDI Group, 221 Lake St. Oak Park, IL. 60302 (708) 848-0135)

A refinement of this model, called Paid On Production, is being used by all three of the major domestic automotive manufacturers. This is the process where payment is made for goods or services based on usage rather than on shipping or receiving records. Until the material is used in actual production, the supplier retains title. Unlike retail consignment or Vendor Managed Inventory strategies that are accounted for on a monthly basis, Paid On Production is accounted for on a daily basis.

Figure 21 provides a representation of a generic Paid On Production system that has been modified for use at GM's Saturn division and at Ford. Like the rest of the business models discussed in this book, few companies have actually implemented the "classical" version due to distinct differences in their internal business environment and their customer and supplier relationships. The models are useful as a framework around which to build a system that works in the practice of everyday commerce.

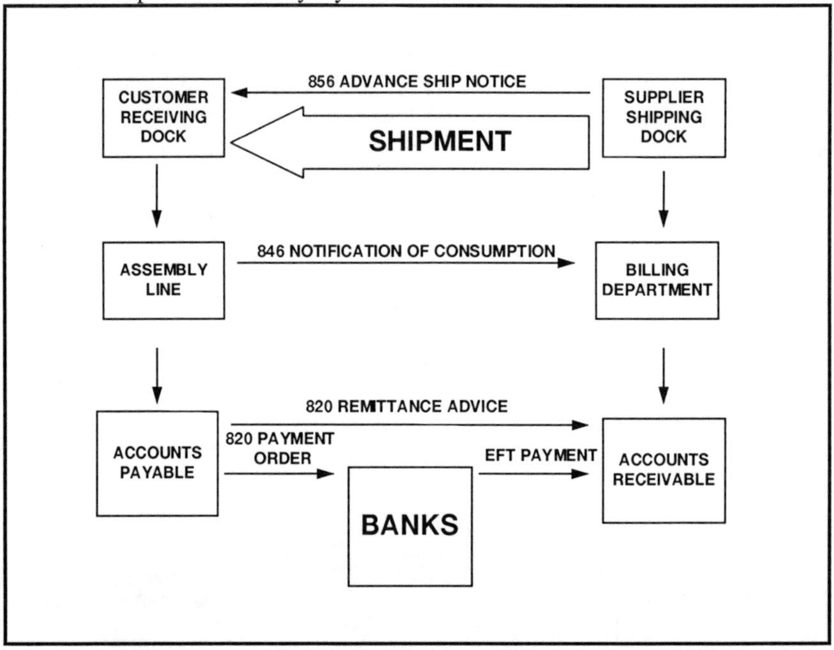

Fig. 21. Paid on Production (Source: Schaap 1991, published by The EDI Group, 221 Lake St. Oak Park, IL. 60302 (708) 848-0135)

This affects the supplier's internal accounting in that revenue cannot be recognized until the material is used in production instead of when it is shipped or received, which is the normal case. Paid On Production suppliers, in addition to being the sole supplier for the material involved, must also have processing systems of sufficient complexity to cope with such differences in accounting and paperwork between the companies.

It is possible for several different relationships of this type to exist at the same time, since a company can be a POP supplier to both GM and Ford. This usually necessitates the installation of new computer systems and processing procedures. In addition effort is required to maintain the existing customer base under the old systems. This can entail substantial cost in money and corporate staff effort, and the supplier must be certain of a continued association before proceeding.

GM's Saturn division's Paid On Production system is structured so that material is ordered on a replenishment basis as production proceeds, much like QR in Retail, but with a JIT focus and a shorter time scale. Saturn's "Material Replenishment System" (MRS) is driven by the concept of material being "pulled" through the Saturn plant by the production process, instead of being "pushed" through the plant by the planning process, such as either a sales forecast or an order-point inventory management system would do.

In Saturn's version of Paid On Production, the supplier receives an 830 forecast schedule so that he may plan for his own production. When the 862 product release is issued by GM, the supplier ships to the appropriate Saturn plant and creates his own record of the consigned inventory. This inventory record is relieved by Saturn's 846 inventory status record indicating consumption in production. Saturn then sends an 820 remittance advice to the supplier indicating which material the accompanying payment is related to and creates an 820 payment order to the bank to transfer funds to the supplier's account.

Ford's version of Paid On Production begins with an 862 product release to the supplier, who would ship the material and send an 856 advance ship notice to Ford. As Ford consumed the material it would send an 861 receiving advice to the supplier indicating the transfer of title. Payments would be made each Wednesday based on the preceding week's receiving advices generated in production. Relief of supplier inventory is the same as with the GM implementation, except that the actual EDI message is different.

Ford was able to reduce its plant inventory significantly, and Saturn expects to reap benefits in quality due to smaller, more controllable shipments. The supplier base benefits because ERS and POP require them to modernize systems and become more efficient in production processes. Suppliers also benefit from better and faster payment terms, and increase profitability by achieving higher inventory turns.

In these examples, the core process that drove the payment to suppliers was the production of vehicles and not order management, inventory management, receiving, or accounts payable. There is a significant set of process changes required to accommodate this type of arrangement on both ends. First, there must be informed agreement by the senior management of both parties. Secondly, there must be a significant amount of education and training. Third, there must be a complete revision to the way in which the internal manual and computerized systems function.

All of the processes that are being superseded must now have two streams of activity, one manual for the existing set of suppliers, and one electronic for the Paid On Production set of suppliers. New methods of tracking and controls must be put in place to ensure that the system works properly. Accounting methods must change to accommodate the changes in transfer of title and recognition of revenue.

Instead of title being transferred at time of receipt, it is now transferred when the unit is actually used in the production process. Instead of the supplier being able to recognize revenue based on shipping and receiving documents, it can now be recognized only at the time of consumption or production of the finished goods. Recognition of assets is calculated in a similar fashion.

Domestic Health Care (WEDI report 1992, 1993)

The Workgroup On EDI (WEDI) is a task force established in 1991 to respond to the challenge of reducing administrative costs in the health care system. In July, 1992, WEDI submitted a set of recommendations to the Bush Administration that included the widespread use of EDI in the health care industry by 1996. WEDI envisioned a health care industry using electronic communications to exchange standardized information across the various groups of payors, providers, suppliers and institutions in an unstructured, any-to-any environment. The diagram in **Figure 22,** on the next page was published in the original 1992 recommendation to illustrate this concept.

In 1993, WEDI reconvened to resolve some of the implementation problems that had been identified in the 1992 Report, and to strengthen the understanding and commitment of the policy makers in the health care industry. Also they wanted to develop a strategy to facilitate quick transition to EDI across the entire health care industry.

WEDI estimates that the cumulative net savings to the year 2000 will be over $42 billion, allowing healthcare enterprises to reallocate administrative funds and resources to the core business of patient care. There were 11 recommendations, centering around standard data formats for patient records, provider identifiers, and coding structures for transactions, legislation to address security and privacy of information issues, and automating the "coordination of benefits" process.

WEDI proposed the adoption of several health care EDI transactions in the area of claims submission and payment as the first step in the major cost reductions described above. These X12 Transactions are described in **Table 17** below.

Table 17
WEDI Health Care EDI Transactions

834	Benefit Enrollment and Maintenance
270	Health Care Eligibility/Benefit Inquiry
271	Health Care Eligibility/Benefit Information
274/275	Patient Information Request/Response
837	Health Care Claim
276/277	Claim Status/Response
278/279	Health Care Service Review/Response
835	Health Care Claim Payment
(no #)	Coordination of Benefits
(TBD)	HMO Reporting

Source: WEDI 1992

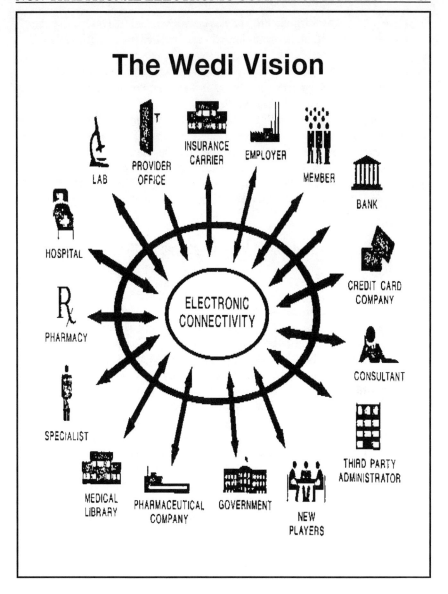

Fig. 22. The WEDI Vision (Source: WEDI 1992)

In 1992, WEDI sponsored three EDI demonstration projects as follows:

- AT&T implemented the 834 benefit enrollment to exchange employee eligibility information with their insurance carriers, Empire Blue Cross/Blue Shield, Travelers, and Prudential.

- The Virginia Project was commissioned to demonstrate the rapid implementation of eight new EDI transactions as above.
- The Twin Cities (Minnesota) project combined two different EDI systems and served an 11-county region around Minneapolis and St. Paul.

The activities and influence of WEDI represent the highest level of business process engineering to date. It encompasses the re-engineering of an entire industry, even though it is not in the core business of health care itself. Like the other paper-replacement strategies, this should pave the way for the industry to concentrate on its real core processes of providing health care. This is a sweeping effort and will take many years to have a significant effect on the industry.

Blue Cross/Blue Shield Implementation (O'Roark 1993)

Blue Cross/Blue Shield of America (BCBSA) and several of its local organizations (called "Plans") have pilot tested the 837 health care claim. Currently, the 835 claim payment is being piloted for Medicare Part A by the BCBS Plans in Virginia, South Carolina, Utah and New Mexico. Medicare Part B is being tested by Arkansas and Travelers Insurance Company.

Advantis, an EDI Van owned jointly by IBM and Sears, is operating a healthcare claims facility called "EDI USA". They provide VAN services and connectivity to a wide range of payors. The actual processing portion of EDI USA is operated by a firm called Medical Management Resources (MMR) in Kentucky.

Under this system, a provider such as a hospital, sends a claim to a local BCBS Plan, either electronically or manually. Claims for other carriers are separated and sent to the operations center in Kentucky for processing and routing to the appropriate destination. Direct network links to carrier's computer centers allows providers to get eligibility information online.

To date, there has been no concerted effort in North America to deal with the core business of health care. European initiatives have progressed in this area. They have approved several EDIFACT transactions relating to patient information, medical imaging, laboratory testing, referrals and hospital scheduling. When the North American health care system reaches the point where it has addressed the financial details and the cost reduction issues, it will find that there is a large body of experience upon which to draw.

International Business Exchange (Jalinous 1994)

In 1992, the US Chamber of Commerce began an initiative called International Business Exchange (IBEX). IBEX is a computerized global trading system, enabling buyers in one country or locality to conduct business electronically with sellers in another country or locality, including interactive negotiations. The orientation of IBEX is to the needs of the small business with little or no computer literacy. It is initially centered around "purchase and sale of goods" activities, with the first release scheduled for September 1994.

The IBEX system is being sponsored and distributed by the US Chamber of Commerce to its over 3,500 local Chambers of Commerce in the US, and its 160 US Chambers in foreign countries, as well as to various industry groups. The local Chambers will sell, distribute and service its own users of IBEX. The US Chamber will market IBEX to foreign Chambers of Commerce in countries where there is no US Chamber representation. The coverage is expected to exceed 1 million subscribers by the year 2000.

The concept of IBEX is that of an electronic trading floor, where buyers post "buy offers" and sellers post "sell offers". IBEX matches these offers, notifies the respondents, and permits anonymous inspection. When two respondents indicate that they are ready, IBEX places them into a visual interactive negotiation mode that allows them to view the offers side-by-side and resolve the differences. When the offers match exactly, the deal is struck and the parties proceed to conclude the business.

In succeeding phases of IBEX, it is planned to offer an EDI capability providing standardization of functionality with the rest of the electronic commerce community. This EDI capability will begin with those transactions necessary to effect "purchase and sale of goods" transactions. It will expand to encompass the entire business cycle, including order status, shipment notification, receipt of goods, and settlement functions, both domestically and internationally.

This will provide EDI connectivity for a large number of small businesses who had none before. It will permit them to use the IBEX network to conduct electronic commerce with the larger corporations. This will equalize the opportunities for small businesses, and provide the larger companies with access to a much broader range of products and services than would otherwise be available through the normal mechanisms of corporate-based electronic commerce as it exists today.

In its broadest sense, IBEX will exert sufficient influence on business processes across several industries to eventually bring some sort of standardization. There is no attempt to redefine the concept of purchase and sale of goods or of conducting negotiations. There is no explicit BPE component involved in using IBEX, but the widespread usage of the IBEX-standard forms and processes will over time impose a de facto standard on small businesses that will bring them closer to the way in which the larger corporations operate under electronic commerce.

Shared-Resource/Workgroup Computing (DeJean and DeJean 1991)

Another non-traditional approach to electronic commerce is the use of a "workgroup computing" tool to bring knowledge workers together and coordinate their joint output, both internally and between companies. The primary tool available as of this writing is Lotus Notes™ by Lotus Development Corporation, who also developed Lotus 1-2-3.

Lotus Notes is primarily a human-to-human interface that can span organizations and permit workers to operate as if they were all using the same computer. With Lotus Notes, work groups can jointly author documents, make changes, additions and comments. They can manage these documents and view them in any number of ways depending on the need of the person viewing. They can share discussion workspace, schedules, and reports. They can access common information and invoke common software tools to manipulate it. Also, they can connect a widely distributed, ad hoc network of people across organizational boundaries to perform common business functions.

Lotus Notes is in current use at Price Waterhouse (PW), who has 10,000 copies. The first application was in the tax law area, keeping partners abreast of continuously changing tax laws and the impact on PW's clients. PW also uses Lotus Notes in the audit area, which is highly document-driven and correspondence-intensive. For larger audits, the home office regularly corresponds with 50 to 100 other offices around the world. It is a process involving great amounts of detailed instructions and comments flowing back and forth.

With the traditional paper-based audit process, massive volumes of reports had to be managed, tracked, summarized and communicated. Lotus Notes significantly reduced the time lags and information lags that were common under the paper environment. It automated the management and tracking of the correspondence, enabling auditors to come to a consensus more quickly.

Corporate Software of Boston sells PC and Macintosh software, as well as hardware add-ins. They provide extensive after-sale support to their customers, including software evaluations. The company publishes a book called "The Corporate Software Guide" twice a year , evaluating the more than 700 software products it carries. The company uses Lotus Notes to add new products and reviews of new versions of software products and to manage the task assignments of the staff involved in doing the evaluations.

Since two internal departments and three foreign offices are jointly responsible for evaluations, Lotus Notes is used to track the project and coordinate the activities of the separate workgroups. The text was centrally stored and made available to everyone involved in the evaluation. Notes keeps track of product recommendation forms, vendor information forms, market analysis forms, product analysis forms, the product discussion form, and the final evaluation form. With centrally managed information, duplication and omissions are eliminated. The evaluation process proceeds much more quickly. The geographical dispersion of the various groups is transparent to Lotus Notes, and the normal mail delays are not an issue.

Manufacturers Hanover Trust in New York City uses Lotus Notes to share information among product-related sales groups and other workgroups within the company. The first Lotus Notes application was company profiles, which centralized information on clients (addresses, histories, financial summaries) that had previously not been formally managed. The profiles also contain a feature to allow an account representative to file a marketing plan for that client and maintain it with the profile. Lotus Notes is able to present different "views" of these profiles. In this way an account representative can get a listing of clients in a particular geographic area, so that he can structure his client visits with minimum cost in time and travel.

Lotus Notes and other shared resource/workgroup computing products address the human-to-human niche of EC that the more structured technologies such as EDI do not. It would be particularly useful in the service industry or where documents and reports are the product of the business activity. The nature of this tool encourages BPE within an organization, as the traditional concept of the sequential flow of documents over time is altered. With simultaneous processing, electronic authorizations (signatures) and other new features offered by the technology, the processes themselves will change significantly.

Summary

As time goes on, more and more companies are joining forces and coming up with creative uses of existing technology to streamline their operations. These are not fads. Rather they represent brand new ways of doing business using a set of integrated electronic tools and updated business processes to support the conduct of commerce in new and interesting ways.

With the ability to share resources and information across company boundaries, ICBE will be able to help further streamline joint operations. Traditional adversarial techniques of paper communication will disappear when all parties have access to the same electronic workbench. For example, engineering designs, technical drawings, product specifications, laboratory results, and other commonly-used information can now be shared electronically on the "same" computer instead of being photocopied and sent by mail. Communication related to the documents can be stored with the documents instead of being sent separately. Items can be ordered and confirmed, and agreements negotiated directly between the parties involved rather than being artificially distanced through the mails.

New ways of paying for goods and services are made possible through the use of EC strategies such as Evaluated Receipts Settlement and Paid On Production. Value moves through the System much faster. Paperwork and clerical effort are drastically reduced, and much of the "I bill you--you wait 120 days to pay--I take you to court" syndrome is avoided. The companies can now concentrate on doing business instead of avoiding each other or becoming involved in unnecessary conflict.

This use of electronic tools for the conduct of business not only strikes at the core processes, but also at traditional mindsets of the workplace and the functioning of human groups within it. The paradigms that are changing here involve the traditional "moving a physical artifact sequentially over time" orientation of paper-based commerce. These changing paradigms themselves open up new opportunities to question the processes that are being electronified.

Even though the strategies discussed here have been largely motivated by commercial interests rather than altruism, it is nonetheless true that real benefits have accrued to the participants. Cycle times have indeed been reduced dramatically, and costs have tumbled for all participants. It has been proven many times in actual practice that companies can work together toward a common purpose.

While this is the logical next step towards attaining corporate maturity, it is only part way there. Regardless of the progress of a few enlightened companies, these successes are still just the result of two or three unrelated companies working at arm's length to streamline a single process at a single point in the business cycle. The next step is the broader application of the disciplines of ICBE to all parties involved in the Value System, and a deepening of the business relationships between them to the point where they are sharing common goals, common resources and profits.

PART II: THE PRACTICE

There are eight distinct steps to be followed in the ICBE process, shown in their proper sequence below. In the practice of implementing an ICBE project, these steps should be followed in the sequence specified, since each step builds on the results of the step before it. Failure to obtain a proper level of informed management commitment, for example, will limit the success of the remaining steps, and optimum benefits will not be achieved. These steps are:

1. Management commitment
2. Internal readiness
3. Inter-corporate team building
4. Value System analysis
5. Business process design
6. Business process transformation
7. System Pilots and operational adjustments
8. Production and Continuous Improvement

The following chapters will discuss the methods and mechanisms of proceeding through the eight steps, offering examples, insights, tips, sample working materials, suggestions, forms, checklists, and other tools that may assist the implementor of ICBE. These do not constitute a definitive methodology or even necessarily a complete approach. They are merely presented to provoke thought and to assist the reader with tailoring his/her own approach to ICBE. There are many roads to the same destination. The reader must decide which is the best suited to the particular needs of the company and the other Members of the Value System.

CHAPTER IX

STEP 1: MANAGEMENT COMMITMENT

Nothing, but absolutely nothing, will happen without commitment from management. Commitment is more than just throwing dollars at the problem and giving it to someone who isn't doing anything at the moment. Commitment is the planned and directed movement toward agreed-upon goals, with the proper funding and allocation of organizational resources. True commitment stems from an informed knowledge of the problem and its solution, and a strong desire to make it happen in spite of all the obstacles.

The Two Dimensions of ICBE

With ICBE, unlike other corporate programs, management commitment must occur across two dimensions, internal and external. Internal commitment must be achieved at the highest levels. The company must be properly prepared before involving other companies. External management commitment must then be gained at the top levels of the other Member companies during the Team Building process described in Chapter XI. Beginning an ICBE initiative without this commitment is a waste of time, effort, money, and careers. The process described in **Figure 23** on page 97 may assist in gaining informed internal commitment.

The process of gaining commitment, whether internal or external, is essentially the same. The processes, techniques, and mechanisms used in the internal, single-company commitment cycle may be used, (with a few modifications and additions) in the external, multi-company commitment cycle. Working materials developed in the internal exercises may provide input to the broader scope of activities. Also it may provide a set of de facto standards for other companies joining the Member community.   In effect, the internal commitment exercise is a practice run for the "real thing", and can provide the company with some valuable experience along the way.

The ICBE Springboard:

The ICBE initiative has to start somewhere. It doesn't just spring into being by itself with everybody suddenly experiencing a fit of religious zeal, simultaneously embracing the same vision, fired with enthusiasm, and vowing to work together as a unit. It has to be led by someone.

The impetus may come from several sources:

1. It may be internally driven, as management realizes that it is behind the technology curve, or that it needs to compress the business cycle and lower its costs.

2. It may occur as a result of external parties putting pressure on the company to engage in EDI or other forms of Electronic Commerce.

3. It may occur as a company implements some other program such as JIT or ISO 9000, and it becomes necessary to work with other companies to accelerate one or more business flows.

4. Or it may be any number of other externally-driven events.

In any case, the company comes to the realization that it is no longer alone in the business world, and it must take steps to ensure its long-term survival by working closely with others.

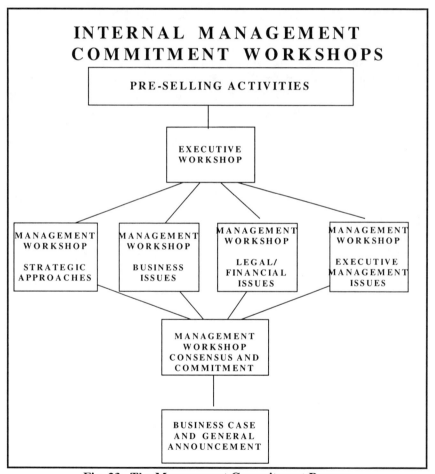

Fig. 23. The Management Commitment Process

Assuming that your company is the first to recognize the situation and take action, then your company must lead by example. This means that, before jumping into a grandiose and probably ill-fated effort to change the way other companies do business, you must first have your own act together. Internal systems and business processes must support what you are trying to do. There has to be a commitment by all levels of your company to the new way of doing business.

The Internal "ICBE Champion":

These types of corporate-change initiatives usually originate with one person, ideally an individual with line operating responsibility who can see the problems clearly and who has the knowledge and ability to envision the solution. This individual is the one who carries the concepts to his/her own management and who provides the spark for leading the other companies to the solution. He or she becomes the "Champion" of ICBE. This is likely a senior-level manager with several years experience in the company; someone who knows how the company *really* works, not how management *thinks* it works. This is called the "Shadow System". This is the individual who provides the ongoing energy and day-to-day attention to detail that will result in permanent change in the organization.

Nothing will happen until this internal Champion is on board and committed, both from a personal standpoint, with the proper funding for his/her time and effort, and with the authority to act. See Fig. 22 & 23 for examples of how to gain the necessary authority. This will take a lot of work and lobbying on the part of the Champion in addition to his/her regular job, and it is not for the faint of heart or weak of resolve. The Champion has a monumental task. It is not just to change the company's way of doing business, but to help change the way several companies do business and to make them work in concert on an ongoing basis.

The Role of Electronic Commerce in ICBE:

The primary goal of ICBE is to facilitate the flow of goods and services through the System. In this light, Electronic Commerce (EC) should be considered to be the primary operating vehicle for realizing that goal. If the company is to proceed with ICBE, then it must first become EC-ready before approaching other companies with a proposal.

In doing so, the company must ensure that it has the technological capability to send and receive EDI transactions, electronic mail, images and electronic forms, handle bar coding and other forms of automatic identification, interface with the proper networks and service providers, and generally deploy up-to-date technology across the company. It must ensure that the underlying business processes and computer systems are able to support the fact that at least some of the company's business will be conducted using these electronic tools, and that there are proper operating controls and security procedures in place to safeguard the company against error.

Achieving a State of Readiness for Electronic Commerce:

The company cannot unilaterally devise business processes and operating procedures for the other Members at this point. There **are** no other Members at this point. It can only develop its own strategic position and ensure its own internal EC-readiness in preparation for when the other Members join the ICBE effort. At that time, the final business environment and operating procedures will be defined for all Members. The company will be in a position to implement its portion of the new System with minimal effort. If for some reason ICBE never comes about, then the company is still in a much better position to cope with EC demand and will be able to undertake a more modest EC strategy without a major investment in time and effort.

To this end, the Champion must acquire a thorough understanding of the mechanics and techniques of EC and of the ICBE process, and be familiar with the implications to his/her company. This can be accomplished by training, directed reading, memberships in EDI associations and other EC-related groups, and detail-level contact with peer groups who are using EC. The Champion must be completely knowledgeable, or Management will never be. The Champion must be able to discuss and promote EC at both the technical level and the business level, and must have the ability to inspire others from a position of knowledge rather than zeal.

The Role of Senior Management:

Senior Management **MUST** be involved from the very beginning. Since EC is a new way of doing business, they are the only ones who are able to make the decisions and wield the necessary influence to get things done. The only way to get them involved and committed is to show them why EC is a business and commercial imperative, and how the company can use it to advantage. There is no alternative.

The following pages will show some of the mechanics of gaining this internal commitment, and some sample working material will be provided. This material may be used as is, customized, or completely ignored, at the option of the reader. Its sole purpose is to provide a conceptual framework for the process of obtaining approval. It is not intended to be comprehensive or even necessarily complete. Imaginative readers will use it as a basis for developing their own methods and approaches to selling EC and ICBE to their own management.

The Champion's Startup Task List:

Here is what the Champion must do:

1.   Send out an announcement to all Senior Management specifying a date and time for an Executive Workshop on EC (clear their calendars first), accompanied by appropriate trade literature and anecdotal evidence of the success of EC in the industry. This should be sent out under the CEO's signature, so the Champion's initial approach will have to be made at that level. At least the CEO should be willing to clear a few hours to discuss an issue of this importance (**Fig. 24**).

2.   Contact each member to ensure attendance and pre-sell the concepts of EC and ICBE. Distribute materials and solicit feedback. If for one reason or another, they are unable to attend, hold a one-on-one session with that person. It is absolutely necessary for ALL Senior Management to be involved. There is nothing to lose and everything to be gained by preparing them beforehand for what is to happen. If there is resistance to the concepts or if there is a hidden agenda with one or more of these individuals, take the time to work it out with them beforehand. This is a chance for the Champion to personally lobby the attendees and settle questions and concerns so that the presentation can be kept on track. The last thing you need is a surprise out of left field.

3.   Prepare the presentation and workshop according to the guidelines in this chapter. Make it specific to the company. Cite actual applications for EC within your business. If there is time, some preliminary analysis may be made of the target areas, but this will be dealt with in more detail later on in the process, by the people who are actually doing the work.

4.   Hold the workshop in the CEO's office if possible or at least the Executive Boardroom. Since it will only be a 2-hour event, try to get them to hold all calls and to be present for the entire time. The CEO should not allow them to delegate attendance to subordinates. This is important for the business, not just another technical presentation, and every action should reinforce that idea.

5.   **Ask for commitment** at the end.   Do not conclude the meeting without a strong commitment--a halfhearted one just will not do.   A sample Announcement is included in Fig. 23, announcing the initiative to the Department Heads and other middle management, soliciting their cooperation in the Management Workshops to come.   Customize it beforehand, bring it to the presentation, and ask the CEO to discuss it with the rest of the team and sign it right then and there.   If they won't, then they either need more convincing or you know up front that the effort will be of limited success.

MEMORANDUM

Date:
To: All Senior Management
From: CEO
Subject: Executive Workshop on Electronic Commerce

Please arrange to attend a 2-hour Executive Workshop in my office (or boardroom) on XXXX at 9:00 a.m.

This workshop will focus on the commercial possibilities of implementing an Electronic Commerce (EC) capability between us and other specially selected companies to accelerate business, cut costs, and stay competitive.

I have included some examples of how other companies in our industry are using EC, and the successes they have achieved. If we are to experience the same levels of success, we must be prepared to commit our full support to this effort, and to do whatever it takes to make it work.

AGENDA:

9:00 -	9:30	Presentation - EC Business Imperatives
9:30 -	10:00	Discussion
10:00 -	10:45	Workshop
10:45 -	11:00	Wrap-up and consensus

This is important to our business, so I would ask that everyone bring their ideas, and avoid outside interruptions while we discuss this issue.

(SIGNATURE)

Fig. 24. Executive Memorandum

Executive Workshop Guidelines

The following outline contains suggestions for discussion material for the Executive Workshop, and guidelines for conducting it. This is an outline only, and there is substantial work to be done in preparation. Here is where the Champion either carries the day or loses his audience.

9:00 - 9:30   Presentation - EC Business Imperatives

This presentation sets the stage for the workshop session which is to follow. The participants should already have been supplied with most of this material beforehand and some of the questions should have already been dealt with. Topics include:

1. What EC is (and is not)
2. General trends in Electronic Commerce
3. Industry-specific success stories
4. "Strawman" strategies for the company
5. The "Alpha Team" and "Inter-Corporate Business Engineering" concepts (from this book)
6. The implementation process

9:30 - 10:00   Discussion

This is to answer any questions or concerns regarding the application of EC to the business, or the soundness of EC in general. The discussion must be carefully moderated to keep on topic and avoid any single individual dominating the conversation. You only have a half hour, and everyone should be heard. Questions may arise in the areas of:

1. Legal issues
2. Control issues
3. Costs
4. Timeframes for implementation
5. Disruption to the business
6. "Horror Stories" and how to avoid them
7. Readiness and willingness to proceed

Most of these issues will be dealt with later in the Executive Workshops, but if there are unanswered questions, note them on a flip chart and commit to getting the answers. It may be necessary to schedule an off-line session for some particularly difficult issues.

10:00 - 10:45   Workshop

This is the opportunity for each of the senior managers to bring their (prepared) ideas to the table regarding how EC could work profitably in their department. Use wall charts, flip charts, whiteboards, etc. to write down the results of the brainstorming session. If necessary, continue on or schedule another session if there are valuable ideas, enthusiasm and synergy occurring. Do not cut off creativity just because the clock says 10:45. In the two previous segments, it was necessary to state ideas crisply and clearly and to be time-sensitive, but here is where the emotional buy-in happens, and it should not be limited by time if there is reason to continue. If you have done your selling job properly up front, you may not be *able* to stop them.

Some of the techniques below may help you facilitate the discussion and channel it along productive lines.

1.   Orient the discussion around Porter's "Value Chain" model below. Each of the functional group heads will then present ideas in the context of their position within the chain. What will result should be full coverage of the business process.

Porter's Value Chain:

    a)   Marketing and Sales (Mktg., Sales, Product/Service Development)
    b)   Inbound Logistics
    c)   Operations
    d)   Outbound Logistics
    e)   Support

2.   Draw a "pipeline" style diagram consisting of a) to e) above. Alternatively, write each title on a separate flip chart page and tape the pages along the boardroom wall in a linear fashion suggesting a pipeline.

3.   Discuss the Value Chain pipeline in terms of the flow of business activity, the relative interdependencies of each of the areas, and the business value of each of the activities. This should have been prepared beforehand, so you should be able to just obtain confirmation at this point. Write the participants' EC ideas under each segment and discuss.   Discuss these ideas in light of the implications of inward-directed vs. outward-directed strategies.

4.   Re-draw the pipeline according to business value, and focus on the "highest and best use" for EC in the company as a whole. For example, if it is determined that the company's success rises and falls with its ability to sensitize the customer to new product offerings, then the Marketing and Sales activities will likely provide the highest and best use for EC. If the Logistics capability is the most critical, then Procurement or Transportation may be the highest and best use initially.

5.   Develop general EC strategies in descending order of priority. The above activities will serve to point the way by highlighting the type of ICBE that should be undertaken. This will in turn drive the selection of the potential Members. These EC Strategies are high-level ideas **only** at this stage. This is not the definitive and final EC strategy, this is merely providing general direction subject to further definition and justification.

10:45 - 11:00   Wrap-up and Consensus

The ideas and strategies presented should be summarized, and the question should be asked "Assuming that the details can be worked out, is this something that we feel we should be doing?". If the answer is no, then two options exist: a) drop the subject and go back to doing business as usual; or b) find out what the problems are, fix them, and start over. Do not proceed if the answer is no.

If the answer is yes (and it should be at this point), a series of Management Workshops should be scheduled with the various functional group heads to resolve management-level issues specific to that group.

These Workshops should include, as depicted in **Fig. 23**:

Session 1 - Strategic Approaches

Session 2 - Business Issues

Session 3 - Legal/Financial Issues

Session 4 - Executive Management Issues

Session 5 - Consensus and Commitment

These same Executive and Management Workshops will be held during the "inter-corporate team building" activities, except that the scope will be broadened to include multiple companies. Materials developed in these internal Workshops may be re-used as well, and will provide a basis for detailed discussion.

The Wrap-up and Consensus portion of the meeting should:

1.   Summarize and restate initial priorities.

2.   Present the "EC Announcement to Middle Management" and achieve consensus. The CEO (at the minimum) should sign, and copies should be distributed immediately. See **Figure 25** for a sample.

3.   Discuss and approve the Management Workshop outlines as discussed later in this chapter.

4.   Set up a schedule for the Management Workshops and conclude the meeting.

ANNOUNCEMENT

DATE:
TO: All Department Heads (and other middle managers)

FROM: CEO (Senior Management names and titles optional, but
                    strongly encouraged)

The Executive feels that it is necessary to provide better business communications between ourselves and the companies we deal with, to accelerate our business processes by eliminating the overhead and delays associated with excessive paperwork, and to reduce the overall costs of doing business.

To this end, we will proceed immediately to develop an action plan to prepare us for the use of Electronic Commerce as the strategic cornerstone for achieving these goals.

This activity will be led by XXXXXXX, and will involve us all in a coordinated exercise designed to flesh out this plan and to develop a prioritized approach to meeting our goals.

This activity is budgeted for (dollars or staff days), and should result in a business case and an Electronic Commerce Readiness Plan, delivered to the Executive no later than xxx xx, 19xx.

(SIGNATURE)

Fig. 25. EC Announcement to Middle Management

Management Workshops

Session 1 - Strategic Approaches

This workshop is by far the most critical of all. This is where the management team is brought to the point of defining specifically how EC is going to work in the company over both the short term and the long term, and how it fits into the overall priority scheme. If not given the proper degree of attention or time, the entire strategy may be compromised and the full benefits of EC may not be realized.

This does not mean that the planning process must be lengthy, merely that all aspects have been considered and dealt with in advance. If adequate preparation is done by the Champion beforehand, this process may be compressed into a few hours or a few days. Hopefully, some of the more obvious strategies have already been discussed as a result of the Executive Workshop.

Both inward-directed and outward-directed strategic models must be fleshed out at this time, describing the overall environment and placement of electronic commerce. This will consist of **The Electronic Commerce Vision**, a set of pictorial models depicting:

a)   the strategic directions and priorities established in the Executive Workshop

b)   the business relationships, current and future, between the company and its key Trading Partners (some of whom will hopefully become Members)

c)   the EC strategies to be applied, such as Automated Procurement, ECR/Quick Response, ASAP, Vendor Managed Inventory, Logistics Management, and others.

The EC Operating Environment:

At this point, the next level of detail must be developed. Specific business transactions (such as purchase orders, invoices, etc.), the companies involved, and the relative priorities must be discussed and approved by the management team before proceeding. This, once again, is a high level summary plan only. It is intended to fix a strategic direction for later discussion with the other Member companies. This will likely change as other companies become involved, and the priorities will (hopefully) become clearer through discussion.

The Big Board Process Model:

To assist in the process, there are some examples provided, specifically: The "Big Board Process Model" (**Fig. 26** on page 107). It depicts the relationships between the participants in the business cycle, the "Strategic Programs" worksheets and the "EDI Model" diagrams showing the flow of transactions for specific business functions such as procurement. This vision will drive everything else. The Big Board will be used again later when the Members are on board and they are ready for ICBE activities to begin.

This should be a high-level diagram depicting the entire business cycle from the consumer through to the supplier, including all participants AS IT IS NOW. Commercial relationships between participants in the chain should be identified with arrows showing the flow of business transactions and other communications involved in dealing with the company, along with the timing of the movement of transactions, goods and services.

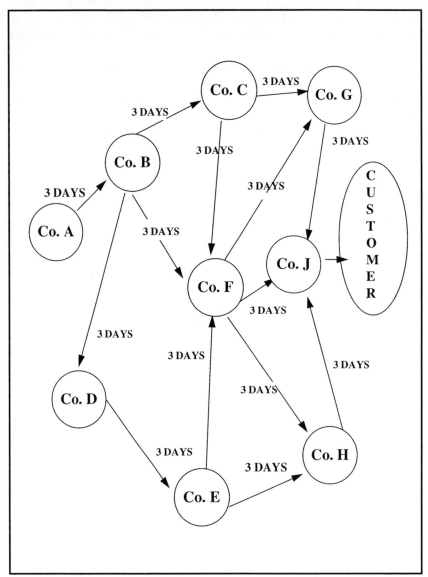

Fig. 26 The Big Board Process Model

This model will form the basis for defining the core inter-corporate business processes (for later refinement) and will help focus on the weak points or bottlenecks in the chain. This will either confirm or redirect the strategies and priorities set in the Executive Workshop, will enable the company to determine where to concentrate its efforts, and will form the starting point for ICBE.

Once these core business processes are defined, e.g. Engineering data, procurement, order management, etc., the company can take a first cut at assessing the feasibility of using various EDI-based strategies for accelerating the flow of bulk information through the System. Other elements of EC such as FAX, E-Mail, etc. can be included during the refinement stages, but it is advisable to begin with well-known and successful strategies such as Quick Response or JIT Release and to determine if they will add value.

Strategic Programs:

The examples in **Table 18** are not exhaustive. They exist only for the purpose of illustration and providing guidance for the thought processes. The company-specific programs must be defined by the Champion before presenting to the management team.

Table 18
Strategic Programs

PROGRAM	PARTNERS	PRIORITY
ENGINEERING/PRODUCT DATA:		
Technical specifications	Customer A	3
Drawings	Subcontractor B	3
	Supplier C	
Formulas/recipes		
Image data		
Price catalogs		
SALES ORDER MANAGEMENT:		
Purchase Orders/Acknowledgments	ABC Co.	1
	XYZ Co.	2
Quick Response Replenishment	Wal Mart	1
Vendor Managed Inventory	Food Lion	3
Direct Store Delivery	Food Lion	4
Evaluated Receipts Settlement	Wal Mart	2
JIT release	Ford	2
	GM	2
	Chrysler	3
Invoicing	Customer Q	3

Table 18: Strategic Programs (cont'd)

PROGRAM	PARTNERS	PRIORITY
PROCUREMENT	*(Fill in the blanks)*	

PROCUREMENT
Price Catalogs
RFQ/Response/Award
Purchase Orders
Shipment Status
Automatic ID
Receiving

PRODUCTION
JIT release
Planning Schedule
Receiving Advice
Order/Claim status Inquiry
Benefits Query

WAREHOUSE/INVENTORY MANAGEMENT
Purchase Orders
Inventory Status
Ship Notice
Material Safety Data Sheets

TRANSPORTATION/LOGISTICS
Customs/Excise documents
DEA/FDA documents
Route Scheduling
Bills of Lading
Freight Billing

FINANCIAL MANAGEMENT
Invoicing/Claims management
Automated Payment/Remittance
Tax filing
Automated debits/credits

RECORDS MANAGEMENT
Patient Records
Benefits enrollment

EDI Models:

Once the Strategic Programs have been selected and prioritized, the company may then begin to flesh out the top two or three on the list, in terms of the specific information flows that will be required. The following EDI model is based on the procurement process. Other process that may be modeled include distribution and logistics, finance, claims and benefits processing, JIT scheduling, and many more. (See also the Business Model diagrams in Chapter VI).

Table 19
EDI Model - Procurement Process

COMPANY SENDS:		SUPPLIER SENDS:	
		832	Price Catalog
		879	Price Change
		888	Item Maintenance
		889	Promo Announcement
816	Organizational Structure		
840	Request For Quotation		
		843	RFQ Response
845	Price Auth/Negotiation		
		845	Price Auth/Negotiation
836	Contract Award		
830	Planning Schedule/Release		
850	Purchase Order		
841	Specifications/Technical Info.		
		855	PO Acknowledgment.
860	PO Change		
		862	Shipping Schedule
		856	Ship Notice
869	Order Status Inquiry		
		870	Order Status Report
854	Shipment Delivery Discrepancy Info.		
842	Nonconformance Report		
894	Delivery/Return Base Record		
		895	Delivery/Return Adjustment
861	Receiving Advice/Acceptance Cert.		
		859	Freight Invoice
		810	Invoice
820	Payment Authorization		
829	Payment Cancellation Request		
		824	Application Advice
		827	Financial Return Notice

The proposed EDI models should represent the entire business cycle for the appropriate function as above. The actual strategy decided upon may in fact be a subset of the model., since not all functions need to or should be implemented. The model will serve to highlight the possibilities so that an informed decision can be made.

When presenting and discussing the models, it is prudent to emphasize that these transactions require time to implement, and that they should be implemented in blocks of related functions. Industry experience indicates that it can take 2 to 3 years to implement a block of functions so that it returns benefits. Senior management should know that the seemingly simple model may in fact take years to realize full benefits.

Session 2 - Business Issues

This Workshop discusses the proposed EC strategies within the context of the other business imperatives in progress in the company at the moment, and assigns a relative importance and priority. This is a free-form brainstorming session with a flexible agenda. General categories covered should include:

1.   **The regulatory/legislative environment**: Is this application of EC subject to regulation or covered by legislative rule? What are the restrictions, if any, on the company's ability to conduct EC?

2.   **The competitive environment**: What are our competitors doing? Are they successful and if not, why not? Are there competitive gains to be had?

3.   **Leadership vs. responsive positioning**: Do we want to be driving an EC initiative or do we want to plug into someone else's? Based on our products and services and our positioning within the primary Value System for our industry, does it make more sense to adopt a leadership position or a supportive/compliance position?

Are we going to plug into the primary Value System effort (the upstream) if one exists. Are we going to start one if it doesn't exist, or are we going to try to gain control of our own downstream operations? If we are going for control of the downstream (our own suppliers, etc.), then which of them has an EC initiative going already, and what are their requirements? Are the rest of them capable of joining the effort to the extent that it will be worth the cost of implementing it?

These questions must be answered by the management team before any effort begins. Depending on what position is chosen, the commitment levels will differ. There may be many valid reasons why your company cannot or should not lead such an effort. The bottom line is, which of the opportunities will yield the best results over the shortest time with the least cost and effort?

4.   **Niche:** This is directly related to the above issue. Based on what we are trying to implement, do we want to/should we be a Hub operation, a Spoke operation, or do we want to conduct EC in a many-to-many environment? The policies, procedures and architectures will differ depending on the answer. If the company is plugging into an existing initiative, then a Spoke arrangement is usually indicated. If a leadership position is adopted relative to the downstream suppliers, then it will likely be a Hub arrangement. If the company's business arrangements are unstructured and involve different respondents based on situational conditions, then an "any-to-any" niche is indicated.

A given company can be both a Spoke and a Hub, as well as an "any-to-any" EC player, but this is a complex environment and is usually the end result of evolution rather than an initial implementation. The initial implementation is best advised to follow the simplest and most direct path. Complexity can come later, when you know what you're doing.

5.   **Existing initiatives:** What else is going on in the company right now (such as ISO 9000, MRP, JIT, TQM, EDI, etc.) and what are the relative priorities? If the company has already made a major commitment in time and resources to implementing ISO 9000, for example, then is the EC effort important enough to compete with it, or should EC be included in the next quarter or fiscal year plans? Is this a good time to be taking on another major effort?

6.   **EC's relevance to or support of these initiatives:** Does EC fit naturally in with these or does it invalidate some or all of the work that has been done? Are there deliverables from these ongoing initiatives that impact on the company's abilities to deliver an EC solution or that are prerequisites to successful EC implementation. If so, what is the timing of these deliverables relative to the EC implementation? Do we need to regroup or perhaps modify some of the results of these activities to maximize the EC benefits? How do we align the efforts so that they can work together? Do we already have an EDI initiative going, and if so, can we leverage off the investment?

7.   **Degree of effort:** Ballpark, how much work do we think this is going to take? Is it something we are even capable of addressing right now, or do we need to rethink some of the other things we are doing?

8.   **Reassessment of priorities:** This is where all the cards are laid on the table and the entire set of corporate initiatives are prioritized, including EC. Some of the management team will likely use this opportunity to advance their pet projects or to try to stop the EC effort for the wrong reasons.

The Facilitator must keep an even hand at this point, and ensure that hidden agendas are minimized, and that an honest verdict is reached based on facts, not FUD (Fear, Uncertainty and Doubt). If necessary, then the CEO must be brought in to arbitrate.

Session 3 - Legal/Financial Issues:

1.   **Regulatory Issues**:   An in-depth look at the legislation and regulations governing this type of EC is required at this point, if any exist. Appropriate documentation should have been examined beforehand, and the company's counsel should prepare a formal opinion for management review.

2.   **Purchase and Sale of Goods Implications**:   Are there implications regarding interstate or international purchase and sale of goods? What about Sales Tax Exemption Certificates and other possible hitches in the legality of EC for purchase and sale? Once again, the corporate counsel should have examined UCC 4A (Uniform Commercial Code) and other relevant legislation, and have rendered an opinion for management review, including solutions to problems discovered.

3.   **Records Retention Requirements**:   What are the issues surrounding records retention requirements? Are electronic records acceptable to the authorities governing this type of EC? Will the EC system be able to competently handle these requirements?

4.   **Filing Requirements**: What are the Federal State and local requirements for filing of documents related to commercial activity, and can the EC system be set up to comply with those requirements?

5.   **Privacy Law Implications**:   Is there sensitive information such as medical records involved that are governed by Privacy laws and what is required by the EC system in order to comply?

6.   **Competition Law Implications**:   Is there a possibility of Competition Law infringement either domestically or internationally? What needs to be done to address the concern? Once again, the Corporate Counsel should prepare an opinion for management review.

7.   **Security, Secrecy and Audit Requirements**: What are the management requirements for security and secrecy of business information, and what do the auditors want to see in an EC system?

8.   **The Trading Partner Agreement**: Review a basic Trading Partner Agreement with the Executive Committee, and construct a company-specific version. In some instances, a Trading Partner Agreement may be replaced by some simpler mechanism such as an on-line Code of Conduct.

Session 4 - Executive Management Issues:

1.   **Status of the industry and externally-driven expectations**: What's happening out there, who is doing what, and what do our customers and major suppliers expect us to do?   Are these expectations of sufficient importance to drive our efforts in and of themselves?   Do these external expectations make sense in light of our ability to respond, or should we be directing our efforts in another area?

2.   **Level of commitment required by executive management**: This is where it must be made absolutely and abundantly clear to top management that this is an intensive hands-on executive effort. Do not attempt to downplay their involvement or the time it will take out of their schedules. If it is not established up front, the energy level will deteriorate very quickly. By now, it should have been clearly understood by all that this is a new way of doing business, and that it is of equal or greater importance to the other issues that consume executive attention.

3.   **Responsibility for management of inter-corporate relationships:** Who is responsible for recruiting and interfacing with the other companies (whoever they may be) that will join the Membership? What authority does this individual have for developing relationships? This is where the topic of the Executive Torchbearer arises. The role of the Torchbearer is outlined below.

4.   **Business opportunities**:   This is a free-thinking session aimed at cementing the concept that EC presents genuine business opportunities. These opportunities should be discussed and documented for as long as it takes to generate enthusiasm. Additional ideas can be supplied by the Champion, who is facilitating the session.

5.   **Key objectives**: As a company, exactly what are we trying to achieve? There should be no more that 4 or 5 Key Objectives, stated simply and clearly. These Key Objectives will drive out the tactical approaches and will help define the measurement systems to ensure that the Key Objectives are met. Some examples of Key Objectives are:

- "To increase Sales volume by 20% through EC"
- "To increase the volume of inbound Purchase Orders by 43% as a result of EC"
- "To reduce the time required to process an incoming Purchase Order by 80%",
- "To reduce the number of inbound Invoices by 50% and outbound Invoices by 75%"
- "To reduce average Receivables to 5 days"
- "To reduce the procurement time for widgets to 2 days"
- "To reduce widget inventory to 2 days supply"

6.	**Critical Success Factors**: What are the things that we have to do or have in order to be successful? How can we achieve them? These are the things that the EC effort cannot succeed without. List them and develop plans to achieve them. Some examples are:

- Management Support
- Legislative compliance
- Adequate technology
- Proper training
- Adequate policies and procedures
- Trading Partner compliance

7.	**Measurements**: How are we going to measure the success of the EC system? Are our existing measurement systems adequate or should we develop or adopt new methods such as Activity Based Costing? What will tell us if we have succeeded or if we are losing our shirts? What are the key performance and financial indicators that we need to measure? How do we snapshot our initial position. How do we evaluate it against industry "Best Practices"? How do we put an ongoing measurement system in place? Are the systems we have in place up to the task, or do we have to develop new systems and processes to measure what we are doing?

The other question is that of how to measure Managment's performance, and provide proper incentives for meeting the goals. Altruism is fine, but most executives will act (understandably) in whatever manner will best reflect their performance at year end. If they are measured (and paid incentive) on their ability to control costs and keep the machines running at 100% utilization, then that is exactly what they will do, regardless of whatever fancy new theories the boss tries to force on them. It is very important to spend time to understand how to tie the goals of EC and ICBE to the manager's compensation, and how to measure their performance against the new goals, NOT the old goals.

8.	**Resources, roles and responsibilities**: What physical, financial and human resources are we going to put on this effort and who is going to do what? Who carries responsibility for what aspects of the EC system?

Session 5 - Consensus and Commitment:

1.   **Strategy Presentation**: This is where the management team takes turns presenting their strategic plans to the CEO. All efforts in the Management Workshops should be directed toward preparing them for their presentation. This gains commitment like nothing else can, since they are presenting their own ideas and solutions to problems they have identified.

2.   **Review and Adjustment**: This is the chance for the management team and the CEO to perform a final sanity check on the strategy and adjust as necessary. The output from this exercise will be an informed understanding, a team decision, and a complete buy-in from all concerned.

3.   **Consensus**: This is a formal vote conducted by the Champion or Facilitator. Once all are in agreement, it is recorded in the Minutes of the meeting, and the EC effort is formally constituted to go forward.

4.   **Signing of the Enabling Act**: The CEO appoints an Executive Torchbearer and signs the Enabling Act (see sample in **Figure 27**).

The Executive Torchbearer:

In a wide-ranging effort such as this, there must be an Executive Torchbearer, a top-level executive with the connections, drive and ability to get out there and work with other companies to make things happen. The Torchbearer must have the authority to make business deals on behalf of the company and to manage the ongoing relationships in whatever way necessary to ensure success. The Torchbearer should be the one to lead the internal EC-readiness initiative for the sake of continuity of effort and for the appearance that management is really serious about this.

Once the desired level of internal EC-readiness has been achieved (See Chapter X), the Torchbearer and the Champion form an ICBE Implementation team. The Torchbearer leads the external recruiting effort, builds the Alpha Team (See Chapter XI) and works with the other Members at the executive level to resolve issues on an ongoing basis, perhaps serving on or chairing the Steering Committee. The Champion works with them and his/her own company at the operational and technical levels, perhaps leading the Project Management Team (See Chapter XI).

EXECUTIVE MEMORANDUM

TO: All Department Heads, supervisors and staff   DATE:

FROM: CEO and Senior Management names and titles

As technology grows in leaps and bounds, the business world is constantly being challenged to keep up. New technologies offer new opportunities to improve and enhance the business environment, and the majority of our competitors are using them to seize the advantage.

As senior management, it is our responsibility to maintain the competitive position of this company. In order to accomplish this in such a rapidly changing world, we must change the way we do business. We must streamline business communications between ourselves and the companies we deal with; we must eliminate the costly overhead and unnecessary delays caused by excessive paperwork and outdated practices; we must reduce the overall costs of doing business for everyone along the chain, including our suppliers and distributors; and we must find new ways to accelerate the flow of goods and services to our customers. This is the formula for our future success.

As the first step, we plan to develop an EC (Electronic Commerce) capability as one of the strategic cornerstones for achieving these goals, beginning with the deployment of tools such as EDI (Electronic Data Interchange) to standardize and expedite the flow of inter-company business information. We also plan to involve some of our key customers and suppliers in aligning their business processes with ours and in designing a smooth, end-to-end business cycle so that we can all achieve the cost reductions and speedy deliveries that are so crucial to remaining competitive.

XXXXXXXX has accepted the challenge of bearing the torch for this activity, and will lead the effort to get us ready for this task. The internal activities to support this plan are now underway, and everyone is encouraged to actively contribute their ideas and support as we continue with the process.

We feel that the ability to conduct Electronic Commerce will be crucial in the years ahead, and that there are already significant business opportunities to be pursued. Accordingly, we will develop a formal "Strategic Plan for Electronic Commerce" that will focus on the following areas:

a)
b)
c)
d)

Fig. 27. The Enabling Act (cont'd)

-2-

THE EC TASK FORCE:

Effective immediately, an EC Task Force is hereby chartered to prepare an EC Startup Plan that will allow us to develop a basic level of competence in this area and to move confidently toward our strategic goals. This Task Force will consist of Senior Management, Department Heads, and staff, operating in cross-functional teams with the mandate to:

a) Identify all internal and external issues involved in implementing EC

b) Take all steps necessary to resolve internal obstacles to implementation

c) Identify issues to be resolved by Senior Management

d) Identify external Trading Partners and business transactions

e) Identify anticipated costs and benefits

f) Prepare and submit a formal business plan for EC

g) Create an EC Readiness Plan and obtain Department-level commitment

h) Oversee the implementation of the Plan across all departments

The EC Task Force will be structured as follows:

Task Force Leader: (should be the Torchbearer)

Human Resources Member/Title:
Finance/Accounting Member/Title:
Engineering Member/Title:
Production Member/Title:
Sales/Marketing Member/Title:
Administration Member/Title:
Information Systems Member/Title:
Support Services Member/Title:
Other (Legal, external auditors, etc.)

We look forward to seeing the results of your combined ideas and efforts, as we work together to keep this company competitive and successful. Thank you for your support.

(SIGNATURE)

Figure 27. The Enabling Act

The Enabling Act:

This is a document with teeth. It sets up a Task Force, establishes leadership, a structure, and a mandate. It formally charges the Task Force to do "whatever it takes" to accomplish the job of getting the company ready for EC. This cannot be taken lightly. It should mean exactly what it says. If there are barriers encountered, the Task Force has the authority and obligation to remove them, regardless of what they are or what political toes get trod upon.

This is sometimes easier said than done, but this is serious business, and nothing can be allowed to get in the way. That is why the Senior Management must drive the effort. Middle management, however dedicated, messianic or well-meaning they may be, cannot exert the authority to act across functional lines, to break deadlocks, or to make decisions that affect the company's internal and external business dealings.

The Internal Business Case:

Once the internal issues are identified and understood, it should be possible to construct a rough-cut Cost/Benefit Analysis and prepare a Business Case preparatory to fleshing out a formal EC Readiness Plan. While the Cost/Benefit Analysis portion should not be by itself the deciding factor in pursuing EC, it is still important to get an "order of magnitude" figure for costs, so that they may be budgeted for. Benefits must be quantified so that there is some basis for establishing expectations, and the expectations themselves must be understood so that there is some way to measure the degree of success.

This need not be exhaustive or long-drawn-out affair, but should give upper management some sort of yardstick to come to its decisions. The Business Case should deal with:

1. Capital costs
    Projected capital requirements (new office equipment, etc.)
    EC Computer Hardware
    EC Software
    Additional telecommunications equipment
    Other automated equipment and systems (bar-coding equipment, etc.)
    Disposal of outdated systems, supplies and equipment
2. Operating costs
    Organizational costs (additional management and staff, etc.)
    Systems support (Help Desk, additional staff, supplies, etc.)

Operating Expenses (leased office space, ongoing communications costs, etc.)

3.   Staffing costs

Additional staff hours for EC operation

Education and training

Professional assistance (consulting, publishing, etc.)

4.   Implementation costs

Trading Partner incentives (cash payments, subsidies, discounts)

Process Engineering costs (staff time, documentation costs, retraining)

Systems integration costs (system and program modifications, new application software)

Professional assistance

Implementation expenses

Travel and living expenses

5.   Other costs

Memberships

Publications

Conferences

Market surveys

Other miscellaneous costs

6.   Risks

Liberally apply Murphy's Law to your specific company and business situation. Quantify if possible. This is a good chance to get concerns out in the open.

7.   Benefits

Quantify if possible. Benefits should be expected in some or all of the following areas:

a)   Material savings

Inventory impact ($ amount of inventory reduction expected)

Revenue impact ($ of increased revenue due to increased sales and improved delivery)

Overall business impact (contribution to the Bottom Line)

b)   External savings

Transaction-oriented savings ($ savings per PO or Invoice, for example)

Volume-oriented savings ($ savings due to the ability to handle increased volumes)

Operational savings ($ savings due to expedited operations and reduced paperwork)

Delivery savings ($ savings due to faster and more efficient delivery mechanisms)

Product/service differentiation
Market penetration
Leadership
Survival
Increased responsiveness
Better product/service planning

c)   <u>Internal intangible benefits</u>
Better utilization of staff
Simplified administration
Growth avoidance
Better service/production planning
Reduction of "error-based processing" environment
Coordinated information
Coordinated supply channels
Employee empowerment vs. clerical labor
Better utilization of financial and other assets

8.   <u>Contribution to other strategic objectives</u>
TQM
MRP II
JIT
DRP
ERS

9.   <u>Expectations:</u>
Critical Success Factors
Benchmark of current environment
Goals and measurements
Timeframe

The EC Readiness Plan:

The EC Readiness Plan will deal with all of the activities that need to come together to get the company ready internally in terms of physical and human resources, roles and responsibilities, task lists, and action items. This is a detailed project plan down to the task level. It ensures that all aspects of EC-readiness are covered. Chapter X will outline some of the elements of an EC Readiness Plan, and will present tools for putting one together.

Since the Readiness Plan may be quite involved and require a significant amount of time to implement in its entirety, other aspects of the ICBE effort may proceed in parallel with it. For example, the company's strategy may call for an Automated Replenishment capability to support a

Quick Response requirement from a major customer. The Readiness Plan may then, among other things, call for a Client/Server implementation of new EDI-capable manufacturing software and its integration with existing mainframe applications. It may also require that QRM ("Quick Response Manufacturing" Suri, 1995), be put in place to gear up your manufacturing operation to support this Automated Replenishment function. These by their nature are long-term implementations and should not necessarily hold up the process of Member recruitment, Alpha Team building, or Value System Analysis (See chapter XI).

Summary

In any ICBE initiative, there must be an initiating Member who starts the ball rolling. This Member is usually the provider of the core product or service in the Value System in question, the first to recognize the benefits of ICBE, and the driving force behind the ICBE effort. For this company, internal commitment and corporate readiness are absolutely essential. A company cannot expect to go out into the inter-corporate world and drive an ICBE initiative until it has its own act together internally and can demonstrate its sincerity, credibility and ability to deliver.

Since the primary goal of ICBE is to isolate and close the Response Gaps across the Value System, a mechanism is required to allow Member companies to synchronize business signals and pass information back and forth across those Gaps. To this end, Electronic Commerce (EC) is both the enabling mechanism and the operational cornerstone of ICBE. The technologies that surround EC (EDI, E-Mail, bar-coding, etc.) provide the primary tools for accelerating inter-corporate business communications. The business strategies and disciplines that surround EC (Quick Response, Evaluated Receipts Settlements, etc.) provide the models for business process change across the Member community. For this reason, the initiating Member must attain a basic level of internal EC-readiness before proceeding with an external ICBE initiative.

This does not necessarily mean that all changes have to be completed in their entirety before you start talking to other companies about ICBE. Some initiatives (such as systems integration, technology upgrades, etc.), may be significant and costly, and may take a relatively long time to implement. Certain initiatives (such as applications integration or QRM), may be affected by unfolding events during the ICBE effort itself, and they should be planned accordingly. All that is necessary at the beginning is to have the basic capability to conduct EC in a reasonably automated, safe and secure fashion, that you have an achievable EC game plan, and that you seriously expect to be fully EC-functional by the time you start transacting live EC business with the other Members.

Senior Management commitment is essential. Middle management is not equipped or authorized to make the internal policy decisions or the external business decisions required. Senior Management is the only body that can commit the resources and funding of the company to initiatives with such broad implications as EC and ICBE. To this end, an internal Champion must conduct a series of top management presentations and workshops to address the strategic and business issues, gain the informed consensus and commitment of top management, and put together a corporate game plan.

Executive decisions must be made regarding the EC business models to be implemented, internal systems and technology architectures, changes in internal processes, internal resourcing and accountability, and proposed operating principles. Other internal initiatives must be prioritized in light of EC and ICBE, and a rough-cut Cost/Benefit Analysis must be conducted so that expectations, goals and budgets may be set. Management must be prepared to do "whatever it takes" to achieve success.

To this end, an Executive Torchbearer must be appointed and empowered to act on behalf of the company in inter-corporate negotiations and in the ongoing operation of the "extended" business. The Torchbearer is the individual who makes things happen both internally and externally, and stickhandles organizational problems between companies on a daily basis. This individual is crucial to the effort, and no company should proceed without a committed and duly empowered Torchbearer.

The Torchbearer, assisted by the Champion, must develop and oversee a coordinated "EC Readiness Plan". This Plan should be designed to provide facilities for the conduct of "basic" EC with other companies over the short term, while building procedural and systems infrastructures that will support a full EC capability over the long term. The EC capability that results must be able to respond quickly to changes in operating philosophy and business practice resulting from the implementation of ICBE, and from ongoing changes in the industry.

Once internal commitment has been achieved and the company has reached a sufficient state of internal readiness to present a credible proposal to the outside world, the Membership Drive may begin.

Developing the Tactical and Strategic Plans for EC:

Internal readiness needs to be achieved at both tactical and strategic levels. "Getting something up fast" does little good unless it is part of a broader strategy. Without a direction or focus, the effort will fail or achieve only limited success. Developing a long-term strategy does little good if there is no practical way to get there. There must be some short-term, measurable successes to keep the emotional momentum going and return some hard dollars for re-investment in the program.

To start things off, however, there must be a basic infrastructure put in place that will support whatever direction the company's EC strategy moves. This is the "EC Startup Plan". From that point on, the EC Strategic Plan should be supported by a series of EC Tactical Plans that work together to intelligently schedule the implementation of EC functions to occur exactly when they will be needed. **Figure 28** illustrates this concept.

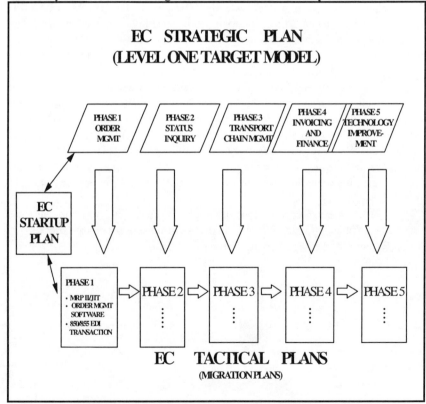

Fig.28. The Tactical and Strategic Plans for EC

The EC Startup Plan answers the question , *"What do we need to put in place right now in order to do the basics of EC with the outside world "*? The goal of the Startup Plan is to ensure the safe, secure and competent conduct of basic EC over the immediate term by implementing the necessary systems, technologies, procedures, equipment and training. This is what the Enabling Act (Chapter IX) refers to when it directs the Task Force to prepare an "EC Startup Plan".

A typical Startup Plan may include such things as:

1. The installation of a PC with EDI Translation software
2. The implementation of an EDI Policy, clerical procedures and controls for handling EDI business.
3. Preliminary data modeling and file mapping for EDI transactions.
4. Linking the PC to the mainframe.
5. Developing a utility program for transferring flat files back and forth between the EDI Translator and the mainframe.
6. Developing programmed "EDI hooks" for the applications software.
7. Installing a corporate-wide E-Mail facility.
8. Choosing a VAN and getting connected; etc.

This should be as simple and inexpensive as possible. It should leave the door open for the important changes to come later, and not paint the company into a corner by making "lock-in" technology decisions. The Startup Plan quickly positions the company to begin sending and receiving electronic transactions, but does not implement any specific EC strategy.

The EC Strategic Plan, by contrast, answers the question *"What do we need to put in place over the long term to support the company's EC direction, and how do we ensure that we can respond quickly and efficiently to changes in the EC marketplace?"* Even though the company's EC strategy may be modified by the results of the ICBE activities to come (The Level One Target Models), management must have a general game plan in mind before it begins.

The objectives of the EC Strategic Plan are:

1. To document, and to direct the implementation of the EC strategies established during the Management Workshops.
2. To establish a robust and flexible internal EC environment that intelligently exploits emerging technologies to the company's benefit.
3. To position the company to respond rapidly to changes in the external EC environment.

This "internal EC environment" will hereinafter be called the company's "Electronic Commerce Environment", or ECE, and it will be discussed at greater length later in this chapter.

In the example in **Figure 28**, Phase 1 of the EC Strategic Plan (as laid out in the Management Workshops) has designated Order Management as the first EC activity to be implemented. It is followed by electronic "inventory status" and "order status", inquiries in Phase 2, Transport Chain management in Phase 3, an electronic invoicing capability and financial EDI in Phase 4, and Technology Improvements (such as the introduction of bar-code scanners) in Phase 5. Initially, these subsequent Phases are not defined in detail, due to the fact that the EC Strategic Plan will likely change dramatically as other companies become involved during the ICBE process.

To support this, the Phase 1 Tactical Plan calls for the implementation of certain aspects of MRP II such as:

1. Bill of Material review, inventory accuracy and cycle counting procedures
2. The installation of Order Management software and cleanup of the relevant data files.
3. Customization of relevant EDI Transaction sets and business procedures.

The initial version of the Phase 2 Tactical Plan might call for further MRP II functionality (such as production scheduling), the implementation of additional EDI transaction sets, and additional supporting procedures.

This initial EC functionality, however, still supports only the company's individual situation. It would be further subject to tailoring, massaging and customization as many times as necessary during the ICBE exercise, according to the needs of the company and the other Members as the joint implementation unfolds. ICBE, in fact, imposes a higher level of EC Strategic Plan, one which includes and affects all Members. This higher level Plan might call for changes as a result of factors which cannot be anticipated by the company's internal planning exercises.

As these external changes are made, they can affect and modify subsequent Phases of the company's internal EC Strategic Plan. As a result, the Tactical Plans for Phases 2 through 5 will be modified accordingly. In this way, the company's evolving EC functionality is developed in response to and in lock-step with the actual implementation of ICBE, with fewer wasted efforts or blind alleys.

Purely internal considerations such as education and training, legal and financial review, audits and controls, technology infrastructures, and internal policies/procedures may be dealt with in detail, but anything that involves the external world should be approached cautiously until the overall Value System has been designed and the other Members are ready to implement their portions of the Plan. Detailed work may then proceed in conjunction with the other Members, ensuring better coordination of effort and a smoother implementation for all concerned.

Developing the EC Startup Plan:

The Task Force works with the department heads and operating staff to resolve the internal company issues involved in conducting EC, and to develop an action plan aimed at achieving an initial state of EC-readiness. The internal issues discussed here originally appeared in "Strategic Positioning For Electronic Commerce: Introducing EDI Into The Organization", also by the author, and they are expanded upon here. These issues would normally include but not be limited to:

A. Corporate culture and human resource factors:

1. Policy-level barriers: Are there policy-level issues in areas such as corporate centralization, financial policy, signing authorities, etc. that would need to be changed to allow the free exercise of EC? Are there new policies that need to be created? A company should develop a specific "EC Policy" detailing how EC will be conducted, with whom, and under what conditions. This Policy then becomes the authority and guidepost for EC implementations.

2. Barriers to employee acceptance: Are there cultural barriers such as fear of technology, fear of personal obsolescence, fear of loss of job, the "we've-always-done-it-this-way" attitude? Are there educational barriers due to the skill or training level of the labor force, the inability or unwillingness to learn new skills or retrain for a new job? Are there going to be issues with the unions? Have the employees seen this all before and are they skeptical? Have they carved out a niche for themselves by complicating their jobs to the point that no one else can do what they do? Employee acceptance or lack of it can make or break any new initiative. Ways must be found to make it easy for employees to accept and enthusiastically support the new order.

3. Barriers to implementation: Is there a lack of time? Do we have enough human or material resources? Do we have the right facilities? Is there a lack of funding? Do we have the right technology?

4. Changes in staff deployment: Will there be changes in organizational structure? Will there be the need to re-assign people? Will there be lay-offs? What are the schedules and details of staff deployment? Who actually goes where, what do they do when they get there, and when do they do it?

5. Employee education and training: Who needs to go on what training courses and what is the schedule? Is there specific On-the-Job training that we can do for the administrative and clerical staff? Is there another company who is doing this that will let us "sit in" with their people and learn? What are the needs for technology training and management training?

6.. Organization for EC What new positions should there be to accommodate the needs of an EC environment? How do existing positions change? At the minimum, there should be an EC coordinator and various Departmental coordinators to ensure that the EC business is given due care and attention and that all issues are dealt with quickly.

Functions should be segregated so that no one individual has care and control of the entire EC environment and can therefore affect the results, financial or otherwise. The EC coordinator position should be separate from the network or systems administrator position to ensure proper security.

B.   Process Flow:

1.   Current flow: How does it work right now ? Draw process flow diagrams, Entity-Relationship diagrams, etc. to illustrate. Include actual forms and documents as appropriate, with the names of departments, workstations and individuals, along with authorizations or approvals required along the way. The existing system, with all its flaws, must be thoroughly documented and understood.

2.   Proposed flow under EC: How would we like it to work ? Draw diagrams as above to illustrate. Walk through the model several times to ensure that the existing flows are not disrupted by the new flows and that everything works in a "conference room pilot". Remember that only some of the company's business is going to be electronic, and that the existing manual systems will be around and coexisting with the new systems and processes for some time to come. They should be compatible with each other, and the proposed flow should attempt to eliminate as many steps as possible.

3.   Rationalization/normalization: Fit the diagrams together, review the processes and the paperwork, and change them or develop new processes as necessary to come up with a new system that will work internally and satisfy all parties. This is internal business process engineering (BPE) at the highest level. These diagrams will be used later during the ICBE effort, as the reciprocal and common processes for each of the Members are examined in the effort to reduce overall cycle times.

C.   Internal availability of data:

Is there an approved EDI transaction set in existence that meets or comes close to our information flow requirements? Look at the EDI transaction (for example, Purchase Orders) vs. the data generated by internal applications, systems or processes. Is everything there? Could you build an EDI transaction with existing data from the PO file? Do the existing applications and file structures carry or provide all of the data that we may need to populate other outbound EDI messages or to store the information from inbound EDI messages? How do we capture what we need or how do we accommodate the new data that will be coming in? Can we even use the new data with our existing applications and if not, what do we do with it?

D.   Information flow mechanisms:

Where does the information come from within the system? Use Data Flow Diagrams where appropriate. What applications are involved and how do we link them together? Does there need to be special computer utilities developed to pass the information around or can it be done manually?

E. "Bridging" procedures and mechanisms:

How do we get there from here? Are there some temporary solutions or work-a-rounds we can put in place until the system is functioning properly? An example might be to set up a PC to receive EDI PO's, print them off and then submit them to Data Entry staff for keying. This is potentially dangerous, unless care is taken to avoid the work-around becoming the new system. The temporary nature of work-a-rounds should be clearly understood, and they must not be allowed to remain in place any longer than is absolutely necessary.

F. Phasing-in considerations:

What do we need to do first? Second? Third? What are the dependencies? An example might be that, in order to go to electronic Purchase Orders, it is first necessary to clean up the customer file, the vendor master file, the Parts Master file, and the PO file. This would be followed by the writing of policies, procedures and controls to allow for the generation of PO's for selected vendors and the reception of PO's from selected customers.

This would be followed by the development of "bridging" software that would select out these customers and vendors and direct their transactions to the new applications or to designated human attention. While this is going on, it is necessary to install the PC-based software that will handle the EDI transactions and the communications. This can become complex as activities are laid out and new dependencies are discovered, but every effort should be made to keep it as simple as possible.

G. Contingency plans:

What do we do when the EC system breaks? Do we have backup procedures? Are we able to re-integrate our EDI transactions into the manual transaction stream? What are these procedures and how do they work? How are they invoked, who does them and how are they controlled?

H. Facilitating mechanisms:

What tools do we have, such as EDM (Electronic Document Management), E-Mail, Workflow Management, etc., that directly relate to the success of this effort?. What other tools do we have that should work in conjunction with EDI? How can we deploy them over the short term to support our EC effort?

I. Technology platforms and systems issues:

1. Internal platforms and technical architecture: What systems and technology architecture is needed to support EC in-house ? Is a stand-alone PC sufficient to get started with until we have a more substantial plan in place? Do we already have an EDI system on the host that we can use, or do we have to start fresh? Is there a connection available between the PC and the mainframe? Do we need special software and utilities? Will it be hooked into the LAN as a Client, or will it be an EDI Server on its own?

What are the memory and storage requirements?

2.   External technology platforms: Are there any platform requirements we want to or need to impose on the Trading Partner community (such as Windows vs. OS/2, vs. Unix, etc.)? This should be avoided if at all possible. These kinds of issues should be decided by the Membership during ICBE, not unilaterally.

3.   Hardware interfaces: Are there any special hardware requirements such as bar code equipment, RF equipment, special printers, scanners, readers, communications hardware, special cabling or phone line service, etc.?

4.   Transmission requirements: What transmission volumes are we expecting, and what are the associated requirements in terms of speed of service, time windows for transmission (such as lower rates for transmitting between midnight and 2 a.m.), etc.

5.   Information   Management/data   collection requirements: How can we get the information into our applications from outside the company? Is there any special point-of-sale of point-of-use equipment required, such as hand-held scanners, portable computers, etc.? What actual information requirements are we trying to satisfy? How do we import the information into our applications?

6.   Software and translation interfaces: What EDI Translation software most closely meets the needs ? What are the file structures and/or other interfaces between the Translator and the rest of the systems ? Do we have access to mapping tools to automate the process of data transfer to the applications?

7.   Application system interfaces: Are there special requirements for interfacing directly with the existing applications? Are they batch-oriented, and if so, does that satisfy the needs of the new EC system? Can batch-oriented applications be converted to "fast-batch" applications that are invoked several times a day instead of on an overnight schedule? Can existing data bases be populated directly with EDI transactions, or are there special time-sensitive transactions that need immediate attention from the application? Is there a way to isolate and report on EDI transactions Vs batch transactions? Are there special programs or new utilities required?

8.   Maintenance/support of standards levels: How many old revisions and different versions of the standards do we support ? Who maintains the standards and what are the mechanisms for ensuring the applications are kept in synch ?

9.   Security and integrity of transmitted data: How do we ensure security? Who has access to the EDI system, the network and the applications? How do we control access to the systems and equipment such that there is no unauthorized access? How do we keep the data from being intercepted and tampered with en route? How do we know that the data got through exactly as it was sent?

10.   Diagnostics: How do we check out the network when there is a suspected error? How do we verify and re-verify that the Trading Partners' systems are sending and receiving information correctly? How do we trace application errors through the EDI system if necessary?

11.   Error recovery and backup mechanisms: How do we back up the system and recover lost information or transmissions? What if the EC system goes down--do we have a backup system that will continue to operate and minimize our down-time?

12.   Network response requirements: Are there certain EDI messages that require faster turnaround or faster processing through the network than others? What are the timeframes for turning these around and how do we handle these transactions?

13.   Network service requirements: What are the products and services that we expect the network to provide to assist with EDI operations? What are the fee schedules? Are there management reports that we can get that show the traffic volumes and give demographic information? Do we need Functional Acknowledgements? Is there a "broadcast" capability that will save us money? Can we exclude certain postings? Should we utilize the in-network translation features until we decide on a Translator of our own?

J.   Internal audits and controls:

1.   The control function is central to any EC initiative. The following material on EC system controls is discussed more fully in "The EDI*Control System", also by the author. While these refer specifically to EDI, they are the same for an EC system in general. In summary, the company must exercise extra care to ensure that:

a)   Proper authorizations and controls are in place (both manual and electronic)

b)   Transactions are generated and processed correctly

c)   Errors are detected and isolated in time to minimize damage

d)   All activity can be traced for verification of system integrity.

2.   A complete EC Control System must address, at the minimum:

a)   Originating System controls

b)   EDI structural controls

c)   EDI logical controls

d)   Security, Operations and Administration controls

e)   Network, transmission and third-party controls

f)   Destination System controls

3.   This consists of:

a)   establishing adequate General controls and Application controls to ensure the *prevention*, *detection*, and *correction* of errors;

b)   establishing adequate mechanisms to ensure security of access and compliance to internal policy and external regulations;

c)   and establishing mechanisms to ensure the integrity of the content and business intent of all transactions.

4.   The following is a (partial) list of some commonly implemented controls. They may not all be necessary for any given company, so the company's audit staff should select the ones that are most appropriate and cost-effective.

a)   Preventive Controls

*Establishing appropriate authorization levels for selected EDI transactions

*Segregating clerical functions relating to generating and handling of EDI transactions

*Designing human intervention points into critical processes

*Ensuring adequate system backup and maintenance procedures

*Ensuring adequate system development and system change control procedures

*Identification of external regulations, filing, retention and legal requirements

*Establishing authorization profiles for privacy of information

*Use of Trading Partner Agreements

*Use of recognized EDI standard messages

*Use of standardized EDI Translation software

*Establishing System Administrator, EDI Administrator, and Departmental Coordinator positions

*Establishing and monitoring VAN compliance checking and pre-delivery controls

*Logic checking of inbound transactions

*Establishing clear policies for recognition of accounting events

*Controlling access to EC equipment and software

*The use of encryption and electronic signatures

b)   Detective Controls:

*Creating the ability to separate, summarize and report EDI transactions from normal input

*Maintaining unaltered logs of EDI transactions

*Establishing a formal archival policy

*Maintaining audit trails of data conversions and media transfers

*Maintaining access logs for sensitive or private information

*Maintaining multiple sorted logs of EDI transactions, controlled by functional staff

*Source document logging

*Special identification of EDI transactions

*Source Event logging

*Maintaining an EDI suspense file

*Linking EDI control numbers and internal control numbers

*Monitoring VAN reports

*Use of Functional Acknowledgement transactions

*Establishing document matching and reconciliation procedures

*Use of Receipt Verification transactions

c)   Corrective Controls:

*Establishing formal Disaster Recovery procedures

*Maintaining unaltered logs of EDI transactions

*Monitoring error reports - VAN, Translator application

*Maintaining an EDI Suspense file for reconstructive purposes

*Selective VAN re-transmission of transactions in error

The degree to which a company undertakes to implement these recommendations depends on its own assessment of the risks it faces in EC operation, the actual need for specific controls as applied to its unique situation, and a balancing of the value of the controls versus the costs of achieving them.

At the conclusion of these planning exercises, there should exist a collection of documentation that may be grouped generally under the following headings:

1.   Issues identified and the resolutions to be undertaken
2.   Unresolved issues requiring senior management attention
3.   Proposed actions and organizational impact
4.   Technology plan
5.   Audit and control plan
6.   Internal cost/benefit analysis

7   Preliminary budget for planning purposes

8.   Implementation schedule

These should be consolidated into a cohesive, structured, detailed plan with dates, deliverables, and staff assignments. This includes a budget that provides basic figures for capital costs, restructuring costs, expenses and resourcing levels. The Startup Plan, including the budgetary numbers, will be presented to the Executive for approval and follow-up action.

The EC Strategic Plan:

The objectives of the EC Strategic Plan are to:

1.   Document, and direct the implementation of, the preliminary EC strategies established during the Management Workshops

2.   Establish a robust and flexible <u>internal</u> EC environment that intelligently exploits emerging technologies to the company's benefit

3.   Position the company to respond rapidly to changes in the <u>external</u> EC environment as dictated by the needs of the ICBE initiative.

To accomplish this, it is necessary to implement both an Operating Strategy and a Technology Strategy. The format of the EC Strategies arising from the Management Workshops is not as important as the content and cohesiveness of the strategies contained in it. Many companies have their own format for outlining a Strategic Plan. These should be adhered to wherever possible for the sake of continuity with the rest of the operation. EC Strategies should generally not extend beyond a 1-2 year period. There is no way to foresee what ICBE will come up with as it progresses, but the document serves as a useful guidepost for internal implementation of EC.

The Operating Strategy:

A company's Operating Strategy may choose different approaches. One approach is to follow the sequence in which most companies traditionally automate their processes such as:

1.   Order Management

2.   Status Reporting

3.   Logistics

4.   Payment

5.   and Support.

Another approach is to analyze their Value Chain and implement those EC functions that provide the highest payback over the shortest period of time, such as gaining control over supplier deliveries or eliminating transportation paperwork. The approach depends greatly on the company's core business and its position in the overall Value System.

In fact, a company may choose to begin with a short-term EC strategy that has nothing to do with the ICBE initiative. An example would be where it was determined that there was value in automating PO's with several high volume customers and suppliers in order to immediately cut costs and pay for an integrated ECE (Electronic Commerce Environment). The customers and suppliers in question may not be part of the targeted ICBE Membership. However, there is a substantial amount of corporate experience and cost savings to be had by doing this before undertaking ICBE. This also gives the company a measure of credibility and a successful track record when it begins its Membership Drive. It now has a story to tell.

The Operating Strategy should consist not only of the outward-directed strategies, but also the inward-directed activities needed to support them. An example would be where the outward-directed strategy calls for automated replenishment through electronic PO's (Purchase Orders). The inward-directed strategy might call for the implementation of EDI PO's supported by:

1.   an MRP II system to handle the material ordering and production scheduling activities for that customer's product set;

2.   a TQM process to ensure high quality of the product;

3.   and a BPE (Business Process Engineering) activity that seeks to reduce the overall time to market for that product set.

The Technology Strategy:

Objectives 2 and 3 of the EC Strategic Plan can be facilitated by implementing an ECE (Electronic Commerce Environment) as the company's Technology Strategy. The ECE, as pictured in **Figure 29** on page 136, is primarily focused on achieving internal EC readiness for a company by integrating all of the internal physical, technological, and procedural elements necessary for the conduct of Electronic Commerce.

The ECE is a self-contained, fully integrated technological, administrative and operating environment that covers all aspects of the implementation and conduct of EC. It is implemented over the medium-to-long term through the various Tactical Plans, and is modified as necessary during the ICBE process. It accommodates both the existing Legacy systems as well as new and future systems and technologies. It allows for maximum re-use and portability to the "Inter-Enterprise Architectures" of the other companies involved in the Value System. **Figure 29** illustrates the concept of the ECE.

The ECE "Infrastructure" links the company's core business applications and "Legacy" systems to the "Technology", "Information", "Connectivity" and "Architecture" dimensions of the ECE model, while the ECE "Processes" ensure proper direction-setting and planning, a controlled implementation and rollout, and a secure ongoing operation. All are necessary.

The ECE model must be customized to the company's specific needs, assembling and configuring the appropriate components to provide a seamless EC capability both for the applications and for the users themselves. In addition, the business processes that surround EC must be streamlined so that the maximum benefits will be realized from the new system. These are as much a part of the ECE as are the hardware and software.

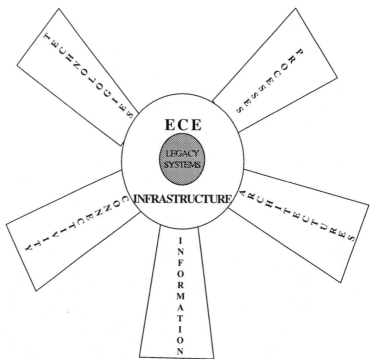

Fig. 29. The Electronic Commerce Environment (ECE) Model

The ECE concept may be easily expanded to include the other ICBE Members. The ECE becomes even more effective when applied to multi-corporate commerce, using common "Inter-Enterprise Architectures". This leverages the investment in resources and capital across several players and reduces the overall fixed costs of the Value System.

The Six Dimensions of the ECE:

As illustrated in **Figure 29**, the ECE consists of six "dimensions" that must be fully integrated together to form a cohesive and harmonized whole. Some of components of these dimensions are physical and some are conceptual, but all must work together as if they were designed as one unit. These dimensions are:

1.   Processes. These are the guiding principles, practices, procedures and mechanisms under which Electronic Commerce is to be implemented and conducted.

2.   EC Infrastructure. This consists of the necessary software,

hardware and intelligent internal/external System Agents ("Smartbots") to interface core applications and legacy systems to the other elements of the ECE and to the outside world

    3.   Architectures. These are the physical and logical components that execute the business functions of the Electronic Commerce system and determine its topology, configuration, and interrelationships with other Trading Partners.

    4.   Connectivity. This provides seamless dialog with the outside world for both the applications and the users themselves.

    5.   Information. These are the mechanisms by which information is captured, represented, stored, standardized, converted, and communicated within the Electronic Commerce marketplace.

    6.   Technologies. These are the present and future technologies that systems developers and end users will employ to interface with the ECE and related applications, and to personally direct the conduct of Electronic Commerce.

An ECE Scenario:

    As an example, Company X's ECE may manifest itself in the following way. The Purchasing and Finance Departments have jointly re-engineered the Order Management process to accommodate electronic ordering, receipt of goods, and payment from the company's MRP II system. From this, the Suggested Orders file is generated. Within the computer system, a specially-created "Smartbot" periodically checks the file and retrieves orders for those suppliers who are EC-capable and who otherwise meet the criteria previously set by the EC Policies and Procedures established by Purchasing and Accounting. Based on a set of rules, the Smartbot either presents the Suggested Order to the Purchasing manager or automatically generates an EDI PO to the supplier. For certain suppliers, however, the order is posted directly into their shared database and results in immediate action.

    Company X's Sales agents in the field use palmtop computers to enter in their customer orders. This is transmitted by wireless communications, and is routed by the appropriate System Agents to the application software that handles call-in customer orders. The credit-check application is invoked automatically. The results are passed back to the sales agent in the field. At the same time, the order is passed to the manufacturing application to schedule production of the order. Expected ship dates are transmitted automatically back to the field sales agent.

    Company X's receiving dock receives a shipment of parts from its supplier and scans it in at the dock using a hand-held bar code scanner. This automatically updates the Order Management system and payment is authorized for the goods received.

    The Marketing Department's PC's have automated access to public data bases and commercial information services. They use the Internet as a strategic tool to do market analysis and to advertise and sell the company's products to the general public. Forecast software on the marketing department's PC is fed with this information, as well as with order fulfillment statistics from the mainframe applications (via Smartbots). The resulting forecasts are fed directly into the Production Scheduling application.

With its high-volume paper-based processes, the company scans them into the system and uses OCR (Optical Character Recognition) software to convert them from images back into documents. Those documents that are human-oriented are then accessed by a Word Processor. They are handled by Document Management software that indexes them and collates them according to pre-established criteria. Annotations and attachments are "clipped" to the documents. The Workflow Management software routes them to the appropriate managers for digital signatures.

Documents that are application-oriented (such as paper Purchase Orders) are extracted and stored in a data base for the applications to deal with. Smartbots see these as well, and take action as necessary, according to their rule-based logic.

The entire coordinated set of hardware, software, systems, applications, methods and procedures that enable this scenario to happen constitute the company's ECE.

Characteristics of the ECE:

Dimension 1: Processes:

These are the guiding principles and management mechanisms under which Electronic Commerce is to be implemented. Without the supporting processes and guidelines in place, the other dimensions of the ECE will not be as effective. The processes encompasses Internal EC-readiness: This is the more detailed process of revising or rebuilding internal systems and processes to fully prepare the company for the conduct of EC. This is the most time-consuming and resource-intensive activity, as well as one of the most critical. The process of achieving full EC-readiness consists of :

1.   EC policies and procedures: These are the day-to-day procedures necessary for the internal departments to conduct EC, and the general policies required to support any differences in procedure from the existing manual systems. These are *in addition to* any policies and procedures put in place as a result of the Startup Plan, and should coincide with them.

2.   Business Process Engineering for EC: This encompasses the redesign or re-invention of existing processes to be able to conduct EC in an efficient and effective manner (such as redesigning the AP/AR systems to be able to cope with electronic payments as well as manual payments) Some of the BPE issues may have been identified at Startup, and a plan or timeline developed. for implementation at this point in the process.

This also includes the invention and design of entirely new processes to exploit the potential of EC, such as customer service enhancements, new marketing and forecasting tools and methods, or the design of new products and services for the Internet audience.

An example of this might be a publishing company who wishes to develop an electronic magazine with an entirely different format and characteristics from the newsstand version, for sale to the online audience. Another example might be that of a financial services company that develops online loan applications over the Internet or develops Internet-based payment products such as secure credit card payments or "electronic cash". This is exploiting the medium to its fullest potential in a positive, contributive sense.

3. Internal System Linkages: These internal links co-exist with existing paper-based systems for companies not conducting EC. These linkages pass information back and forth between EC systems and Legacy or special-purpose application systems. The questions and issues were raised as a by-product of the Startup Plan, and they may be more fully addressed here.

4. Internal Systems Readiness: The modification or rebuilding of internal systems and applications support the changes required for the conduct of EC, including the installation of the required architecture (discussed later).

5. End-to-end Security and Control Systems: The system of security, audits and controls that ensure the smooth flow of business transactions through the system, ensure that the EC system does not either generate or accept unauthorized or runaway transactions. It also ensures that all Trading Partners have received and processed all transactions correctly.

Once again, this was dealt with to some degree in the Startup Plan, but may be addressed in more detail and in a broader scope here. The major issues should have been identified during Startup, and a plan may already be underway to institute the audit procedures and controls. These should be coordinated with the rest of the effort.

6. Education and training: There should be an ongoing program of EC education for management and staff, and the hands-on training necessary to perform the functions of operating an EC environment on a continuous basis.

7. Trading partner recruitment, liaison and relationship management: This is the process of identifying prospective new Trading Partners for the EC program, negotiating terms and conditions of business, identifying specific management, operating and technical contacts between the companies involved, and managing the ongoing business relationship. This subject will be dealt with more fully in Chapter XI.

8. Pilot Projects: Controlled joint ventures involve specific business processes between companies. They are designed to establish "proof of process", to work out the operating environment, and to solve implementation problems before proceeding into full production. Each set of business functions should be conducted as a Pilot project, regression testing as appropriate. This will be dealt with more fully in a later chapter.

9.   Acceptance Testing and Licensing: A formal exercise ensures that all aspects of the multi-corporate operation are thoroughly tested for error-free compliance with the original objectives of the project. It ensures that the Trading Partners are fully competent both technically and operationally to proceed. Upon successful completion, a "License To Trade" is issued as the certificate of entry into the EC Trading Partner community.

10.   System rollout: The rollout of a successful Pilot project across an expanded base of Trading Partners includes the identification, liaison, EDI-readiness issues for the new Trading Partner, the Acceptance Testing and Licensing process, and the ongoing relationship management. This is performed for a potentially new set of Trading Partners as each new Pilot project is completed.

11.   Third party services: This includes the management of outside services necessary to the conduct of EC such as Value-Added Networks (VAN's), banking services, backup & recovery, asset management, auditors, logistics management services, and others.

Dimension 2:   EC Infrastructure:

The EC Infrastructure is specific to the company, and consists of the necessary software, hardware and intelligent internal/external System Agents ("Smartbots") to interface core applications and legacy systems to the other elements of the ECE and to the outside world. The infrastructure consists of:

1.   "Back-office" EC-enabled systems: These are specific to the customer's industry, and reflect the "core process" applications conducted by that particular company, Division, or office. For example, it could be a Physician's office, an automobile dealership, or a motor assembly plant. These applications are EC-enabled, meaning that no additional effort or software, apart from entering basic configuration parameters at installation time, is required for them to conduct EC through either EDI, E-Mail, Smartbots, or other mechanisms.

2.   Mapping and conversion utilities: These are the suite of (usually third-party) utility programs that map data back and forth between the formats used by application programs, and the formats used by external communications such as EDI messages, SQL scripts, or Internet searches. In addition, they can be used to convert or map data between different applications on the same system. They can be used either by human operators in creating data maps, or by Smartbots in the performance of their duties.

3.   EDI translation software: EDI Translation software is normally a third-party product that assembles and disassembles EDI transactions in both directions. Usually it contains the latest standards libraries, communications software and a basic level of message management. Sometimes it includes mapping and conversion capabilities.

4.   E-Mail and mail interface/conversion software: This provides a single mail facility for the entire Environment, with links to mail-enabled applications and conversion facilities for "foreign" E-Mail from outside the organization such as cc:mail, Eudora, or mail formats from other networks such as the Internet, CompuServe or America Online.

5.   Technology bridges: These are specialized drivers for such technologies as voice response systems, automatic identification systems, Personal Digital Assistants (PDA's), automatic sensing devices, and other tools of personal EC or high-tech applications

6.   Specialized configurators: Systems tools configure an individual's system according to a set of rules based on his/her function within the Environment. A remote sales person with a laptop or a palmtop would require a substantially different configuration from a clerical worker, a department manager, or a systems developer.

7.   EC development and testing tools: This suite of tools, such as GUI (Graphical User Interface) front-ends and re-usable objects, permit systems developers to customize or configure the EC software. The tools, such as script generators or EDI transaction emulators permit testing of new EC implementations.

8.   EC-specific hardware and software: The remainder of the EC Infrastructure consists of the physical equipment and operating software that links the Legacy systems to the outside world, including the EC Servers, EC client systems, bar-coding and scanning equipment, POS (Point-of-Sale) equipment, and other specialized systems and equipment that enable the conduct of EC.

9.   Smartbots: These are based on the concept of "Knowbots" (Cerf, 1995), which are programs that "move" between computers and invoke action on those computers. "Smartbots" integrate the technologically-diverse ECE with the Legacy systems environment and with the outside world. They are the "brains" of the ECE Infrastructure, and provide the intelligence and "energy" that links the disparate elements of the old and new systems together.

Smartbots may be thought of as the roving "Action Agents" of the ECE.   They are the translators, expeditors, routers, couriers, managers, synthesizers, application launchers, caretakes, butlers, researchers, shoppers, security guards, and other electronic entities that interface with other entities and integrate the various elements of the system into a cohesive whole.

Smartbots "know" the characteristics and requirements of each of the elements comprising the system. They are able to move information and instructions between them.   Smartbots can intelligently determine what information is needed, where it resides, what format it is in, and how to get at it.   The use of Smartbots can enhance a company's ability to couple and decouple applications easily, merely by reconfiguring the necessary parameters.

Smartbots can use rule-based and/or fuzzy logic to interpret and prioritize the results of a search and present the likeliest alternatives to an application or a human being. Smartbots can "learn" by experience and can build other Smartbots out of re-usable components as necessary. Smartbots can convert the experiences to "gestalt memory" for re-use by themselves and other Bots.

Smartbots can carry encrypted information across the networks between companies. Smartbots initiated on one system can invoke "Companion Bots", "Recipro-Bots", or "Mirror Bots" on any of the other systems in the inter-corporate network and conduct a controlled session with these systems. In these cases, the Bots in question are designed, implemented and tested together when the inter-corporate ECE is set up.

Smartbots can also act as Personal Agents (PA's) to individual users in the conduct of their daily business. The PA is specific to an individual user, and establishes that user's preferences, tailored requests, and so on. This can be used to automatically configure the ECE for each user at start-up, and pro-actively execute on his/her behalf according to a set of rules. For example, it can retrieve Dow-Jones information for the user's client list at 10:00 a.m., schedule appointments and other personal activities related to the user's job function, download specific information from the Internet at particular times, etc. Smartbots can be constructed in several ways:

> a) They can be *generalized* and get their input and direction
> from the initiating application.
> b) They can be *specific* to a certain type of request or business
> function
> c) Or, they can be *dynamic,* built by an intelligent EC-enabled
> application or another Smartbot that requires ad hoc
> information.

Dimension 3: Connectivity:

The Connectivity dimension provides seamless dialog with the outside world for both the applications and the users themselves. It ensures the proper management of network resources. This consists of the appropriate combination of:

1. Internet access: Gateway services and TCP/IP communications support, SLIP/PPP connection, World Wide Web browsers, etc. To permit Internet access from Windows, OS/2, UNIX, or other operating software.

2. Internet-related services: These services include Corporate/Departmental Home Page, individualized links to specific Internet newsgroups, mailing lists, or other Home Pages relevant to the conduct of EC for the company, search scripts for commonly accessed functions, automated or "user-friendly" URL's, etc.

3. Commercial network interface: Interface to commercial networks such as CompuServe, MecklerWeb, EINet, America Online, Prodigy, IBEX, etc.

4. Transport (X.400): An X.400 capability for the simultaneous transmission of EDI, images, text, binary files, etc. is sometimes required for doing business with other X.400 capable Trading Partners.

5. Network Directory Services (X.500): This means access to services such as AT&T's Network Directory Services (NDS) or Bell Canada for application-driven searches for information or resources residing on other computer systems.

6. Wireless/Cellular/Satellite communications: This is the ability to accommodate mobile computing or nomadic personal communications. An example is the submission of low volumes of EDI-based purchase orders or order status requests from your sales staff at a customer's site.

7. LAN/WAN/VAN interconnectivity: This ability allows a user on a LAN or an application to connect transparently to the appropriate WAN or VAN for EC purposes. For example, a user or an application that is processing a credit card number may need to access a credit card validation service online to process the card number immediately. Another example is an accounts payable application (or worker) that needs access to a financial EDI VAN for the authorization of funds transfer.

8. Network systems management (NSM) environment: This ability allows remote management of all nodes of the ECE, including servers, desktops and mobile units. Management includes distribution of upgrades and fixes, file management, software installation, remote configuration, remote sensing, and remote diagnostics.

Dimension 4: Architectures:

The ECE architectures are the combination of hardware, software, and systems that implement the Electronic Commerce Environment in practical terms. The ECE architectures bridge the gap between internal Legacy systems and the outside world of commerce. This consists of the appropriate combination of:

1. Distributed Computing Environment (DCE): A computing environment where applications and data are logically and physically distributed, allows inter-operability that is transparent to the users of the system and the computing platforms involved. In an ECE, this means that EC-related functional applications such as sales, production, shipping, and accounting can communicate seamlessly with each other independently of their location, their software package, or the system on which they operate. This can result in the reduction of paperwork and staff effort between departments, and can greatly streamline the operation.

The DCE model can also be used to build an Inter-Enterprise Architecture to implement shared applications and shared data bases between a company and its electronic Trading Partners.

2. Workgroup Computing systems: These systems that logically "centralize" applications and data where the work group is distributed. This is the reverse of the DCE concept discussed above, where applications and data are distributed according to need. In a Workgroup Computing environment, many different individuals can work on a single document or file, according to rules established for version control and security. Examples are the creation of proposals, the design of a new product, sales cycle management, or any other human-oriented effort involving the collaboration of multiple workers.

In an ECE, Workgroup computing could be used for joint product design (possibly including the customer and suppliers), paperwork between shipper and carrier, hazardous material documentation, or laboratory paperwork such as chemical analysis, etc. that accompanies raw materials.

3. Workflow Management systems: This is software that manages processes or "documents" through a series of steps according to established rules. An example is an internal purchase requisition for a software package that requires supervisory, departmental, and corporate approvals, as well as a technical review for compliance to standard. These can involve:

a) complex logic
b) digital signatures
c) selective security
d) interrelationships of various documents
e) voice and text annotation to existing documents
f) attachments of graphic images
g) indexing, and filing.

An ECE may use workflow management systems to streamline those processes that still require paper artifacts or human review processes for electronic commercial activity.

4. Inter-Enterprise Architectures: Inter-Enterprise Architectures are those combinations of hardware, software and processes that permit multiple unrelated companies (EC Trading Partners) to undertake electronic commerce initiatives with each other using shared resources and facilities. These architectures may consist of:

a) Shared computing platforms: Trading Partners can share the hardware and operating software necessary for the conduct of EC between them. This can be accomplished in several ways. It can consist of an actual shared physical platform, where the hardware and software is jointly owned and administered and joint processing is done centrally. It can consist of a DCE arrangement where each Trading Partner's equipment is part of the DCE and the EC system operates as a single company image, using the same systems software. Or, it can consist merely of a mutual agreement to use the same or compatible hardware and systems software platforms and the same configuration parameters, but owned and administered by the individual Trading Partners.

b) Shared applications: This is one of the key concepts underlying an inter-corporate EC architecture. Trading Partners can have the ability to actually share application software, either through a DCE environment, through a shared physical platform, or simply through mutual agreement and installing the same applications software on their systems with a standard set of configuration parameters.

All companies involved in the Trading Partner relationship not only use exactly the same application (such as Financial or Manufacturing software packages), but also share the relevant technologies, processing techniques and business conventions imposed by that application including data structures, account codes and so on. Shared applications still permit the companies to operate each business independently and safeguard their confidentiality, but impose a persuasive influence on the processes.

c)   Shared data bases: This is another of the key concepts in an inter-corporate EC relationship. Through shared data bases, Trading Partners can eliminate much of the time-consuming, transaction-driven activity normally associated with electronic commerce between different companies.

For example, instead of sending EDI transactions for purchase orders, status requests and invoices, a shared data base allows the customer's "inventory stock-out" or "re-order point" situation to generate an event trigger directly to the replenishment application of the supplier. There is no time delay, and no inter-company overhead.

Assuming that sufficient security and controls are put in place, companies may operate from different views of the same data base, either in a DCE environment, or on a shared physical platform jointly owned by the Trading Partners.

d)   Cooperative computing: Cooperative computing is a much more intimate example of shared applications and shared data bases, using either a DCE or a shared physical platform. In this case, the companies not only use the same application software and the same data bases, but use their joint system as if they were different departments in the same company.

For example, Company A's sales records trigger a replenishment order directly to its supplier's (Company B) sales order system, which is maintained on the same database. Company B's shipping schedule automatically posts a delivery notice directly to Company A's inventory management system, including the expected arrival time and any changes. Company A's scanning of the received product then automatically creates a journal entry to transfer the appropriate value directly from Company A to Company B (Assuming that the proper audit trails are in place).

In a less intimate example, the payment process may be decoupled. In this case, Company A's A/P and Company B's A/R are linked so as to post to each other and to the relevant journals, so that invoices and checks are eliminated. Company A's A/P process generates a payment authorization to the bank , and posts the remittance advice to Company B's A/R (to be matched by the bank's remittance advice so that payment is verified). This eliminates a great deal of the "outstanding receivables" problem experienced in everyday business, and dramatically lowers the cost of the total operation. This is the ultimate goal of all EC activity.

Dimension 5: Information

The Information dimension consists of the methods, techniques and structures for capturing, representing, storing, retrieving, and moving data and other information around the ECE. An integrated ECE environment will consist of a uniquely tailored combination of the appropriate information elements listed below:

1.   Point of Sale (POS) systems: Typically, consumption data is captured at the point of sale during the act of scanning the item's bar coded label across the cash register or other POS device. This creates sales information at the SKU (Stock-keeping unit) level, which can be summarized by the store's computer and sent via EDI to the suppliers of the items. This can act as a replenishment signal to the supplier, causing a new shipment to be sent to the store.

This implies a standard method of representing the item information such as a bar coded label, a standard method of encoding the information to several different suppliers (EDI) and a standard means of responding to the information when it is received at the supplier's system (a rule-based replenishment algorithm).

2.   Bar coding and scanning: The means of encoding and retrieving meaningful information about an item, using an external identifying mechanism that physically accompanies the item. Supplier and product information contained in the computer system is represented in the bar code label, which is scanned at the other end or at points along the journey, automatically entering the same information into the other system without re-keying.

Bar code labels can also be used to contain entire EDI transactions. These are printed at the shipping site, scanned in at the receiving site, and completely eliminate the need for an EDI VAN for those transactions. The EDI transaction arrives with the shipment, instead of after it, and scanning eliminates the need for key entry. The shipment may then be reconciled on the spot and sent to the sales floor immediately instead of waiting for the EDI transaction to come in through the VAN, which can take up to a full day or longer to reach the shipping dock.

3.   Automatic ID tags: Automatic ID (most commonly Radio Frequency, or RF) tags, convey information that can be used to locate shipments, identify serial numbers, or carry detailed cargo or other information in situations where bar coding is not feasible. Read by special scanners, the data is once again entered into the system without the need for manual keying.

Examples include trucks or railroad cars that are subject to grime and soot build up, stacked crates that may have the bar code labels hidden, conveyor belts where the containers are placed randomly, or other situations where the physical orientation of the coded label cannot be guaranteed when unloading and scanning.

4.　　Imaging/OCR/Pattern Recognition: Documents that come in from other companies (such as purchase orders, etc.) can be scanned in as images (or faxed into a fax server) and OCR (optical character recognition)) techniques or pattern recognition techniques applied to extract data from known positions on the document. This is less reliable than EDI or other electronic means of transmitting data , but it can be useful in situations where there is a large body of documents that come from sources that are not technologically advanced and can only use paper.

5.　　E-Forms: E-Forms are the electronic version of the above. Companies send data such as purchase orders or requisitions via electronic forms whose structure is known to both the sender and the recipient. The sender activates the E-Form on his system, fills in the blanks, and sends it via E-Mail or other mechanism to the recipient. At that end, the E-Form is reconstructed and populated by the data. This is used primarily where the data is generated and processed by humans rather than directly by applications. There are many human-based EC systems built around the use of E-Forms, including Lotus Notes™.

This technique is quite useful where there is a limited number of partners that share the "form" that is being used. When additional partners are added, it is necessary for them to subscribe to the use of this "form", causing extra work on their part, or possible incompatibilities in data or in process. By its very nature, this restricts the technique to those who are willing to abide by yet another "Standard", whereas with EDI, the "Standard" is already in place, and generally accepted by a wide body of users.

6.　　Document management systems: These are forms-based systems that categorize, sort, manage and control forms as they "move" electronically from work station to work station within a company. In cases such as loan processing, claims adjusting, or patent approval, where human processing is the driver for the system (rather than the contents of the form itself), document management systems can reduce delays in processing and process changes are easier to identify and implement.

Document management systems are capable of simulating all of the normal paper-based document processing activities such as sorting, indexing, file foldering, stick notes, annotations (text and voice), keyword retrieval, in and out-baskets, tickler files, and so on. The difference is that document management systems retain only one copy, and can route that to several different respondents at once, each seeing only that portion of the form that is relevant to the job at hand. Sequential processing models can easily evolve into parallel processing models, where the document can be worked on simultaneously by several different participants.

7.　　E-Mail data transfer mechanisms: Data can be transferred through the E-Mail mechanism by "attaching" a data file or a form to the

E-Mail message, sometimes with the ability to encrypt. This mechanism is different for each type of E-Mail facility. It may necessary to employ a utility to convert or encode/decode attachments between differing systems.

8.   Hybrid messaging: Hybrid messaging refers to the carrying of a mixture of data formats within the same message structure, such as E-Mail, forms, EDI messages, graphic images, video and sound. An example would be an X.400 message that contains:

a)   A mail message from the Engineering Manager of Company A to the Engineering Manager of Company B confirming the plans for joint product development between the two companies and discussing schedules and resources.

b)   An EDI Item Master transaction for the part in question

c)   An EDI Technical Specification transaction for the part

d)   A drawing of the part

This neatly delivers all of the related documentation to the receiver in a single transmission, eliminating the delays and "re-construction" effort that would ensue if they were each sent separately and arrived at different times.

9.   Mail-enabled and EDI-enabled applications: These are business applications such as Manufacturing, Distribution, Inventory Management, Hospital Admissions, etc. that have the capability and the necessary data structures to create and receive EDI messages or to send/receive information via a direct E-Mail interface.

10.   Smart cards, Swipe Cards and other personal storage devices: Data can be recorded to, and retrieved from, Smart Cards and other such devices. This can include medical insurance coverage, credit limits, bank balances, and other information of a personal nature that is used as input to or output from the electronic commerce process.

An ECE that includes public access to the company's products or services may incorporate these devices into their system architecture in one form or another. For example, hospitals may use Smart Cards to read a patient's insurance information and limited medical history. This is captured electronically and now may be used by the hospital's system.

Retail outlets that accept ATM or credit cards can automatically capture account information and sales information and for use by their system. They can use this information to automatically initiate a funds transfer from the bank or credit card company. Public telephones, gasoline pumps, automatic dispensers and other electronic purchase/payment mechanisms have the same capability to capture information directly from the cards and eliminate re-keying.

11.   Palmtop Computers, PDA's and other personal computing devices: These devices can capture sales information, inventory requests, and scheduling information in the field, access corporate data bases such as Lotus

Notes™, and otherwise communicate with servers, desktops and laptops. This can be accomplished either by direct connection upon return to the office, transfer of files by diskette, or by remote connection (Notes, in-house E-Mail, Internet ftp, EDI through a VAN, etc.)

12. EDI and OpenEDI: EDI is by far the most widely used mechanism for the reliable exchange of high volumes of standard business transactions between companies. Over 50,000 companies in North America use EDI on a daily basis to transact business with their major Trading Partners.

One of the difficulties of EDI has been the emergence of industry-specific standards. For example the EDI Purchase Order transaction, while it has a standard framework, differs significantly between industries such as Manufacturing, Pharmaceuticals, and Grocery. OpenEDI is an attempt to resolve these issues, and will become more prominent as it matures.

13. Real-Time EDI: Normally, EDI is a store-and-forward mechanism that uses mailboxes maintained by a Value-Added Network (VAN) to exchange transactions between Trading Partners. This can involve time delays ranging from minutes to hours before the exchange of an EDI transaction is complete. In some cases, this delay is not acceptable.

The primary example is that of a hospital Emergency Room. The medical staff cannot wait for minutes or hours for information regarding a patient's medical history or insurance coverage. The need for information is "Real-Time". In this case, mailboxing is not used. Rather, the VAN creates a virtual circuit between the requestor and the supplier of the information. EDI transactions are exchanged over the circuit in real time.

14. Proprietary data interchange formats: Some of the major retailers such as Wal-Mart and Food Lion use EDI with their suppliers, but do not use a publicly approved standard such as X12 or EDIFACT. Since they were among the pioneers of EDI, they evolved their own proprietary EDI transactions, and require their suppliers to use these in all transactions. While these companies are in the process of migrating to public standards, it is a slow process and will take some time and effort to complete.

This forces the suppliers to maintain the proprietary standard as well as the public standards, and to differentiate the use of them according to the Trading Partner they are communicating with. An ECE will need to be able to support both public and proprietary EDI standards into the foreseeable future.

15. Public data bases: Part of a company's information portfolio may be contained in public data bases that are created and maintained by other companies or government agencies. If the information content and access methods of these data bases are known, then the ECE can be designed to make use of the information contained in them as though they belonged to the company. They may be made available to applications or to individuals through an on-line query facility if the database has that capability.

16.   Subscription information services (D&B, S&P, Gartner, Dow Jones, etc.): These data bases are characterized by their high degree of volatility. The information contained in these data bases or subscription services is primarily of value to a human reader accessing through on-line query. However, the subscription service can periodically download information such as currency exchange rates that can be used directly by the company's applications. The ECE should be designed to include this type of access to information, along with the procedures required for its deployment and optimum use within the company.

Dimension 6: Technologies

These are the current and emerging technologies that will be used by people to conduct their personal Electronic Commerce business through the ECE and by systems developers to configure flexible EC systems.   These technologies include:

1.   Language translation - Verbal and written language conducts personal business across international boundaries and differing economic systems.

2.   Speech and pattern recognition - Used in personal interface to applications.   System commands and data entry can be verbal, and pattern recognition can assist in handwritten input.

3.   Remote sensing - Used to establish an empty or stock-out condition in storage tanks, containers or shelves, eliminating the need for taking physical inventory for ordering purposes. Replenishment orders can be generated automatically, and delivery can be scheduled efficiently. Remote sensing could also allow a customer to establish the status of his order while in production.

4.   Remote manipulation - Used for such activities as automated stock picking or movement of materials by robotic devices.   Remote manipulation can also be used in a virtual reality environment to allow a customer to inspect a sample item for purchase.

5.   Shop Floor CIM (Computer Integrated Manufacturing) interfaces - This type of interface would allow an application program to download an electronic specification directly from an EDI message into the shop floor device that is to produce the part.

6.   Locator mechanisms - These allow a user to fix the location of a shipment of goods or a physical asset such as a PC. This enhances the scheduling activity and the management of assets.

7.   Automated route mapping mechanisms - These facilitate the logistics side of commerce by planning the route of the shipment and providing a real-time electronic map to the driver during delivery.   The shipment destination information is processed by the application software. The resulting route plan is loaded into an on-board computer on the truck, which displays the optimal route. If used in conjunction with a locator mechanism, it could

facilitate the process of fleet management.

8.   Personal messaging, digital assistants - These are the wallet-sized palm tops or PDA's that have limited storage capacity, but support basic word processing, spreadsheets, and schedules. These may be integrated in both directions, to download information collected by the individual during the day, or to upload information to the individual as needed depending on the situation (such as a particular word processing document, contract, spreadsheet, cost estimate, etc.)

9.   Pericomputers or "Ubiquitous Computing" (Weiser, 1995) - These are computers that are embedded into traditionally non-computing devices such as conference room display screens, traffic flow monitors, dock sensors, conveyor belts, and so on. These may be integrated with display or graphics software, or scheduling software.

10.   Pen-based computing - These are devices that are useful for gathering handwritten signature type information in situations where it is necessary to establish proof of delivery or of personal authorization. This type of computing is presently being used by UPS (United Parcel Service) in home delivery. The ECE would contain the software drivers and internal data delivery mechanisms necessary to interface this information with existing applications.

11.   Multi-media applications - These permit the inclusion of graphics and sound into an application. This would be useful in a situation such as an engineering drawing or a patent application, where there would be text, graphic images, motion video, and voice-over describing the product. The multi-media application would need to be able to store, retrieve, manipulate, and integrate the data into other applications.

12.   Video conferencing and ad-hoc conferencing - This would allow the company to initiate personal conferences either over dedicated lines (for specific sites on a repetitive basis) or over a medium such as the Internet for ad hoc or one-time conferences. This can include full-motion video (not on the Internet for some time yet, however), file transfer, document exchange, joint workspace, interactive presentations, shared whiteboards, and other tools that facilitate human communication.

13.   Expert systems - Expert systems may be integrated into the ECE to assist with routine diagnostics and problem-solving. These are based on rule sets developed by experts in various areas and may be applied in areas such as Help Desk, software and systems support, and others.

14.   Home computing systems - These must often be integrated into the systems environment in such a way as to become invisible to the operation. Documents, spreadsheets, presentations, data files, and other products of home computers must be made seamlessly available to the systems on the corporate LAN or mainframe, just as if they were connected locally. This requires specialized "remote" software and specialized setup.

By the same token, the products of LAN or mainframe processing must be made seamlessly available to remote users as required to perform their jobs. Sending diskettes back and forth or "downloading" files is too cumbersome and time-consuming to be efficient, and these problems must be solved via an integrated ECE.

15.   Object-oriented tools - Object Oriented Programming (OOP) is seen by many as the wave of the future for developing systems and for establishing new ways of thinking about processes. The ECE must provide the ability to exploit the latest in Object Technology for the support and enhancement of existing systems and processes, as well as for the rapid and easy development of new systems.

16.   System Development tools - The ECE must allow for the latest in system development tools, data modeling tools, and other such aids to rapid application development and prototyping. The ECE must accommodate new tools quickly and easily, must facilitate the transition from old to new, and support a varied application development environment.

17.   EC emulators - These are testing tools designed to simulate an EC environment and to generate transaction traffic. This permits the analysis and debugging of the EC system, including the applications links, the EDI or E-Mail package, the EDI Translator, the communications software, etc. The ECE must provide for its own diagnosis and treatment.

Summary:

In order for a company to conduct Electronic Commerce with external parties in a safe and secure manner, it is first necessary to attain a state of internal EC-readiness by undertaking those internal activities that will equip it to handle EC effortlessly and flawlessly along with its existing paper-based processes.

The first step is to develop an EC Startup Plan that will institute a basic EC capability and ensure that the company is at a state of technological, procedural, and organizational readiness. The next step is to develop the EC Strategic Plan. This is a set of integrated strategic and tactical plans that will position the company for flexibility and responsiveness in the EC marketplace over the longer term.

The top level of the EC Strategic Plan is developed in the Management Workshops. It is given shape and definition as the Task Force does its more detailed investigation The EC Strategic Plan consists of two components, the "Operating Strategy" and the "Technology Strategy". The Operating Strategy specifies the general sequence and timing of EC functionality. The Technology Strategy specifies the general systems and technology environment that will support the Operating Strategy. This is known as the company's "Electronic Commerce Environment", or ECE.

The Tactical Plans follow the individual Phases of the EC Strategic Plan. They specify the corporate programs that need to be in place to support this functionality, the policies and procedures, and details and the timing of the systems and equipment to be deployed. These will be constantly modified and refined during ICBE, because other Member companies are involved, each exerting influence on the other Members. Only the first Phase of the company's EC Strategic Plan will exist in any level of detail until the actual ICBE process begins. It is still wise, however, for the company to have an initial game plan in mind before it becomes involved in ICBE with other companies.

An ECE consists of six "dimensions", fully integrated with each other, with the Legacy systems currently in place, and with future core business applications. These are:

1. Processes. The guiding principles, practices and mechanisms under which Electronic Commerce is to be implemented and conducted.

2. EC Infrastructure. The software, hardware and intelligent internal/external System Agents ("Smartbots") needed to interface core applications and legacy systems to the other elements of the ECE and to the outside world

3. Architectures. The physical and logical components that execute the business functions of the Electronic Commerce system and determine its topology, configuration, and interrelationships with other Trading Partners.

4. Connectivity. This is the seamless dialog with the outside world for both the applications and the users themselves.

5. Information. The mechanisms by which information is captured, represented, standardized, converted, and communicated within the Electronic Commerce marketplace.

6. Technologies. The present and future technologies that systems developers and end users will employ to interface with the ECE and related applications, and to personally direct the conduct of Electronic Commerce.

Taken together, these six dimensions provide a tailored "environment" that is unique to the company, its internal processes and style of business practice, its systems, its hardware and software configuration, and its culture. Every element within the "environment" is configured to operate together. It is focused on the conduct of EC within the company and with outside parties.

During the ICBE process, the lessons learned from the ongoing evolution of the company's ECE can be passed on. The other Members can develop their own ECE's to achieve compatibility of systems and operations. In its ultimate expression, a single ECE can span organizations, streamlining the conduct of commerce among them.

Once the company has achieved a state of internal EC-readiness, it may then turn its attention outward to the business community within which it operates, and move on to the next phase, that of Inter-Corporate Business Engineering.

CHAPTER XI

STEP 3: INTER-CORPORATE TEAM BUILDING

The Membership Drive: Recruiting Candidates

As difficult and arduous as it has been to bring the company even to an initial state of EC-readiness, you have at least had some measure of control over your own staff up to this point. The minute you step outside your door and try to convince other companies to work with you, it's a whole new ball game. They have absolutely no motivation except money. They don't think the way you do. They don't have the same values or corporate culture as you. They haven't been through the rites of passage that you just have. They don't have your newly found evangelical fervor, and they have their own agendas that hardly ever line up with yours.

Your company is embarking on an entirely new enterprise. You are now venturing into unfamiliar territory, and this requires a steadfast commitment from the top. That is why it was so important to build internal management commitment before beginning your own EC-readiness exercise. You need your top management to gain the commitment of their top management. Now is the time to stop thinking just in terms of EC as it relates to your company. Start thinking of EC in the context of ICBE within the end-to-end Value System. That is what you have been preparing for.

This presents a high degree of difficulty, compounded by the fact that there are usually several companies to work with, each concerned with its own best interests. There is absolutely no way to accomplish ICBE alone, so the enthusiastic participation of all Members is essential for success. The high degree of difficulty, instead of discouraging the Members, should strengthen their resolve to find ways to do it right the first time and to make the effort profitable for all concerned. If it's that hard to do, you don't want to have to do it twice.

The ICBE Champion Company:

Recruiting other companies and gaining their commitment is the most difficult and time-consuming activity of ICBE, and has no measurable payback in and of itself. As the "Champion" company for ICBE, you must be fully informed, understanding, patient and committed to the results or the entire ICBE process will fail (just like the internal Champion). If you are expecting immediate ROI, you are likely to be disappointed. It is going to take time to achieve meaningful and permanent results. If you have done your homework, though, you should have a good idea what those results will eventually be, and you will be prepared to see it through.

In any ICBE process, the "Champion" is the Member who initiates the exercise, the one who is responsible for the bulk of the activities in the Value System. The "Champion" provides the core material or service, or is most closely associated with the end consumer of the product or service.

Even though all Members should have a co-equal voice during the ICBE process, and corporate personalities should not dominate, this Member's needs should be the focal point, since they most closely represent the true needs of the marketplace. This keeps the attention where it should be, on the customer, instead of on the individual companies and their priorities.

Focusing on this Member's needs results in a "pull" of goods and services through the System based on actual need, as opposed to the traditional "push" based on forecasts or the (perceived) need for maintaining discretionary inventory. This is where quantum benefits are realized. The end consumer's *buying action* dictates what is produced by the Value System, instead of everybody in the chain trying to guess or hedge their bets against unforeseen inventory demand.

If your company is not the one closest to the final consumer, but you are still planning to be the ICBE Champion within your particular Value System, then you will likely have to approach ICBE in 2 stages:

1.   First, you must Champion ICBE for your "supply side" Members (your downline suppliers or service providers) by using EC and ICBE to align their business processes with yours to achieve a smooth delivery function in and out of your operation. In the eyes of your upline customers, you shouldn't even be talking to them about "shrinking the business cycle" or "closing the Response Gaps" until you can deliver what you say when you say. If they're going to pump time and money into the effort, they can't afford to fail because you haven't gotten control of your own supplier base or delivery network.

2.   When that has been achieved, you can approach your "demand side" Members (your upline customers) and use ICBE to align your business processes with theirs and plug smoothly into the "supply side" of their operation. Even if your upline customer is a giant like K-Mart and declines to participate with you, your downline ICBE efforts will still have given you the advantage of a smooth, optimized delivery operation. You will be way ahead of your closest competitors.

If you are indeed the one that is closest to the end consumer, then you still want to start by Championing ICBE for your supply-side Members. The only difference is that when you have achieved this, you have no formal "upline" to go to except your consumer base. While you may enact customer-based strategies that include consumers in your product planning cycle, that goes beyond the scope of ICBE itself. Further iterations of the ICBE process may result from this, however, as the Members seek to refine the Value System. ICBE should be thought of as an ongoing "Process", not as a "Project" that has a beginning and an end. This is a whole new set of business relationships and a new way of doing business. It should be expected to continue on for as long as there are Response Gaps in the System.

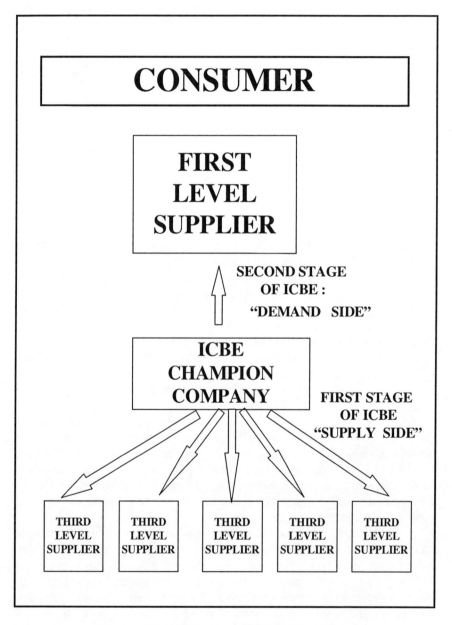

Fig. 30. The Position of the ICBE Champion

Now, we move on to the first step in the ICBE process--gaining control over your downstream suppliers and service providers. You are their upline customer. You are closer to the end consumer, and you are the one with the most at stake. They should already see you as a leader, because you have already given this some thought. Also you have done some demonstrable work in this area, and you have insight and experience that can add value.

Potential ICBE Membership Candidates

Potential ICBE Members are drawn from the first tier ranks of your company's closest partners in the Value System in question. These are likely to be a few well-known companies that have long-standing relationships with you, and who have an evident stake in the success of ICBE.

If you have done your preliminary cut at the "Big Board" model during the Management Workshops, the ICBE candidates should be fairly obvious. The goal is to eventually recruit all of the participants in your Value System, in the order of their impact on the flow of goods and services to you.

To state the obvious, you should not recruit suppliers who are also your direct competitors, even if they do not compete with you in this particular line of business. Their presence on the Team could open the initiative up to suspicion. Suppliers of yours who also supply your direct competitors should be recruited with caution for the same reason. There may be the potential for competitive misuse of commonly developed systems and services.

All relationships should be clearly demonstrated to be at arms length and free of collusion. Collusion, as defined by Webster, is "a secret understanding between two or more persons prejudicial to another" and is intended to limit or eliminate competition in an unfair manner. If two competitors are involved in any joint strategic endeavor such as ICBE, it could give the appearance of collusion. This must be avoided at all costs.

The CEO's Sales Pitch:

Senior management is indispensable in this recruiting effort. Anyone of a lower rank than CEO or Vice President simply won't be taken seriously by other companies. The ideal situation is for the CEO to make the initial contact with the other CEO's (one-on-one) over lunch or at a private meeting (not just a phone call). Set up a "meeting of the minds" on the subject of a joint EC initiative and the ICBE activities required to get there.

The CEO should have the facts and figures at hand, and be able to convince them to agree in principle to the concept of ICBE with your company. Their CEO and senior management team should be invited to attend a high-level presentation and site visit at your company where they can see for themselves what you have achieved (a "Discovery Day"). The details can then be taken over by your Torchbearer and the rest of your management team, each working with their counterparts in the other companies.

The biggest mistake would be for the Champion company's internal staff such as the MIS Director, Engineering Manager or Purchasing Manager to make contacts at his/her level, since those counterparts will not be empowered to make the kinds of commitments that need to be made. They can't allocate the necessary funds. They can't make corporate policy, and they can't commit corporate resources. Driving ICBE from a technical or functional perspective also sends the wrong message. It needs to be driven from the corporate level.

Overcoming Resistance to ICBE:

When you start recruiting, there will be resistance. You may have to get past some stiff objections. If you've been down this road before, you may recognize some of these:

1.   **We're too small and undeveloped to benefit from EC**. It is more effort and cost than it is worth to them. In these cases, it may be advisable to develop a cheap and easy EC work-around or permit manual "paper-based" communications such as Fax or E-Mail if the Member is of sufficient importance to the Value System. This will at least return some quick benefits to both parties and demonstrate your sincerity in arriving at a real solution instead of just peddling a new theory.

2.   **We have no resources to undertake any kind of program at this time**. We have other things on the go that are more important to our survival. Once again, depending on their importance to the System and the validity of their objection, it may be advisable to make funding or resources available to them, for later recovery out of the savings.

3.   **We already have an EDI program in place and we want YOU to comply with IT**. Depending on the program and their importance to the System, they may very well be right. Even though they are your supplier, they may be bigger than you are, and may be further along in EC. Leverage off whatever you can or make the necessary accommodations wherever possible. Don't ask them to reinvent their own wheel. If they become working Members, they may contribute some valuable experience and insights to the System. Over the long term, they will likely end up making whatever changes are reasonable and correct in any case.

4.   **We are not convinced that there are real benefits, or that your company is serious about following through**. As mentioned above, you should get their senior management into your premises for a one-on-one "Discovery Day" with your own senior management (see "The CEO's Sales Pitch" above). Share the cost / benefit analysis figures (as much as you can). Go through the work that has already been done by senior management in your own company. Talk about their place in the Big Board model and ask them to plug their numbers into the model to satisfy themselves that there are benefits

be had. Share your company's formal plans for ICBE and the rationale behind them. This will show them your level of corporate commitment and will hopefully go a long way toward alleviating their concerns.

5. **This is just a flash in the pan, another management fad that will fizzle out and leave us holding the bag for a lot of wasted time and effort.** If they have been through a failed effort before, such as MRP II, JIT, TQM, etc. then they will understandably be "gun-shy" and doubly hard to convince about any new theories. Here is where your own senior management, particularly the CEO, needs to be rock-steady in the resolve to pursue ICBE. He/she has to make it crystal clear that your company is willing to make the commitment to proceed, and that the effort certainly will not fail on your account. It needs to be communicated that ICBE and EC are not themselves the goals of the exercise. They are only the tools. The goals are **streamlining the business cycle** and **reducing costs** across the Value System. Once a company can focus on to the concepts and the expected results rather than on the methods and the buzzwords, this objection will hopefully disappear. If you can't convince them, re-examine your own level of commitment. Maybe they're right.

6. **We want to wait and see how the others do and what mistakes are made before we jump in.** Observers are fine. They will soon become participants when they see successful results. The problem is that some observers tend to want to run things without contributing, since they have nothing at stake. This must be carefully managed. They should be invited to join the team every time they express an opinion. Hopefully, they will soon get the message. At the very least, they'll go back to their companies and make some of the changes you have been talking about in the ICBE sessions so that they are almost up to speed when they do join in. This benefits everyone.

7. **We supply the same products to your competitors. Why would you want to help us be more efficient so that we can supply them better ?** Here is a very good question. You might not want to deal with these companies at all. If you do deal with them, you should make certain that whatever you do does not impact their ability to serve your competitors now or in the future. At the same time, you must ensure that you are providing value to them that your competitors do not (more about this in Chapter XIII, under "Best Practices"). While your competitors may enjoy some of the benefits of your labor by the fact that the supplier has improved his operation, they will not gain the direct benefits that either you or the supplier will. You may provide some of the tools for the supplier to serve them faster, but at the same time you are forging a closely-knit and growing strategic relationship that they are not. You may wish to negotiate terms that relate the contribution of these companies to the value that they receive from the exercise.

8.   **We don't believe that we need to make any changes or put
out any extra effort. If you want our business, you have to do it our way.** If
this objection cannot be overcome by any of the above techniques, then it may
be time to look elsewhere for a Member to fill that niche in the System. This
may not be realistic in all cases, but a Member who is not willing to work with
others will be a liability to the System and will likely not be successful over the
long term. This may be a good way of tightening up the System by weeding out
the old bottlenecks and recruiting new Members who are all ready willing and
able to work with each other toward a common goal.

Obviously, some companies have developed this attitude because they
are the Wal-Marts of the world. They have enough clout to get their own way
because they are the end customer. A successful ICBE process will be flexible
enough to deal with these companies in whatever way they dictate. It will
accommodate their needs as a part of the overall System.

The Alpha Team

ICBE, since it is a multi-corporate effort, requires the active
participation of senior management from each of the Members, working as an
"Alpha Team". The Alpha Team is a special multi-corporate construct,
existing above all other organizational issues and apart from individual
organizational constraints.   It consists of the Chief Executives and
Torchbearers of each of the Members, working together as a Steering
Committee for the ICBE process and all that follows.

The Alpha Team should be properly constituted as an operating body
with decision-making authority, and formally chartered to "do whatever it
takes" to achieve its stated objectives relating to inter-corporate commerce. It
can either be jointly funded by the Members as a temporary working group or it
can be set up as a separate organization. The format and content of the
operating agreements is up to the Members and their preferences or legal
requirements, and the subject is beyond the scope of this book. The important
elements, however, are the Alpha Team's independence from the political and
operating constraints of individual Member companies, and its empowerment
to make decisions and achieve cross-corporate results.

It is important that all Members be co-equal partners. Such equality is
mitigated only by the extent of their personal stake in the results or their
contribution to the core process. It may be advisable for the Alpha Team to
engage an independent facilitator to drive the activities and to adjudicate
differences in opinion or direction among Members. Even though there will
likely be a dominant Member, possibly the one who initiated ICBE and
recruited the other participants (the Champion), this Member cannot be
allowed to exert an undue influence on the interests of the group as a whole or

distract the group from the primary goal of streamlining the business cycle for the end consumer. In this regard, the Facilitator can be of value only if he/she exists outside all of the organizational influences of the Members. **Figure 31** shows a suggested Alpha Team structure.

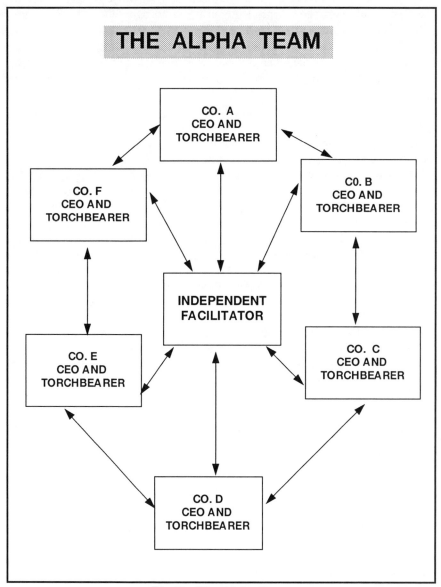

Fig.31. The Alpha Team

This model places each of the Members in a non-hierarchical "round table", each with equal weight in the process. At the center is the Facilitator, who drives the activities, schedules events, moderates discussions, helps resolve issues of contention, produces deliverables, and maintains the integrity of the overall process. It is critical that the Facilitator be properly empowered to break ties and to operate independently or the effort will fail. If the Facilitator can be overruled or removed at whim the effort will be seen to be a sham. If the Champion is seen to be dominating the proceedings and the Facilitator is seen simply as a clerk, the other Members will soon lose interest and go back to business as usual. This has to be a legitimate joint effort, led by an impartial entity.

The existence of the Alpha Team distinguishes ICBE from all other "project" oriented activities that the companies have engaged in previously. Many companies have, over the years, implemented joint "EDI projects" that involve one or more parties. Joint ventures are nothing new. These projects or joint ventures, however, do not usually promote a team spirit. They consist merely of a number of separate organizations that work together for a period of time to achieve a single well-defined goal and then go their separate ways, allowing the gains they have made to deteriorate over time. These projects fail to align the companies from an ideological perspective. They fail to make lasting changes in business processes, and generally favor the initiating party. These projects have a beginning and an end. The players change from one "project" to the next--there is no overall game plan that spans all the participants. The Alpha Team, by contrast, provides:

1.   **Identity**: The very fact of having a name, a structure and a charter provides a sense of identity and tends to give the initiative a sort of "life of its own". The Alpha Team has the ability to achieve the status of an independent Going Concern that survives for an indefinite period for the benefit of all concerned.

2.   **Partnership**: Having the senior management of each Member company as part of the Alpha Team fosters a sense of partnership among the Members and reduces the chance of one Member realizing the bulk of the benefits at the expense of the others. It is much more conducive to a "All For One, One For All" mindset.

3.   **Synergy**: The ability of the Alpha Team to make inter-corporate decisions and to deploy resources and expertise among all Members promotes a synergistic effect. What one company could not accomplish by itself, it can accomplish with the aid of the other Members. With the existence of an "immortal" Alpha Team, the initiative can take advantage of continuous improvement of the processes and practices and realize greater returns than if they had acted as single companies.

4.   **Continuity**: The Alpha Team survives any and all individual Pilot projects or other joint business initiatives. Its goal is to remain a guiding

force for the duration of the relationships among its Members and to provide a continuity of style and direction. While individual Members may come and go as the Value System changes, the Alpha Team retains its individual members and thus its overall focus.

Duties of the Alpha Team

The Alpha Team is the first line of experimentation. New business concepts are developed here. They are tested out operationally "in vitro" before proceeding with a full scale roll out to the Membership's other electronic trading partners. As each business function is introduced, it can be operated in a controlled pilot project environment to solve the problems associated with implementation (more on this later).

The Alpha Team is the overall "Steering Committee" for the ICBE process, and these terms will be used interchangeably from here on. Its Members establish the business intent, the grand vision and key objectives for ICBE. They set the overall operating parameters, monitor progress, and make adjustments as required. The Alpha Team should consist of two representatives from each Member company: the CEO or equivalent, and the Executive Torchbearer. With small companies, these may well be the same individual, but their roles on the Alpha Team are different.

The CEO of each Member company is responsible for the strategic, financial, and operating decisions relating to his or her company, and for contributing to those same decisions as they apply to the entire Alpha Team. The types of strategic decisions that are made at this level can include such things as:

1.   Streamlining the procurement cycle through strategies such as Automated Procurement, Quick Response, Efficient Consumer Response, Vendor Managed Inventory, etc.

2.   Gaining better control over the logistics and delivery operation through partnering and strategic alliances with transportation providers, Direct Store Delivery, Evaluated Receipts Settlement, electronic customs and brokerage interfaces, etc.

3.   Automating payments through Financial EDI, Paid On Production, Electronic Cash applications, etc.

4.   Sharing plant and equipment resources such as computer equipment, software and staff.

5.   Developing new products and services centered around the EC marketplace, such as electronic catalogs, online ordering, Internet-based marketing and product support, etc.

6.   Setting goals for financial return, and for the reduction of the business cycle.

7.   Developing new approaches to EC in general

The CEOs retain oversight responsibility and final decision-making authority, and are the source of funding for the ICBE process. The CEOs need not be devoted full-time to ICBE, since in the real world, there are many other things going on that require the same or higher level of attention. By the same token, however, if they fail to give the necessary attention and support, the effort will not be successful. In the final analysis, the degree of success or failure is directly attributable to the CEOs of the Member companies.

The Torchbearers, on the other hand, are the day-to-day operating managers of ICBE. As such they should be more committed in terms of their time and involvement. They make the tactical and operating decisions, and are responsible for such things as:

1.   Developing the overall business plan for the strategic approaches identified by the CEOs

2.   Recommending changes in strategic approaches to the CEOs based on unfolding circumstances or events during actual implementation

3.   Analyzing the Value System and identifying the Response Gaps

4.   Developing tactical solutions to close the Response Gaps

5.   Establishing specific objectives and measurements for these tactical solutions

6.   Creating Migration plans and Business Pilot Project Plans (more on this later)

They then oversee the efforts of the various multi-corporate ICBE implementation teams that are charged with achieving the results. These Business Pilot Projects and the ICBE implementation teams will be discussed in more detail later.

Building Executive Commitment in the Alpha Team

As with the "internal commitment" exercise, this may be a lengthy process and is by far the most important. Without full conceptual buy-in and funding from the Membership, ICBE cannot work. As with the "internal commitment" exercise, this buy-in can be achieved through a series of joint strategy workshops, facilitated either by the Champion or a third-party facilitator, and involving the senior management of the companies involved.

Once again, these workshops will typically deal only with executive-level concepts at this point. This is not the definitive EC strategy for the System. This is introducing the players, starting the dialog, introducing some basic ideas, obtaining agreement in principle and providing general direction subject to further definition and justification.

By now, the Champion company has experience in the use of the tools and understands the mechanisms. The best way to go forward is by employing exactly the same techniques as were used to gain internal commitment. If your internal executive could be convinced of the feasibility and cost-effectiveness of the exercise, then the same evidence should convince other CEOs to join the effort. In addition, you already have most of the material, and it should be easier to customize it than to develop new material from scratch. Much like the internal EC-readiness exercise, the sequence of events will consist of:

1.   Pre-Selling Activities
2.   CEO's Workshop
3.   Management Workshops
4.   Consensus and Commitment Workshop
5.   ICBE Business Plan and General Announcement

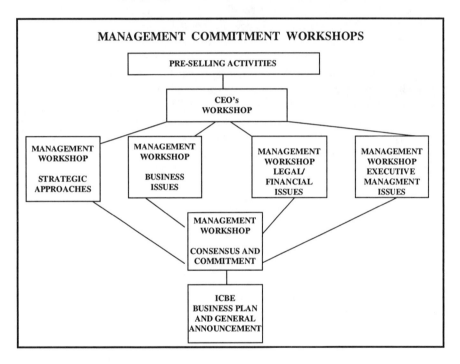

Fig.32. The Alpha Team Commitment Process

Figure 33 presents an example of a letter of invitation from the Champion company's CEO to the other CEO candidates, announcing the CEO's Workshop. This should be sent out just after the one-on-one sessions and the Discovery Day visits. The ones that have responded favorably to the concepts of ICBE and who have taken the time and trouble to attend the Discovery Day are at least conceptually on board and are ready for the next step. The time has come to roll up the sleeves and start work.

Date:
To: CEO's of "Member Candidate" companies
From: CEO, Champion company
Subject: Executive Workshop on Electronic Commerce

As per our earlier discussions, we would like to pursue the possibilities of conducting a joint Inter-Corporate Business Engineering (ICBE) effort with the objective of reducing the overall business cycle and cutting costs for everyone involved. To this end, you are cordially invited to attend a 2-hour CEO's Workshop in "XXX facilities" on XXXX at 9:00 a.m.

This workshop will focus on the commercial possibilities of implementing an Electronic Commerce (EC) capability between our companies, and aligning our joint business processes to accelerate business, cut costs, and stay competitive.

I have included some examples of how other companies in our industry are using EC, and the successes they have achieved. If we are to experience the same levels of success, we must be prepared to commit our full support to this effort, and to do whatever it takes to make it work.

AGENDA:

9:00 - 9:30   Presentation - Business Imperatives

9:30 - 10:00   Discussion

10:00 - 10:45   Workshop

10:45 - 11:00   Wrap-up and consensus

This is a very important exercise, so I would ask that everyone bring their ideas, and avoid outside interruptions while we discuss this issue.

(SIGNATURE)

Fig.33. CEO's Workshop Announcement

CEO's Workshop Guidelines

The following outline contains suggestions for discussion material for the Executive Workshop, and guidelines for conducting it. This is an outline only, and there is substantial work to be done in preparation. As with the "internal commitment" exercise, here is where the Champion (now the CEO of the initiating Member company) either carries the day or loses the audience. The identical presentation and visual materials from the internal workshop may be used here, with audience-specific modifications where necessary. This session should be chaired by the CEO, with assistance from the Torchbearer as necessary.

9:00 - 9:30   Presentation - Business Imperatives
This short presentation sets the stage for the workshop that follows. The participants should already have been supplied with most of this material beforehand and some of the questions should have already been dealt with. Topics include:

1.   What EC is (and is not)
2.   General trends in EC
3.   Industry-specific success stories
4.   "Strawman" Value System strategies (as developed in the "internal commitment" phase)
5.   The "Alpha Team" concept (as outlined in this chapter)
6.   "Inter-Corporate Business Engineering" concepts

9:30 - 10:00   Discussion
This is to answer any questions or concerns regarding the application of EC, or the soundness of EC in general. The discussion must be carefully moderated to keep on topic and avoid any single individual dominating the conversation. You only have a half hour, and everyone should be heard. As with the internal workshop, Questions may arise in the areas of:

1.   Legal issues
2.   Control issues
3.   Costs
4.   General timeframes for implementation
5.   Disruption to the businesses involved or impact on existing programs
6.   "Horror Stories" and how to avoid them
7.   Readiness and willingness to proceed

Most of these issues will be dealt with later in the more detailed Alpha Team Workshops, but if there are unanswered questions, note them on a flip chart and commit to getting the answers. It may be necessary to schedule an off-line session for some particularly difficult issues.

10:00 - 10:45   Workshop

Use wall charts, flip charts, whiteboards, etc. to write down the results of the brainstorming session. If necessary, continue on or schedule another session if there are valuable ideas, enthusiasm and synergy occurring. As with the internal commitment workshop, do not cut off creativity just because the clock says 10:45. Here is where the emotional buy-in happens. It should not be limited by time if there is reason to continue. Some of the techniques below may help facilitate the discussion.

1.   Facilitate the discussion around the "Big Board" process model developed in the internal commitment exercise, and modify the model as necessary. Each of the Members should feel free to present their own ideas in the context of their position within the chain. What will result should be a full understanding of the Value System by everyone. It doesn't need to be in great detail at this stage, because these are the CEOs and they should understand the big picture quite well. This Big Board model will be carried forward into the ICBE activities to follow. It will form the basis of the Value System Analysis and the Migration plan design.

2.   Discuss the Value System in terms of the flow of business activity, the relative interdependencies of each of the areas, and the business value of each of the activities. Write the participants' EC ideas under each segment and discuss. Use consensus to arrive at a dominant strategic approach to be taken, such as Quick Response or Paid On Production.

3.   Develop general EC strategies that support the dominant strategic approach and rate them in descending order of priority, such as:

        a)   Point of Sale data capture,

        b)   sharing of production scheduling information,

        c)   or automating purchase orders.

This will serve to point the way by highlighting the type of ICBE that should be undertaken, and will consequently point each Member to the internal readiness activities they need to focus on.

4.   Focus on the "highest and best use" for EC in the Value System as a whole, in light of the dominant strategic approach. For example, if the dominant strategic approach is a Quick Response implementation, and the System's major bottleneck is the ability to move finished goods or perishables quickly and at low cost then the Transportation capability will likely provide the highest and best use for EC. If the Manufacturing process is the bottleneck, then Procurement and Logistics may prove to be the highest and best use. This will help select the proper EC Business Models to use in the Analysis phase to come.

5.   Discuss and validate the Alpha Team structure using Figure 28 as a model, (name the individuals) and adopt or modify the Team Charters for each of the functional teams (see **Figures 34-38**).

Once again, these are high-level ideas **only** at this stage. This is not the definitive Electronic Commerce strategy. This is providing general direction subject to further definition and justification. During further investigation, these priorities may change.

10:45 - 11:00   Wrap-up and Consensus

The ideas and strategies presented should be summarized briefly. Just as in the internal workshop, the question should be asked, "Assuming that the details can be worked out, is this something that we feel we should be doing?". If the answer is no, then two options exist:

1.   Drop the subject and go back to doing business as usual.

2.   Find out what the problems are, fix them, and start over. Do not proceed beyond this point if the answer is no.

The Alpha Team Management Workshops

If the answer is yes, then the Alpha Team Management Workshops should be scheduled with the various Member companies involved to resolve management-level issues specific to the operation. These Alpha Team Management Workshops consist of the Torchbearers and other relevant operating-level executives of the Member companies, chartered to delve further into the details and establish the application of ICBE within this framework of Member companies and this particular Value System. The sessions may follow the general guidelines laid out in Chapter IX.

Briefly, these workshops should cover all aspects of importance to the business cycle. Their purpose, apart from fleshing out the plans, is to remove the uncertainty and doubt on the part of the operating management of each of the Members, to finalize and solidify the concepts in everyone's minds, and to achieve complete buy-in. The deliverable from these workshops is the ICBE Business Plan. The workshops should cover such details as:

1.   Strategic approaches identified in the CEO's Workshop, e.g.:

a)   Quick Response/Efficient Consumer Response, Vendor Managed Inventory, Evaluated Receipts Settlement, etc. From a conceptual standpoint relating to this particular industry

b)   How these strategies apply specifically to the Members' situation, product lines to be implemented, sequencing of events, etc.

c)   Issues to be resolved

2.   Business issues, e.g.:

a)   The regulatory/legislative/competitive environment

b)   Existing initiatives (MRP II, TQM, etc.)

       c)   Degree of effort and level of commitment required from each Member

       d)   Preliminary budget estimates for each Member and for the total ICBE exercise

3.   Legal/financial issues, e.g.:

       a)   Purchase and sale of goods implications

       b)   Records retention and filing requirements

       c)   Security, secrecy and audit requirements

       d)   Inter-corporate control systems for EC

       e)   Details of the trading partner agreements

4.   Executive management issues, e.g.:

       a)   New business opportunities arising from EC

       b)   Key business/financial objectives

       c)   Critical success factors and measurement systems

       d)   Resource allocations, roles and responsibilities

5.   Consensus and Commitment:

       a)   ICBE Business Plan Presentation

       b)   Review and Adjustment

       c)   Consensus

       d)   Signing of the Letter of Intent and the General Announcement

The ICBE Business Plan

The ICBE Business Plan sets high-level objectives and unifies the focus for all Members. This is analogous to the EC Strategic Plan developed internally by the Champion company. The Champion can in fact use their own EC Strategic Plan as a discussion model for the ICBE Business Plan. This would be useful in two ways:

1.   It would facilitate discussion around a formal structure instead of allowing it to drift.

2.   It provides the opportunity for the Champion company to modify its own internal EC Strategic Plan to conform to the real-life requirements of the Membership.

The ICBE Business Plan does not need to be an involved, detailed document at this stage, since the actual ICBE process has not been started and the details have not yet been worked out. It should, however, set out the strategic direction of the Membership in clear terms, such as specifying a Quick Response initiative followed by Evaluated Receipts Settlement, followed by Financial EDI . This is just an example, yours may be different. The Business Plan portion should lay out the anticipated costs and benefits, the guidelines, and the measurements for success. The Analysis phase will provide the tactical approaches to achieving them.

Once the Alpha Team has ratified the ICBE Business Plan, then each

Member may begin its own internal EC-Readiness program, perhaps benefiting from the experience and insights gained by the Champion. Once again, this can be a long and involved process for the individual Members, and they should be kept focused on those activities that will support the ICBE Strategic Plan. In other words, they should be encouraged to implement a basic EC Startup Plan as opposed to developing their ECE. It may also be wise for each Member to subscribe to a Letter of Intent, outlining the ideals that are to be achieved, and formally committing their resources to the initiative. An example is provided in **Figure 34** below. This is for illustration purposes only, and it definitely should not, repeat, **SHOULD NOT** be used as is. As with any legal agreement, corporate counsel of all parties should be involved before anything is signed.

LETTER OF INTENT
RESPECTING ELECTRONIC COMMERCE

ABC, XXXX, VVVV, and YYYYY intend to form a business relationship with the aim of using Electronic Commerce (EC) for improving the timing and control of the exchange of business documents and related information.

In respect of the above, ABC, XXXX, VVVV, and YYYYY, ("The Parties") propose to enter into one or more arrangements respecting the communication of such business related documents or messages.

The first of such arrangements will consist of ...., and will be conducted as a joint "Pilot" supported by the senior management of all of the Parties.

All Parties will operate in good faith, using their best efforts to ensure that appropriate resources are dedicated to this task, and that a high priority is accorded to all activities involved.

Each of the Parties will bear its own costs of preparation and participation, with expectation of future benefits.

ABC, XXXX, VVVV, and YYYYY have executed this Letter of Intent each on the date below the signature of its duly authorized representative.

ABC Co.	XXXX Co.	VVVV Co.	YYYYY Co.
-----------------------	-----------------------	-----------------------	----------------------
Signature	**Signature**	**Signature**	**Signature**
----------------------	----------------------	----------------------	----------------------
(Print name)	**(Print name)**	**(Print name)**	**(Print name)**
----------------------	----------------------	-----------------------	----------------------
Title	**Title**	**Title**	**Title**
----------------------	----------------------	-----------------------	-----------------------
Date	**Date**	**Date**	**Date**

Fig. 34. Letter of Intent Respecting Electronic Commerce

GENERAL ANNOUNCEMENT

DATE:
TO: All Department Heads, supervisors and staff (of each
                 Company)
FROM: CEO and Senior Management names and titles (of each
                 Company

As technology grows in leaps and bounds, the business world is constantly being challenged to keep up.   New technologies offer new opportunities to improve and enhance the business environment, and the majority of our competitors are using them to seize the advantage.

As senior management, it is our responsibility to maintain the competitive position of this company and its partners in business. In order to accomplish this in such a rapidly changing world, we must change the way we do business in general. We must streamline the flow of goods, services and communications between ourselves and the companies we deal with; we must eliminate the costly overhead and unnecessary delays caused by excessive paperwork and outdated practices. We must reduce the overall costs of doing business for everyone along the chain, including our suppliers and distributors. We must find new ways to accelerate the delivery of our products and services to our end customers. This is the formula for our future success.

As the first in a series of bold steps, we plan to involve some of our key customers and suppliers in aligning their business processes with ours and in designing a smooth, end-to-end business cycle so that we can all achieve the cost reductions and speedy deliveries that are so crucial to remaining competitive. These companies will join with us in a combined effort that will span organizational boundaries and result in a smoother operation and better profitability for all concerned.

The companies that we will be working with are: XXXX, VVVV, and YYYYY. We have met with the senior management of these companies over the last few weeks, and we all feel that we can benefit from such an arrangement. We have begun to put the wheels in motion to design better ways of working together, and we would like to request your assistance in making this a successful endeavor. Thank you for your support.

(SIGNATURE)

Fig. 35. General Announcement to the Membership

ICBE Implementation Team Structure:

Once the ICBE Business Plan has been developed, attention must turn to implementing it through application of ICBE principles. This requires a multi-corporate, multi-disciplinary team of individuals that can follow through from Value System Analysis, through developing the Migration plans, through planning the Business Pilot Projects, through final implementation and rollout.

The following Team structure (**Figure 36**) is suggested as the most effective method of controling a simultaneous implementation involving multiple Members. The underlying principles are those of **separation of function** and **concentration of focus.** So even though the same individual may work on different teams at different times (and they do), the mandate of that particular team is sharply defined, and team activities are tightly focused on only that function and none other.

This separation and concentration prevents, for example, the Project Management Team from being distracted by detailed technology problems or systems development issues are the sole purview of the Technology Team. When the Project Management Team (PMT) meets, they are focused solely on the job of Project control and decision-making, and the meeting agenda is designed to reflect that. When the Technology Team meets, they focus solely on the job of defining the technology architectures, integrating the software, designing the EDI message structures and so on, and are not distracted by issues of process engineering, the mechanics of shipping and receiving with electronic documents, or EC-based accounting. Once again, the meeting agenda is designed to reflect that focus and none other.

The key to the success of the implementation teams is that all Members are represented on each of the teams, reporting to a strong "Implementation manager" acting as expediter and decision-maker. This individual is accountable for the project results, and likely will come from the senior ranks of the Champion Member (possibly, but not necessarily, the Torchbearer) or from a third party facilitator. The Implementation Manager is not likely to be the same person as the Alpha Team Facilitator, since different skill sets are involved for each of these tasks. The Implementation Manager is usually a hands-on operations-oriented person, while the Alpha Team Facilitator is more of a senior-management level visionary. Team efforts are coordinated and integrated, by the Implementation Manager, assisted by the Planning and Facilitation Team (PFT).

The key to the success of this approach is the setting of the scope and authority for each of the teams, and ensuring that these are not exceeded as the team fulfills its mandate. This technique ensures that the time is well spent as opposed to getting off on side issues that the team is not capable of addressing.

A unique feature of this structure is that, while the number of different teams may look awkward and imposing, in actual practice only a few individuals need to be involved from each Member. For example, one person may sit on the Project Management Team, lead the Planning and Facilitation Team, lead the Technology Team, and sit on both the Operations Team and the Audit and Commissioning Team. Rather than confusing the issue, this lends continuity to the process and increases the individual's understanding and contribution.

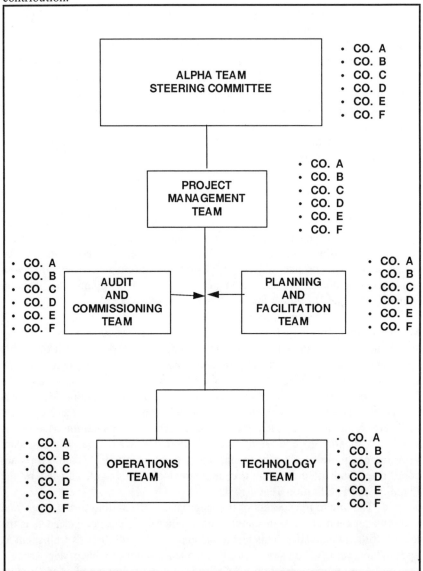

Fig. 36. ICBE Implementation Teams

ICBE Implementation teams are set up along functional lines. Most of the teams discussed below are not full-time, but are working groups that are convened at need when there is activity within their specific domain. While individual members may serve on more than one team, the functions performed by each team are clearly separated, allowing key project members to focus on one project element at a time. This team structure would consist of:

1.   **Alpha Team Steering Committee**. The Steering Committee consists of the senior management staff from the Members, those being the CEO and the Torchbearer. This committee provides high-level direction, makes financial and operating decisions, arbitrates disputes and is the final acceptor and owner of the completed project. The Steering Committee may meet periodically or at need.

2.   **Project Management Team**. The Project Management Team (PMT) is the key working entity of the implementation project. It consists of an overall (independent) Implementation Manager and joint representation from each of the Members involved. This should consist of a senior manager to make decisions and to act as team leader for that Member, one operations manager, and one technical manager who can commit resources on behalf of the Member. This team should meet at least once per week, making day-to-day operating decisions regarding the project and dealing with progress-related issues (see **Figure 35**).

3.   **Planning and Facilitation Team**. The Planning and Facilitation Team (PFT) supports the PMT by:

a)   developing, maintaining and coordinating the ICBE project plans and the associated reporting functions;

b)   setting the agenda and preparing materials for PMT meetings;

c)   facilitating the ICBE sessions;

d)   liaison with other project teams on behalf of the Implementation Manager.

The PFT manages the involvement and contribution of support groups within each organization such as legal, audit, accounting and finance. This team consists of one manager from each Member on a part-time basis, led by the Implementation Manager. These managers should be skilled in planning, project management, and BPE, and be able to bring value to the process (see **Figure 36**).

4.   **Operations Team**. The Operations Team (OT) consists of the business managers from each Member organization, who are responsible for implementing the new processes within their departments. These managers should also serve on the PMT, so that the true needs of all Members' operating departments are reflected in the final implementation. The team develops the final overall implementation plan as well as their company-specific implementation plan, and assists with the operational aspects of the Pilot (see **Figure 37**).

5.   **Technology Team**. Reporting to the respective Team Leader, the Technology Team (TT) is specific to each of the Members and consists primarily of its internal MIS technical staff. It is responsible for the internal applications and the technical levels of the implementation such as installing the communications links, applications software, and other supporting technologies. These teams meet or correspond as necessary to establish the necessary inter-enterprise coordination of technology and systems. This team is key to the success of the implementation of the project. Care should be taken to avoid placing too much emphasis on technology and not enough on the business needs (**see Figure 38**).

6.   **Audit and Commissioning Team**. The Audit and Commissioning Team (ACT) reports to the Implementation Manager and is independent from all other influences. The function of the ACT is to develop audit trails and control mechanisms across the board, perform pre and post-audits, develop system acceptance tests, impartially conduct and record the results of such tests, and provide objective evidence to the PMT to authorize the issuance of a License To Trade to the Members.

The ACT should be an objective third party, or individuals from Members who are not affected by the results. However, the ACT can and should be involved in the details of the project so that they may have insight into what is being tested (see **Figure 41**).

Once the direction is set, commitment is confirmed, preliminary funding has been allocated to support the initial ICBE design effort, and these teams are in place, the real work of ICBE may begin.

The Team Charters in **Figures 37-41** are intended to reflect both the generic responsibilities of the Teams, as well as to provide a vehicle for granting specific authority to those Teams. If desired, one of these Charters might be completed for each Business Pilot Project developed from the Migration plans in the Value System Analysis phase (See Chapter XII).

CHARTER
PROJECT MANAGEMENT TEAM (PMT)

SCOPE AND AUTHORITY:

The PMT is the sole authorized management control group for the implementation of those projects or initiatives designated below: (*This Team is made up of the Torchbearers and other senior management of the Members. It need not be a full-time activity, but time requirements for each of the Members will escalate as implementation project approach crucial points*)

1.   (Pilot Project) - *provide a short description of the key objectives of this project. This could be a strategic initiative such as Quick Response, Evaluated Receipts Settlement, Transport Control, Automated Procurement, or other business oriented project as defined under a Migration plan.*

2.   (Business Process Engineering Project - if applicable)
3.   (Systems Development Project - if applicable)
4.   Other related projects or sub-projects

RESPONSIBILITIES:

1.   Coordinating the goals and objectives of all initiatives
2.   Setting performance objectives and implementation schedules
3.   Monitoring progress-to-plan on a regular basis
4.   Expediting or assisting Members with their internal implementations
5.   Decision-making regarding:
    a)   Schedule adjustments
    b)   Project scope, objectives and measurements
    c)   Operational adjustments
    d)   Joint policies and procedures
    e)   Corrective action

6.   Maintenance of the Project Plan, acceptance of all project deliverables, and issuance of the Certificates of Compliance and the final Completion Report.

7.   Managing and coordinating Project Teams, Working Groups or spin-off Task Forces.

Fig. 37. Project Management Team Charter

CHARTER
PLANNING AND FACILITATION TEAM (PFT)

SCOPE AND AUTHORITY:

The PFT is a Working Group responsible for the overall planning and coordination of the Projects approved by the PMT. This group is responsible for establishing and instituting the appropriate planning methodologies and controls necessary for smooth implementation, and for facilitating activities on a day-to-day basis on behalf of all of the Members.

RESPONSIBILITIES:

Reporting to the Project Manager, the PFT will:
1. Provide a long-term perspective and a formal structure to the planning process.
2. Provide Strategic Planning and Project Planning expertise to the PMT, Working Groups and Project Teams.
3. Ensure visionary consistency of the various plans across all Members.
4. Customize and maintain the "ICBE Business Plan" documentation and the "Level Zero" Project Plan.
5. Monitor all projects and other initiatives on a regular basis to ensure compliance with the scope, intent and direction of the overall plan.
6. Establish the control systems necessary to track performance-to-plan, operating results and compliance with the terms and conditions of the various agreements respecting electronic commerce.
7. Facilitate the scheduling and conduct of Team meetings and provide a standard reporting mechanism.
8. Provide the vehicle for day-to-day communication between the PMT, Working Groups, and Project Teams.
9. Facilitate the achievement of Project Plan activities within each Member.
10. Escalate problem issues in a timely manner to the PMT or the Project Manager.

Fig. 38. Planning and Facilitation Team Charter

CHARTER
OPERATIONS TEAM (OPT)

SCOPE AND AUTHORITY:

The OPT is a permanent Working Group responsible for providing an operations perspective to the PMT. This group is responsible for defining and implementing the "physical plant" processes and daily operating procedures necessary to achieve the overall business objectives. *(This Team is made up of the people in the trenches who have to make the system work in actual daily operation).*

Business Process Engineering will be the focus of this group as they work to leverage their joint efforts to achieve mutual benefits. Inter-Corporate Business Engineering efforts will be complemented by the internal BPE efforts mounted by each Member, *(These efforts will largely determine the EDI Message Definitions, the Systems Development, the audits and controls, and the Acceptance Testing processes that will be implemented).*

RESPONSIBILITIES:

1.   Design and document joint (External) operational procedures.
2.   Assist with the design and documentation of new Migration plans to address joint operations problems.
2.   Design and document internal business processes, procedures and operations guides to support the new Migration plans.
3.   Implement operational procedures as specified in the operations guide.
4.   Review project plans and provide operational guidance to the PMT.
5.   Collect and report operational performance statistics as required to measure attainment of the objectives.
6.   Assist with internal system training.

Fig. 39. Operations Team Charter

CHARTER
TECHNOLOGY TEAM (TT)

SCOPE AND AUTHORITY:

The TT is responsible for the coordination of the common systems development activities among all Members, as well as for the internal systems development activities within each Member. The TT is authorized to make all technical decisions relating to systems.

RESPONSIBILITIES:

1. Specify the technological and operating environment for the project.
2. Develop specific EDI messages or other EC solutions identified by the PMT.
3. Design and unit-test technological solutions.
4. Install systems and equipment as required.
5. Provide technical assistance to the PMT, Working Groups, and other Teams as required.
6. Develop and administer internal and external training programs as required.

Fig. 40. Technology Team Charter

CHARTER
AUDIT AND COMMISSIONING TEAM(ACT)

SCOPE AND AUTHORITY:

The ACT is the Working Group authorized to institute and maintain proper audit procedures and to administer the process and content of the Acceptance Tests. Upon successful completion of the final Acceptance Test, the ACT will issue a Certificate of Compliance to the successful Members and will recommend to the PMT that a License to Trade be granted.

The ACT will conduct a formal on-site audit at the end of each phase of the project as determined by the PMT, and will present its Final Report at a special session of the PMT prior to project closure.

RESPONSIBILITIES:

1.   Develop and implement mutually acceptable security, audit and control procedures to ensure the ongoing reliability and integrity of the business information being traded and of the systems at each end which generate, utilize or act upon this information.

2.   In conjunction with the PMT, develop the Standard Acceptance Test (SAT) for the project, and maintain autonomous custody of the Acceptance Testing process and the associated documentation and procedures.

3.   Maintain working advisory relationships with the Members during the system development processes and keep the PMT advised of relevant issues..

4.   Provide Quality Assurance by:

a)   Conducting the Acceptance Tests formally in a controlled setting.

b)   Maintaining objective evidence of process integrity through the issuance of Standard Acceptance Test (SAT) reports, Non-Compliance Reports (NCR's), Corrective Action Bulletins (CAB's) and Certificates of Compliance (COC's).

c)   Ensuring that all Members are commissioned in an identical manner.

d)   Ensuring that the SAT continues to reflect the intent and objectives of the project, making adjustments as necessary.

Fig.41.. Audit and Commissioning Team Charter

Summary

Recruiting and obtaining commitment from the Membership is crucial to the ICBE effort. Due to its importance, and the importance of achieving internal readiness, a great deal of attention has been given to those topics in this book. That is as it should be, since the better prepared the Membership is, the better chance there is for ICBE to return the quantum benefits expected of it.

These up-front activities should be expected to take a lot of time without measurable payback. The Champion and the Membership should be mentally prepared for that fact. Immediate ROI is simply not going to happen, and payback will not be achieved until the new processes are in place and operating smoothly. The good news is that once they are, they are in place for the long term, and will be returning dollars over the long term instead of just the short haul.

The Champion company is the one who provides the core product or service, who has the most activities in the Value System, or who is closest to the end consumer. The Champion is the one who recognizes the benefits of EC and ICBE, and who recruits the "supply side" or "downline" partners in the ICBE effort. Once the supply side is under control and operating smoothly, the Champion can then approach the "demand side", or "upline" customers with the hopes of being able to plug smoothly into their "supply side".

ICBE, since it is a multi-corporate effort, requires a multi-corporate, multi-disciplinary team, referred to as the "Alpha Team". This Alpha Team consists of the CEO and the Executive Torchbearer from each of the Members, operating as a Steering Committee in a non-hierarchical Round Table forum to address issues of inter-corporate importance and to ensure that the needs of all Members are met equally and fairly. It is advisable to achieve impartiality in this process by engaging an independent Facilitator that is outside organizational constraints and detached from the daily politics.

The process of gaining the commitment from the Members is the same as that used to gain internal commitment:
1.   The CEO's Workshop
2.   The Alpha Team Management Workshops
3.   A Business plan which is ratified by the Alpha Team.
Cross-corporate, cross-functional teams are set up to do the implementation activities, consisting of:
1.   Project Management Team (PMT)
2.   Planning and Facilitation Team (PFT)
3.   Operations Team (OT)
4.   Technology Team (TT)
5.   Audit and Commissioning Team (ACT)
These Teams work together using ICBE techniques to implement the strategies identified by the Alpha Team in the ICBE Business Plan.

CHAPTER XII

STEP 4: VALUE SYSTEM ANALYSIS

Constructing the Business Model

The first real cut at ICBE occurs here. The executive workshops have identified and confirmed a general direction for ICBE to take, and have identified the operating guidelines and constraints involved. It is now necessary for these concepts to begin to take on shape. The implementation teams are now tasked with putting the new environment together and making it work in practice.

The primary goal of ICBE is to identify and close the Response Gaps across the Value System. Therefore, the first logical step is to identify the overall Value System environment and isolate the problem areas or potentials for inefficiency within the System. This should already have been done on a very high level (Level Zero, Big Board) in the management workshops. Some general directions should have already been identified.

Even though the Alpha Team Steering Committee has identified these general directions, the implementation team must still challenge all assumptions and develop a detailed model of the System for analysis. It is possible that the Steering Committee has not perceived the real problems, has proceeded on unfounded assumptions, and has arrived at false conclusions. If so, these detailed analysis and planning sessions will highlight the real situation for feedback to the executive for resolution.

The first step for the PFT (Planning and Facilitation Team, headed up by the Facilitator) is to conduct a series of ICBE planning sessions with the PMT (Project Management Team), the OT (Operations Team), and perhaps the TT (Technology Team). They should validate the "Big Board" model of the Value System so that it may be used to drive the remainder of the ICBE exercise.

Figure 41 depicts a generic example of a Level Zero "Big Board" model, with flows in a single direction, representing cumulative lead times for products to flow from suppliers to their "customers" in the Value System. The Members may wish to use other means to represent relationships and dependencies, but this model serves to illustrate the basic concepts. The key point is to use an agreed-upon visual tool to arrive at a joint understanding of the structure of the total Value System, and to arrive at ways to isolate and define the Response Gaps.

Analyzing Lead Times:

Lead times are a good place for the Team to start when trying to understand the problems in the Value System. The APCIS Dictionary defines cumulative lead time as

"The longest planned length of time involved to accomplish the activity in question. For any item planned through MRP, it is found by reviewing the lead time for each bill of material path below the item; whichever path adds up to the greatest number defines cumulative lead time."

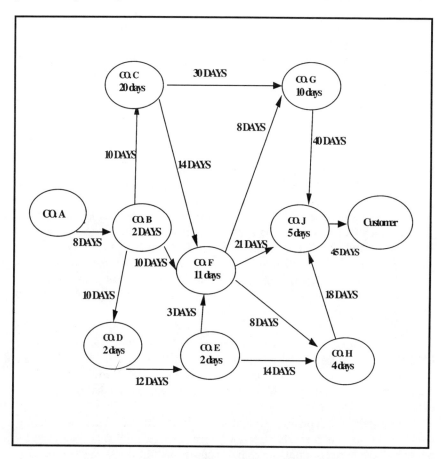

Fig. 42. "Big Board" Cumulative Lead Times

The cumulative lead time shown in this diagram (45 working days) is the total time required to get the product to the end customer. It includes the flow of raw material, parts, and sub-assemblies among all companies involved in producing the end product. The lead times shown between the circles at each stage includes the lead time of all downstream suppliers. The number shown inside the circles represents the time (in working days) for each company to process the material for the next stage. The lead times that the Team uses in constructing the diagram should be those that are quoted by the suppliers, or the "actual" lead times that are experienced by the buyers, whichever is longer. Later examination and discussion may show the commonly accepted times to be wrong or out of date, but they should be used as a starting point.

By looking at the example in **Figure 42**, it is seen that the customer has to wait 45 working days for his product (9 weeks). This breaks down as follows (all times are stated in working days):

1.   Co. J, who is the final assembler and distributor (and, incidentally, the ICBE Champion), waits 40 days for product from Co. G, 21 days for product from Co. F and 18 days for product from Co. H before assembling and shipping the final product to the customer (which takes Co. J 5 days). In this case, the 40 day wait is the longest, and is therefore the cumulative lead time for this Value System.

2.   Following the chain backwards, we can see that Co. G waits 30 days for subassemblies from Co. C and takes 10 days for internal processing..

3.   Co. C has to wait 10 days to get parts from Co. B, and takes 20 days for internal processing and production..

4.   Co. B uses raw material from Co. A (which takes 8 days) before beginning production, which takes 2 days.

Co. J also has to wait 21 days for Co. F, who waits 10 days for Co. B, who takes 8 days to get raw materials from Co. A. In addition, the lead times from Co. H add up to 18 days, so we can see that Co. J is seriously constrained by the lead times of its suppliers. This is complicated by the fact that these suppliers hardly ever meet their quoted lead times in any case. The real cumulative lead time is actually much longer in practice.   If I were the customer, I'd go somewhere else.

The Big Board may be stark and unflattering to some of the Members, but at least it has the ability to highlight the problem areas. In this case, the 40-day "A-B-C-G-J" path defines the cumulative lead time (sometimes called the "critical path"). It will be the primary target for analysis. This means that, if Co. G has everything it needs from Co. C in 30 days, it can produce and ship its sub-assemblies in 10 days.   While this 10 days will itself be analyzed in later ICBE sessions, the Team's attention is focused primarily on Co. C because the Board shows that it has a 20-day internal processing time.

Analyzing the H-E-D-B-A path, it is apparent that the longest process time of any one Member is 4 days(Co. H). The average is around 3 days, so this does not raise any immediate alarms. In looking at Co. F's situation, it is discovered that its longest lead time is 14 days, once again from Co. C, and that it takes an additional 7 days to produce the product for Co. J. This makes Co. C the prime candidate for the first cut at problem analysis and resolution, and Co. G and Co. F secondary candidates.

When analyzing the Value System, the Team should generally try to follow the 80/20 rule, and focus its initial attention on any Gaps where there appears to be an inordinate amount of time wasted, and where 80% of the problem may be solved with 20% of the effort, or 80% of the problem is caused by 20% of the activities. In this example, it is the Gap between C and G.

Mapping the Current Processes

The next step is to develop a Current Process Map at the Gap in question, describing the existing process flow at a Level One degree of detail. Eventually, all Gaps in the Value System will have Current Process Maps associated with them **(Figure 43)**. However, the Team will concentrate first on those that have been identified in the initial analysis.

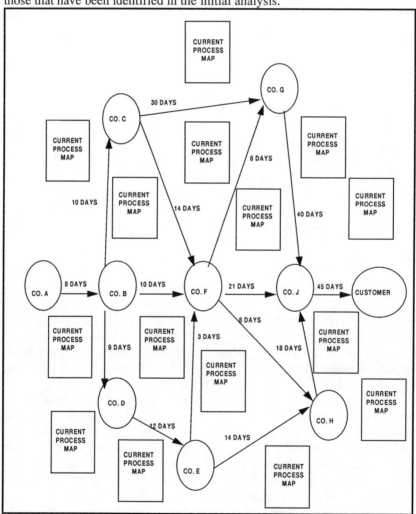

Fig. 43. Current Process Maps

Here is where the Operations Team in particular must concentrate its attention. All members of the Team must work together, stepping through the model, investigating the processes at each Gap, and constructing a detailed process flow model to account for all activities on both ends of the Gap and in between. This helps develop a detailed understanding of the entire process flow from beginning to end. It serves to document what is going on at the moment. At this point, the Team is merely taking a snapshot of the process flows, without making any judgments one way or another.

This is a time-consuming and labor-intensive operation, and involves the Operations Team and the functional staff of the Members at each end of the Gap.

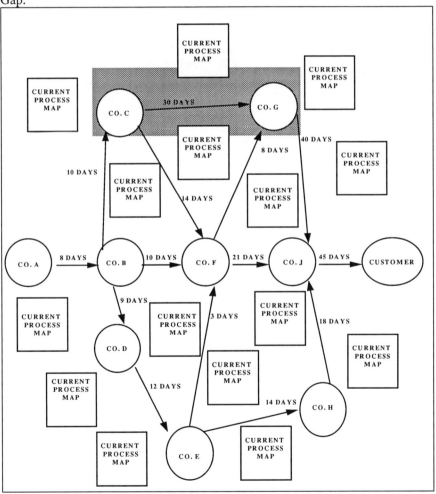

Fig. 44. A Candidate for Current Process Mapping

In this example, Co. G is the manufacturer, and Co. C is its supplier for the parts it requires to fill orders for its product. The Big Board (The "Level Zero Model" as discussed in Chapter IV) shows 30 days lead time from C to G, but it tells us nothing else about the process flow or the specific makeup of the C-G Response Gap (the components being Demand Lag, Process Time, and Supply Lag as discussed in Chapter IV).

At this point, the reader might well ask, " Aren't Response Gaps just a fancy name for lead times?" While it might appear that the two terms are interchangeable, the answer is no. Lead times differ from Response Gaps in several important ways:

1.   Lead time is a rough estimate by the supplier (often padded) of the time required to supply a product <u>after the order is received</u>. The Response Gap is an analytical, fact-based representation of the total time required to identify and satisfy a need, <u>including</u> the ordering process itself. In practice, the two will tend to differ significantly.

2.   Lead times are normally used for production planning purposes (as in MRP or DRP systems). Response Gaps are used as a tool to analyze, re-engineer and measure the Value System on an ongoing basis.

3.   Lead times are expressed at a high level of granularity (usually stated in days) and are insensitive to the processes involved. Response Gaps are process-oriented and can be stated in terms of hours and minutes to assist in process re-engineering.

4.   Lead times are usually static in nature. The Response Gap is expected to shrink over time. Lead times are an expression of one of the symptoms, while the Response Gap is the statement of the overall problem.

5.   Lead times assume fixed processes and the continuation of the status quo. The Response Gap by its very existence, implies that there is an imbalance in the System, a "Gap" that needs to be "closed." The existence of a Response Gap is an ongoing challenge to improve the processes involved.

Even so, this may look like splitting hairs, and some may still wish to use the term "lead time" as opposed to "Response Gap" when reading the material. If that makes it easier to proceed, then by all means do so for now, but we will continue to use these terms to describe two different concepts. The differences may become clearer as we go on.

Figure 45 shows a Level One Current Process Map. The Team can depict the relationships and process flows any way it wants to, as long as they are meaningful and are used consistently throughout the exercise. There are several computer-assisted process mapping tools available, and a description of some of them can be found on the Internet at HTTP://WWW.IE.UTORONTO.CA/EIL/TOOL/BPR.HTML.

CURRENT PROCESS MAP - CO. C AND G
(LEVEL 1)

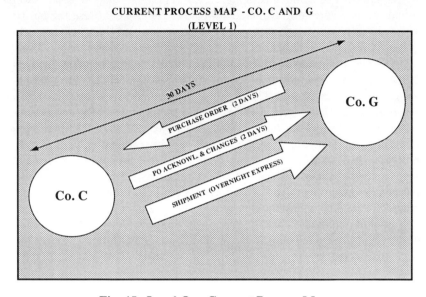

Fig. 45. Level One Current Process Map

The Level One Process Map

        In this simplified example, the primary C-G inter-corporate processes
are:
1.   The Purchase Ordering process, which takes 2 days
          (estimated)
2.   The PO Acknowledgment and PO Change process, which
          takes another 2 days (estimated)
3.   The shipment of the order, which is overnight express.
This adds up to 5 days, and that leaves us with a 15-day internal processing
time as yet to be accounted for.
        There seems to be an obvious technical solution here, one that is
simple to implement. Using EDI, the 2 days for issuing the PO could possibly
be reduced, as well as the 2 days for the back-and-forth exchange of PO
changes and acknowledgments.   Having seen this obvious solution, the
temptation is to cheer loudly, proclaim the analysis a success, and go right out
and implement EDI PO's between C and G. Not so fast. The analysis has
barely begun yet. The Team should not jump at fast and easy "obvious
solutions" until all the facts are in. EDI is certainly a possibility, one of many
that should be noted and addressed during the "Best Practices" workshops to
come later.
        The overnight delivery, while effective from a time standpoint and
good for customer relations, is probably not cost-effective, and tends to distort
the magnitude of the problem. If normal delivery methods were used, the

Response Gap would likely be up to 2 or 3 days longer than it is now, which would be unacceptable to Co. G and would cause Co. C to lose the business. To avoid this, Co. C incurs extra costs to achieve on-time delivery, which indirectly results in a higher price for Co. G and the end consumer.

The Team, having uncovered these issues and problems at Level One of the C-G Gap, now needs to develop Level Two models of the processes at each end (**Figures 46 and 47**) to gain a deeper understanding. To save the Team's valuable time, each Member should be responsible for developing its own Level One and Two models, along with whatever other documentation is relevant to the analysis, so that it can all be laid out together as the analysis proceeds. It is entirely conceivable, even likely, that the processes at one Gap may be similar to those at another, or that they may affect processes at one or more of the other Gaps. The Team may wish to keep the entire System in full perspective as it continues the exercise.

For purposes of this illustration, we will drive down to the lower levels of detail for the C-G Gap, and review their Level Two Current Process Maps, depicting the process flow from right to left for visual consistency with the Big Board.

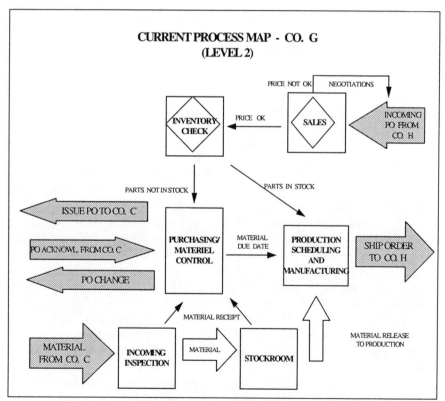

Fig. 46. Level Two Purchase Order Process for Co. G.

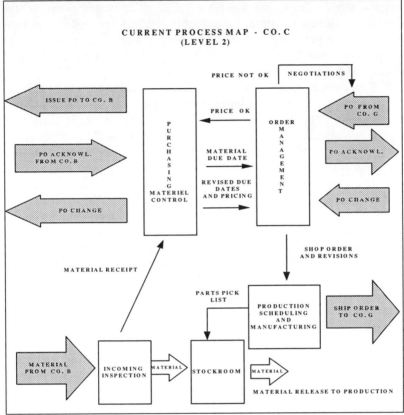

Fig. 47. Level Two Order Management Process for Co. C

The Level Two Process Maps

When completed, these two diagrams may be laid side by side and the shaded arrows matched up to provide a complete picture of the inter-corporate process flow from both sides (a graphic artist may be able to develop them so that they overlay properly). The new diagrams can then replace the circles on the existing Big Board. Gradually the complete picture will begin to develop. The Technology Team may be able to develop a computer-based graphical representation that will link all of these together, and pull up succeeding levels of detail at the click of a mouse button.

By looking at the Level Two models in **Figures 46 and 47**, it is apparent that the two companies are set up quite differently in the way they handle orders and schedule production. Co. G has made its sales force responsible for establishing whether or not there is inventory available, and for issuing the order to the shop floor. The purchasing / materiels department only comes into play when there is no inventory to make the product (by then it's already too late).   Co. C, on the other hand, relies more heavily on the purchasing / materiels department to establish the due dates of the material before issuing the shop order. This would seem to imply better coordination among the order management, purchasing and production functions, but it is much too soon to tell.

Both companies appear to be sharply divided along departmental lines. This implies a rigid structure to internal communications as well as external communications. The Team should be on the lookout for these signs as it progresses through the levels of detail in the Current Process Map. If there are glaringly obvious problems that jump out during the mapping process, they should be noted separately for the "Best Practices" workshops to come.

The Team should also be looking for potential bottlenecks in the internal processes such as incoming inspection and the stockroom. These tend to be non-value-added activities, and can be the source of unnecessary delays in any organization.   Another area of potential concern is when a single department (such as Purchasing) is responsible for the bulk of the activities, and has no accountability to other departments other than informing them when they are finished.

For example, Co. G has responsibility for both incoming inspection and the stockroom.   Problems in either of these areas cannot be well highlighted to the rest of the organization, since they are under control of a single department. Purchasing is a "black box" to the rest of the organization and keeps its secrets safe from prying eyes.   Co. C, however, splits the responsibility. Purchasing is responsible for the material until it is inspected and properly accounted for. The Manufacturing department is responsible for maintaining the stockroom and issuing the material to the shop floor. At this point, it is impossible to say which company is right. In fact, both may be right given the individual circumstances, but this highlights a possible problem area that the Team may want to flag for more detailed analysis with a Level Three model.

The Team should, at this point, begin to develop some empirical data around the model.   Each of the inter-departmental and inter-corporate relationships should be timed, perhaps using a test purchase order that is followed manually from end to end. This will plug actual numbers into the Response Gap, and serve to identify the orders-of-magnitude of the Demand Lag, Process Time and Supply Lag at each of the processes. Once again, this is a time-consuming and labor-intensive exercise, but understanding cannot be achieved without it. Let's continue with our example in **Figures 48 and 49** on page 194 and 195.

Analyzing the Level Two Processes

In this example, the Team has walked through the entire process with the Members from Co. G and Co. C. For the purposes of simplifying the example, we will ignore the PO Change processes, but in real life this is normally where most of the delays and confusion occur. The Team may expect to spend some time analyzing this activity. In the walkthrough, they have found that every process in Co. C takes 2 days to complete except for the mail, the stockroom issue of parts into production and the overnight express delivery to Co. G (once again for simplicity's sake). This example further assumes that Co. C's parts are never kept in stock, but must be ordered from Co. B each time. The Response Gap picture that emerges is:

        1.   <u>Demand Lag</u> of 12 days: 2 days (overlapping each other) in Co G's Purchasing and Co. C's Order Management, 2 days in Co. C's Purchasing (including negotiations with Co. B--another possible overlap), 3 days for surface mail delivery of paper PO to Co. B, 3 days for surface mail delivery of PO acknowledgment from Co. B (price, terms and availability etc.), and 2 days for Purchasing to confirm. Assuming no further back-and-forth negotiation, this is the shortest possible time before the order is firm enough for Co. B to act upon, and for Co. C to schedule production for Co G's order.

        2.   <u>Supply Lag</u> of 14 days: 10 days for material to come from Co. B, 2 days in Co. C's incoming inspection, 1 day in the stockroom, and 1 day for delivery to Co. G. Material handling is not considered to be part of Process Time, since no value is added to the product.

        3.   <u>Process Time</u> of 2 days in Co. C's Manufacturing department. Upon further investigation, it may prove that this can be reduced further using MRP II or JIT techniques, but the real problems appear to be in other areas.

        The total Response Gap for the C-G Gap is 26 days. Remember, Process time does not figure into the Response Gap. It is very close to the 30-day quoted lead time. The other 4 days includes 2 days for the actual production of the goods for Co. G and some built-in slack for PO changes, etc. This indicates that Co. C has already given some thought to its lead time quotation, and has done its homework.

        While the Team Member from Co. C is beaming with pride over the accuracy of his numbers, the rest of the Team begins to ask questions: Why does it take 2 days to work through each department? Why do you rely on surface mail? Why is it necessary to go back and forth over price and terms with your supplier? Why does it take 2 days to inspect incoming material? Why does it have to go into the stockroom and then back out again? Why is it necessary to spend (our) money on courier services when cheaper methods are available? Etc.?

        These questions are not asked in a spirit of aggression, merely to understand the reasoning behind the processes and to uncover potential problem areas. Rest assured, the Honorable Member from Co. C will have his turn to ask questions of others later on.

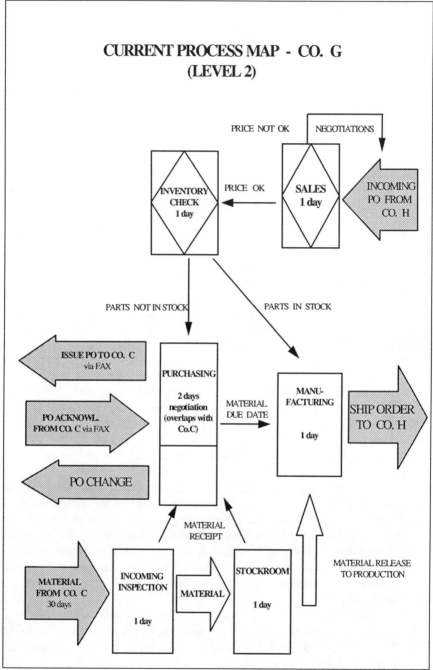

CURRENT PROCESS MAP - CO. G
(LEVEL 2)

Fig. 48 . Level Two Resonse Gap Analysis for Co. G.

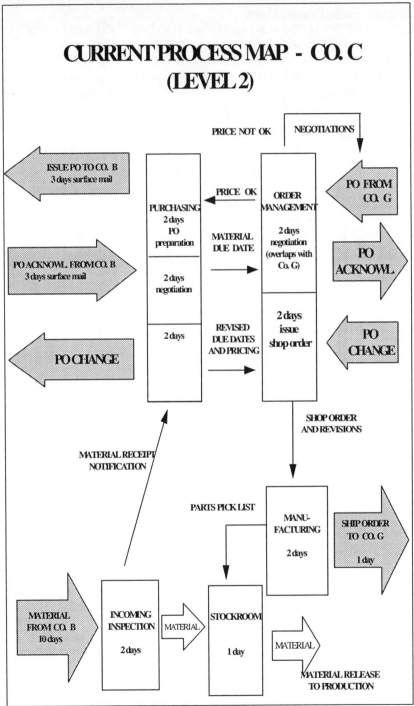

Fig. 49. Level Two Response Gap Analysis for Co. C

The Level Three Process Maps

Once the Team has analyzed the Level Two model to its satisfaction and has noted the areas it wishes to pursue further, the Members may then proceed to develop the Level Three models for each of those areas. Generally, these will explode the selected boxes on the Level Two model into a detailed depiction of the actual processes. As an illustration, let's look at Co. C's Order Management and Purchasing processes.

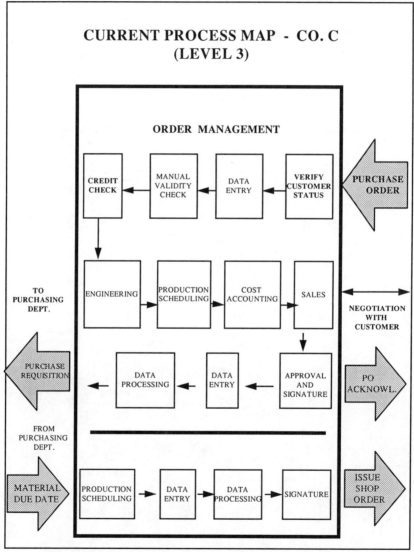

Fig. 50. Level Three Order Management Process for Co. C

Analyzing the Level Three Processes

In the Order Management function, there are 11 separate steps before a Purchase Requisition is cut for the Purchasing Department. These are:

1.   Manual Validity Check: When the incoming PO's are delivered from the mail room (1 hour), the Order Management clerk examines them for completeness and validity, assigns an internal tracking number to them, sorts them by customer name, and sends copies to the appropriate Sales Representatives (2 hours). Total step time: 3 hours

2.   Data Entry: The PO details are entered into the mainframe computer system by the clerk, along with the internal tracking number and salesman information. Step time: 1 hour. Total elapsed time: 4 hours.

3.   Verify Customer Status: The clerk looks up the customer record in the computer, and verifies the ship to and bill to addresses, the status of any outstanding orders in progress, and pre-negotiated price and terms information. Step time: 1 hour. Total elapsed time: 5 hours.

4.   Credit Check: The clerk phones the Accounting Department to perform a credit check on the customer, to verify outstanding balances, credit hold, credit limit information, etc. An approval number is given and entered into the computer. Step time: 1 hour. Total elapsed time: 6 hours.

5.   Engineering: The PO is reviewed by the Design Engineering Department for changes in design, technical specifications, materials, etc., and changes are noted for review by cost accounting. Step time: 2 hours. Total elapsed time: 8 hours.

6.   Production Scheduling: The PO is reviewed by Production Scheduling to determine possible conflicts or delays in production, as well as to review existing orders in progress for that customer. Step time 2 hours. Total elapsed time: 10 hours.

7.   Cost Accounting: The PO, with engineering changes, is reviewed against the customer's existing price agreement. If there is a change in price, it must be negotiated with the customer before approving the order and committing to production. Step time: 2 hours. Total elapsed time: 12 hours.

8.   Sales: The Sales representative assigned to that customer contacts the buyer and either verifies that the order is accepted or re-negotiates prices/terms based on the previous findings.   The PO Acknowledgment is printed out on the computer and sent to the Sales Manager. Step time: 1 hour. Total elapsed time: 13 hours.

9.   Approval and Signature: The Sales Manager approves and signs the PO Acknowledgment, and FAXes a copy back to the customer. The signed PO Acknowledgment is sent to the Data Entry clerk for processing through the computer. Step time: 1hour. Total elapsed time: 14 hours.

10.   Data Entry: The Data Entry clerk re-enters the PO Acknowledgment into the computer, including any changes in price, terms, or delivery. Step time: 1 hour. Total elapsed time: 15 hours.

11.   Data Processing: The computer processes the PO information and creates a Purchase Requisition for the Purchasing Department (located in the plant across town), as well as an update to the Production Schedule. Step time: 1 hour. Total elapsed time: 16 hours (2 days).

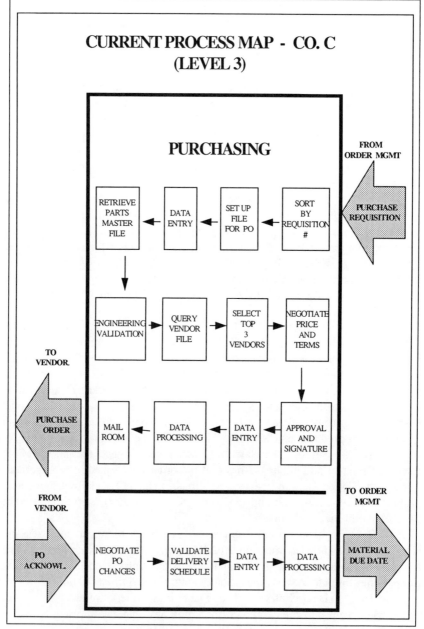

Fig. 51. Level Three Purchasing Process for Co. C.

The Purchasing Department receives the inter-office mail the next morning, and follows a 12-step process before issuing a PO to the final Vendor. These are:

1. Sort By Requisition #: The Purchasing clerk sorts the incoming paperwork by Purchase Requisition # and performs a visual validity check. Step time: .5 hour.

2. Set Up File for PO: The clerk then sets up a file folder for the Purchasing paperwork to follow and attaches the internal tracking number to it. Step time: .5 hour. Elapsed time: 1 hour. Total elapsed time: 17 hours.

3. Data Entry: The clerk enters the PO Requisition information into the plant computer. Step time: 1 hour. Elapsed time: 2 hours. Total elapsed time: 18 hours.

4. Retrieve Parts Master File: The clerk then retrieves the Parts Master File on the plant computer and verifies part numbers, product structure (Bill of Material), preferred vendors, etc. Step time: 1 hour. Elapsed time: 3 hours. Total elapsed time: 19 hours.

5. Engineering Validation: The clerk sends the PO and the paperwork to Manufacturing Engineering who validates the product structures and the technical specifications, schedules equipment maintenance and setup, etc. Any differences in the Parts Master File specifications and the specifications maintained at the sales office are resolved at this point. Step time: 2 hours. Elapsed time: 5 hours. Total elapsed time: 21 hours.

6. Query Vendor File: The clerk looks up the preferred vendors in the Vendor Data Base. Prices, terms and delivery are checked against the existing paperwork. The results are printed out and placed in the file, and the file is sent to the appropriate Buyer. Step time: 1 hour. Elapsed time: 6 hours. Total elapsed time: 22 hours.

7. Select Top 3 Vendors: The Buyer reviews the information in the folder, looks up information in the Parts Master and Vendor Databases as necessary, and selects the top 3 Vendors who can supply the part or parts in question. Step time: 2 hours. Elapsed time: 8 hours. Total elapsed time: 24 hours (3 days).

8. Negotiate Price and Terms: The next morning, the Buyer calls each of the selected Vendors and discusses the Purchase Requisition with them. They negotiate details of price, terms, and delivery. The successful Vendor is selected and notified that a PO is on its way. The information is entered into the file folder and forwarded to the Purchasing Manager. Step time: 3 hours. Elapsed time: 11 hours. Total elapsed time: 27 hours.

9. Approval and Signature: The Purchasing Manager reviews the Purchase Requisition, verifies information as necessary, and signs the Requisition. Step time: 2 hours. Elapsed time: 13 hours. Total elapsed time: 29 hours.

10. Data Entry: The information on the completed Purchase Requisition is entered into the plant computer, including any changes, and including the successful Vendor information regarding estimated delivery

times. Step time: 1 hour. Elapsed time: 14 hours. Total elapsed time: 30 hours.

11.   Data Processing: The computer processes the information and prints out a Purchase Order for the selected Vendor (Co B). Step time: 1 hour. Elapsed time: 15 hours. Total elapsed time: 31 hours.

12.   Mail Room: Packages and sends out the Purchase Order to Co. B. Step time: 1 hour. Elapsed time: 16 hours. Total elapsed time: 32 hours (4 days).

By surface mail, the PO takes 3 days to arrive at CO. B. If it is turned around immediately and acknowledged, it takes another 3 days to travel back to Co. C. This is a minimum of 6 days added to the cycle. The total elapsed time is now 10 days (80 hours) from receipt of the original PO from Co. G. Co. C's Purchasing Department now takes the following steps before issuing a Material Due Date to the Order Management Department:

1.   Negotiate PO Changes: The Buyer (C) and the Vendor (B) discuss any changes that have taken place since the PO was issued, and verbally verify the price, terms, and delivery. When verified, the PO Acknowledgment is stamped by the Buyer and filed back in the folder. Step time: 4 hours. Total elapsed time: 84 hours.

2.   Validate Delivery Schedule: The Buyer contacts the carrier that will be delivering the material to Co. C and books the shipment. Paperwork is created and sent to the carrier, and the carrier confirms the booking. Step time: 8 hours. Elapsed time: 12 hours. Total elapsed time: 92 hours.

3.   Data Entry: The folder is sent to Data Entry who enters all of the information into the plant computer. Step time: 2 hours. Elapsed time: 14 hours. Total elapsed time: 94 hours.

4.   Data Processing: The computer batch run processes the information and produces the material due date listing, including the material due dates for all other parts and materials confirmed that day. This listing is sent back to the Order Management Department via inter-office overnight delivery. Step time: 2 hours. Elapsed time: 16 hours. Total elapsed time: 96 hours (12 days).

When the Material Due Date listing is received by Order Management, the following 4 steps occur:

1.   Production Scheduling: The list is validated against the working records and they are updated accordingly (2 hours). The list is then sent to Production Scheduling who matches it up with the planned order and verifies the upcoming production schedule. A scheduling run is performed through the computer and the order is scheduled for production (6 hours). Step time: 8 hours. Total elapsed time: 104 hours (13 days).

2.   Data Entry: The information is entered into the mainframe computer. Step time: 2 hours. Elapsed time: 10 hours. Total elapsed time: 106 hours.

3.   Data Processing: The mainframe computer does its daily production run and issues a paper shop order and associated production documentation. Step time: 4 hours. Elapsed time: 14 hours. Total elapsed time: 110 hours.

4.   Signature: The VP of Manufacturing signs the Shop Order and sends it to the Manufacturing Department at the plant. Step time: 2 hours. Elapsed time: 16 hours. Total elapsed time: 112 hours (14 days).

This puts the total time from receipt of the original order to the issue of a Shop Floor order at 14 working days, or almost 3 working weeks.

This example is totally fabricated, but it serves to show the detail to which the analysis must be taken in order to understand the inter-corporate processes. The identical exercise will have been conducted at the offices of Co. G, and the Current Process Map will take shape there as well.

Now that the processes have been well documented, the next step in the analysis is that of Problem Definition. Each step must now be looked at from the standpoint of, "Does this activity add value, or does it add time and cost?" Each hand-off must be examined to determine if there are unnecessary steps or unnecessary staff involvement, or unnecessary processes.

Documenting the Results

When the Team examines these Maps and steps through the processes, it is safe to assume that a lot of vigorous back-and-forth discussion will ensue. The Facilitator must be especially vigilant at this stage, and not allow the exercise to degenerate into a finger-pointing free-for-all. The only purpose is to identify the problem areas that need to be fixed, to document the problems, and move on to the design stage.

When analyzing these Maps, the Team's conclusions should be documented in such a manner as to provide consistent input to the design phase to follow. Each Current Process Map for each Member and each Gap between Members should have an "Analysis and Conclusions" report associated with it, describing the pockets of excellence (for the Best Practices workshops to come), an unbiased assessment of the processes and practices, and opportunities for improvement.

When each of the Gaps and Current Process Maps have been examined in this way, the entire Value System is now understood. The Team may now proceed with the design phase of ICBE. It may be a useful exercise, and it might save embarrassment, for each Member to do its own preliminary Analysis and Conclusions report, and present it to the Team. That way, each Member is part of its own solution instead of simply being forced to air its dirty laundry in public.

Some of the Members may feel that the Analysis phase is "taking too long" and that there are no concrete results just a lot of wheel-spinning and fault-finding. The Facilitator must be aware of Senior Management's short attention span and their desire to see quick results. He/she must be able to move the exercise along as quickly as possible without sacrificing due care and attention to detail.

The Analysis phase will take a significant amount of time, particularly if it is done properly, but it provides the foundation for the remainder of the ICBE exercise. If the Analysis is competently done, the design phase will be relatively short and direct.

The Analysis and Conclusions report for Co. C might look something like the example in **Figure 52** below. This is not a complete example, merely a suggested format for purposes of illustration. A similar report would be prepared for Co. G and for the Gap between them, if it involves more activities than were previously supposed.

ANALYSIS AND CONCLUSIONS
Co. C

Background:

Co. C provides component parts for widget handles to Co. G. In an effort to expedite the delivery of these parts, Co. G has been sending Purchase Orders to Co. G by FAX, and Co. C has been sending the parts to Co. G by overnight express. Co. C has a quoted lead time of 30 working days. This analysis is intended to highlight areas in which this time may be reduced.

Analysis:

1.   Organizational Issues: Co. C has separate Order Management and Purchasing functions, housed in different locations, each maintaining its own computer system. This results in some significant duplication of effort and possible conflict of information between systems.

There is a high degree of management intervention, and signing authority is not delegated. It is unclear why it is necessary for the Sales Manager to sign the PO Acknowledgment, the Purchasing Manager to sign each Purchase Requisition, or the VP of Manufacturing to sign each Shop Order.

2.   Process Issues: There are 11 process steps between Order Management and Purchasing, 12 between Purchasing and Co. C's supplier, 4 between Purchasing and Order Management and 4 between Order Management and Manufacturing. This totals 31 process steps before production begins.

There are manual record-keeping processes in place that seem to be holdovers from pre-computer days. These can provide backup in case of computer failure, but are otherwise redundant or in conflict with the computer systems in place.

There is a significant amount of data entry, involving the same or similar information. Documents are entered in their entirety, instead of entering incremental information into a common central data base.

There are unnecessary internal records created. The paper Purchase

(Continued on next page)

Requisition is not necessary if the two computer systems are linked together or if both departments were to use the same computer system.

This section of the report can continue on for several pages, and can be very exhaustive in its detail. For the sake of brevity, a complete analysis will not be performed here, but the reader can get the general idea of the document.

3.   Operational Issues: Co. C relies heavily on the internal Expediter to keep the system going. If there are any delays at any process step, the delivery dates cannot be met.

Engineering is heavily involved in both the Order Management and Purchasing functions. The Design Engineering and Manufacturing Engineering departments appear to   be overburdened with performing unnecessary validations on simple assemblies that seldom change.

There are 3 days between the arrival of the material and its receipt on the shop floor. Incoming inspection appears to be understaffed and this results in a bottleneck. The policy is 100% inspection of incoming materials, but there have been no rejects of Co. B's materials reported in the past six months. In the case of Co. B, 100% inspection may not be necessary.

Once again, this section of the report can be quite detailed.

* High accuracy of manufacturing data (Bills of Material, Routings)
* Modern manufacturing facilities and techniques

Conclusions:

Pockets of Excellence:
        * Competent staff, high morale, structured and disciplined workplace.
Areas for Improvement:
        * Better inter-corporate business communications
        * Organizational redesign between Order Management and Purchasing
        * Redesign of clerical functions to eliminate redundancies
        * Redesign of process steps to combine functions
        * Redesign of computer systems to reduce internal paperwork
        * Elimination or reduction of incoming inspections

Figure 52. The Analysis and Conclusions Report

Brainstorming the Solution

One of the key milestones of the Analysis phase is the brainstorming session that takes place once all of the Current Process Maps have been individually analyzed. Now that each of the Members have had their own moments of truth and have survived the soul-searching and denial, they have had to face up to the fact that everyone including themselves has real problems that need to be resolved. They realize that there is no way of avoiding an overhaul that includes everyone. They are now mentally prepared to look at the overall Value System in an objective manner and get on with fixing what's broken.

In this session, all assumptions are challenged. Nothing is sacred, and no question is forbidden. If the Team asks, "Why do we need Purchase Orders at all?", or "Why not eliminate incoming inspection?", then these must be treated as legitimate questions that require a competent, professional answer that is satisfactory to all of the Team Members.

There can be no cop-outs like, "It's policy", or "We've always done it that way", or "we do it the same way for everybody--why should we change it for you?" These are not acceptable answers. Having said that, these dodges are likely to be tried by Members wishing to avoid having to change things. The Facilitator must discourage "status quo" answers such as these and foster a "breakthrough thinking" style.

What will emerge from the brainstorming session is a truly cooperative, objective analysis of the complete Value System that may then be reviewed against the original direction established by the Alpha Team Steering Committee. It is likely that there will be some major departures from the initial thinking, because now all of the facts are in and the Members are able to assess their strengths and weaknesses much better. The Team should develop an Analysis and Conclusions Report that summarizes the findings and highlights areas for improvement, and present it formally to the Steering Committee.

This will give visibility to the effort, and will give the Committee the opportunity to make adjustments to the grand strategy if necessary. They will have other opportunities to review the progress during the Business Process Design phase, and may make further adjustments at those times. It is crucial to keep the Steering Committee involved at these key points. It reinforces the executive commitment from all Member companies, and keeps the ICBE process from running away with itself.

The next chapter will deal with the selection of Best Practices that the Members wish to adopt, the establishment of measurement systems, and the design of the target Business Processes.

CHAPTER XIII

STEP 5: BUSINESS PROCESS DESIGN

Benchmarking

Now that the current processes are understood and problem areas have been identified, the question is, "What are we going to do about it?". It's all well and good to say that things need to be fixed, and certainly some of the fixes may be obvious from looking at the Analysis and Conclusions reports, but how do we know what we should be doing? Is there anyone out there who has been through this type of exercise and who can provide us with an example of the best way to do things? Are there any measurements that we can use to gauge our performance against theirs, and that we can use as a tool to help us improve our own situation? We already know what doesn't work, but what does work?

The answers to these questions lie in the technique known as "benchmarking". The principle of benchmarking is familiar to computer people. They have for years used industry-accepted performance indicators to evaluate computer systems or software packages. The principle is the same for organizations and for Value Systems; select an industry standard and measure against it. In this case, an "industry standard" consists of successful practices used by companies who are recognized for excellence in certain areas, such as inventory management, logistics and distribution, manufacturing, and so on.

Depending on the reason for doing it, traditional benchmarking can focus on individual areas such as strategies, structures, practices, or processes, or it can encompass all aspects of a company's operation. Benchmarking can be done against internal departments or divisions of a company, against a company's competitors, against the industry in general, or against a cross-section of all industries (Best In Class, or BIC benchmarking). The idea is to weed out the best of the best and adapt those "Best Practices" to the company's operation, resulting in a set of Target Models tailored to the specific needs of the company (See **Figure 53**).

In ICBE, these Target Models are the center around which the new business processes are built. The Migration plans (discussed in more detail in Chapter XIV) lay out a sequence of steps by which the current processes are transformed into the Target Models.

ICBE employs two types of benchmarking to create a Target Model: *Internal,* and *Best in Class* (BIC). *Industry benchmarking*, while it may uncover some interesting techniques for consideration, concentrates only what the other companies in the same industry are doing. Other companies in the same industry are usually operating under the same outdated techniques and artificial constraints that we are trying to improve upon. Using them as models would only serve to enshrine the status quo. ICBE is interested in breakthroughs, not in doing what everyone else is doing.

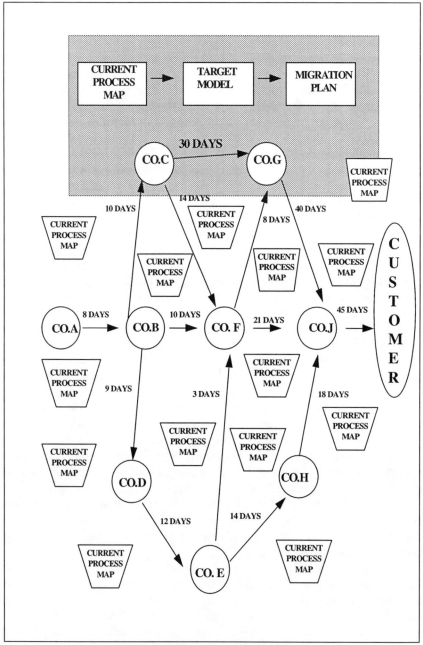

Fig. 53. Target Models and Migration plans

Competitive benchmarking is concerned with what direct competitors are doing, and this only challenges us to be as good as they are. We don't want to be as good as they are, we want to be far and away superior to them. We don't want to beat them at their own game. We want a brand new game, played on our own field, with our own rules.

In Chapter XI, it was pointed out that, if we include suppliers on our ICBE team who also supply our competitors, then we may be indirectly helping those competitors through the increased capability we are helping our supplier build. Theoretically, the supplier could then use EDI with our competitors as well as with us, and this could help streamline the competitors' business cycles as well as ours.

This is absolutely true, and is actually to be encouraged. One of the major selling points for ICBE is that the supplier and other ICBE Members as well gain the ability to deal, not only with us, but also with other Trading Partners in a more streamlined manner, thus amortizing the cost and effort over a larger base and gaining competitive advantage in other areas. They are not locked in to us. The fact that some of these other Trading Partners may be our direct competitors does not change the point of the exercise and should not cause us undue concern. We cannot control the dealings of the entire business community, and sometimes our competition benefits from our efforts. That is a fact of life.

The point of ICBE, however, is to go beyond the mere facilitation of business transactions, and to attain strategic advantage and market dominance by redefining the playing field through cooperative endeavor. We don't care if our competitors can send and receive business transactions faster and cheaper through EDI, if we are eliminating the need for business transactions altogether.

In the years to come, the competition will still be operating under the old "EDI paper replacement" paradigm and struggling to "add EDI Trading Partners" to their "system" for traditional PO's and Invoices, while we are designing entirely new modes of commerce that will leave them far behind. They are implementing current Industry Best Practices, while we are promoting Best-In-Class.

Our common supplier (and customer) may still be "doing EDI' with them, but will be "conducting commerce" with us, and will tend to concentrate the efforts where there is the most payback. Unless the competitors are also conducting an ICBE initiative with this supplier, it is unlikely that their EDI implementation (if they have one) will be as widely encompassing, as sophisticated or as focused as ours. The benefits will just not be there as an incentive for the supplier to give it much attention. The supplier will gain far more by participating in ICBE with us. In the final analysis, we won't really have helped the competition very much at all.

ICBE employs internal benchmarking only for transitional purposes, or for streamlining the detailed processes at Levels Three, Four and Five. It is not always practical to make the radical changes implied by BP's once over a number of different companies all at once. It may be advisable to use the "pockets of excellence" discovered during the Analysis Phase to share existing "Good Practices" among the Membership. For example, Co. H may have an excellent method of billing and collection, Co. B may have an excellent organizational structure for materials management, Co. J may have a good process for managing incoming orders, and so on.

While the Members are gearing up to make the radical Best-of-the-Best BP changes, some benefits might be gained by doing this, especially since the local experts are handy and are able to advise each other in temporarily streamlining the operation. This is called "cherry-picking". It can produce some immediate benefits in cost reduction and/or time savings. It can also show the Alpha Team that some tangible benefits are already accruing as a direct result of mutual cooperation, and that they haven't spent all that time and money for nothing.

The Best of the Best

The best examples for our Target Models are to be found in a cross-section of industries, each with its own strengths. We want the Best Practices (BP's) for our logistics operation to come from a world-class logistics player, such as L.L. Bean or Wal-Mart. We want the BP's for billing and collection to come from leaders in that field, such as American Express or MCI (Camp, 1995, 424); BP's for manufacturing from Steelcase, Black & Decker, or EG&G Sealol; BP's for supplier management from Ford, Sears, or Motorola (Camp, 1995, 427), and so on.

This is not to say that we must slavishly adopt their techniques as is, but that we must adapt the relevant BP's to our specific Value System and to each Member as appropriate. Each company is different in structure and circumstance, so one size does not necessarily fit all. By adapting to individual circumstance, it is possible to improve on the Best of the Best as it relates to us.

With ICBE, several companies are involved, so it would seem that benchmarking for a complex Value System would be a difficult matter indeed. With all of the different companies, it would seem that each one would have to select a different Best Practice to emulate since they all perform a different function, and that this could cause process conflicts among the Members.

This is not necessarily so. The Value System in our example really consists of two main types of Member: the customer interface (Co. J) and the suppliers. In the example, let's assume that the Analysis phase has proved that the problem areas lie principally in the Supplier Management and Order Management functions, and that the inter-company logistics operation is not a significant issue.

In this case, the most that would be required would be three BIC benchmarks. Co. J could employ *Customer Service* BP's from a company like L.L. Bean or Procter & Gamble, and all Members could employ the *Supplier Management* and *Purchasing* BP's from a company like Ford or GM (or the US

Federal Government). In our example, the goal of the ICBE exercise is to streamline the order management process and thereby optimize the supply chain. The focus would be on Supplier (order) Management and Purchasing as the first stage, with Co. J implementing Customer Service BP's as the second stage (see **Fig. 29**).

It is also desirable from a continuity standpoint for all suppliers to follow the same BP models, at least to the level where it impacts inter-corporate commerce (Level One). Remember that the idea is not to follow word-for-word what others have done, but to use the model as a starting point for developing a working Value System that is specific to the needs of the Members.

Where To Find Best Practices

There are several sources for benchmarking and Best Practice information. Below is a partial list. This list is not intended to imply any form of endorsement, merely to inform the reader of some potential sources of information.

1.   In "Business Process Benchmarking", Robert Camp gives several examples summarized by function such as "Customer Service", "Quality", "Supplier Management", etc. He in turn has summarized these from the following publications:

Altany, David, 1991. Share and Share Alike: Benchmarkers are   Providing the Wisdom of Mother's Reproach. *Industry Week*, 15 July, 12-16.

Foster, Thomas, 1992. Logistics Benchmarking: Searching for the   Best. *Distribution* 96 no. 3 (March): 30-36.

Port, Otis and Geoffrey Smith, 1992. Beg, Borrow and Benchmark,   *Business Week*, 30 November, 74-45.

2.   Back issues of *EDI Forum* contain many examples and case studies of best practices and specific instances of re-engineering (see bibliography for the ones used in the writing of this book).

3.   The EDI Group, Inc. (Publishers of the *EDI Forum*) provide directed research in specific topical areas. They may be reached at (708) 848-0135.

4.   The American Production and Quality Center in Houston provides benchmark information, workshops and training courses. (713) 681-4020.

5.   The American Society for Quality Control (ASQC) is a leading proponent of TQM. They publish a monthly magazine "Quality Progress" that contain useful information regarding Quality Management, Benchmarking and Best Practices. They also offer books for sale on those subjects. (414) 272-8575.

6.   Personal contact may be made with the Directors of TQM, QA (Quality Assurance), or anyone who has the word "quality" in their title

within organizations such as Ford, GM, Black & Decker, Steelcase, Motorola, Fedex, or any other large successful company with a reputation for excellence in a particular area. Successful companies usually like to talk about their successes, and they may share some of their Best Practices with someone who is serious about researching the subject.

       7.   In addition to the above, the business models outlined in Chapter VI of this book may be used as starting points for developing Best Practices as they relate to the application of EDI and Electronic Commerce between companies.

Designing the Target Models

We now have the information necessary to begin building the Target Models. Like the previous sessions, this will consist of a series of facilitated workshops involving all Team Members (The PMT, assisted by the Operations Team and the Technology Team) working with the Big Board, developing each level of the Target Model alongside the corresponding level of the Current Process Map. The Best Practices are used as an aid to transform the what-is into the what-should-be. Beginning with the C-G Gap and working outwards from there, the Team constructs Level One Target Models such as the one in **Figure 54** below:

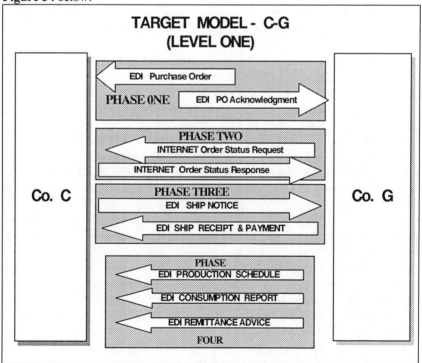

Fig. 54. A Level One Target Model

In our example, the Team determines during the workshops that the desired end result should be a completely paperless system that eliminates the traditional "adversarial" Purchase Order, PO Acknowledgment and Invoicing processes entirely (Phase 4). It is desirable that the customer (Co. G in this case) share its production schedule with the supplier (Co. C) in electronic form, and that the supplier would automatically comply with that schedule without any further authorization required.

Payment would be made to the supplier as the goods are consumed in production. Information regarding the payment and the product consumption (serial #, color, etc.) would be fed back via EDI so that Co. C's production schedule could be intelligently modified according to actual demand (the "Paid On Production" Best Practice model). In addition, Co. C can use the electronic remittance advice to update its A/R system.

Furthermore, the Team sees this strategy being applied to the entire Value System, and directs the other Members to modify this Model for their own Gaps. In actual practice, individual circumstances may dictate that they cannot all use the identical Model, but they should all try to follow the same general strategy. Having designed the basic Target Model seen in the "Phase 4" block in **Fig. 54**, the Team must now design a transformation strategy for Co. C and Co. G.

For instance, Co. C does not have a computerized production schedule yet, much less the ability to share it electronically with either B or G. Other Members are likely in the same position. This capability must be built up in such a manner as not to disrupt the current operation while instituting the processes, disciplines and technologies in each company necessary to implement the model. This could include a joint MRP II/JIT implementation at some point, along with supporting technologies such as bar coding or RF tagging of parts or containers. In our Level One Target Model, the strategy consists of three preparatory phases designed to gradually align the business functions and set the infrastructure in place for the Phase 4 goal of an automated replenishment/Paid On Production system that will move the Value System from an order launching system to a "pull" system based on actual consumption.

In spite of the Team's far-reaching vision, however, this Model is still not the final target. It is only a single step along the continuum of continuous improvement. There is little in the way of conceptual ground-breaking here. It is merely an application of existing technologies to support existing strategies already implemented elsewhere in the EC community. Specifically, this means Automated Procurement, Evaluated Receipts Settlement and Paid On Production). The next pass through will focus on leveraging the infrastructure and experience gained to achieve real breakthroughs such as shared data bases, shared systems, concurrent engineering, and so on.

The Level One Strategy

The Level One Target Model serves as the primary strategic vehicle for ICBE at each Gap. Levels Two and lower tend to be specific to each Member, but Level One is the unifying strategy between them. This particular strategy starts with establishing basic communication facilities via the use of EDI in Phase 1 and the Internet in Phase 2. It goes on through the process of streamlining the logistics and billing functions in Phase 3. It concludes with a full-scale Paid-on-Production environment that completely eliminates the need for traditional business transactions such as PO's and Invoices in Phase 4. In this model, Phases 1, 2 and 3 set up the conditions, processes and practices necessary for Phase 4, which replaces them all. A short description of each Phase follows:

1.   **Phase 1:**   Automates Purchase Orders by using EDI to replace the current paper PO's. The 1 Level 2 and Level 3 Business Models (**Figures 55 and 56**) expand on the details and lay out the new process flows required to support the Level One-Phase 1 Model. The corresponding Migration plans (described later) outline the methods, procedures, policies and other mechanisms that will be used to support and implement each level of the Model. These Migration plans describe the "what" and "how" in detail, and serve as input to the individual company's project planning mechanisms that will decide the "who" and "when".

2.   **Phase 2:**   Makes use of the Internet to facilitate human-to-human status reporting. Once this facility is in place, it can be expanded internally to include marketing, consumer sales, and other company-specific functions (including EDI and secure payments). This is a key element of the EC infrastructure within the Value System. It is well suited for person-to-person communications and other unstructured forms of electronic commerce. The very ability to have universal secure E-Mail across the Membership is in itself a major step forward and can provide the basis for other forms of electronic commerce.

3.   **Phase 3:**   Automates the shipment and receiving process using EDI to implement an Evaluated Receipts Settlement program. The corresponding Migration plan describes the operating details of how the program works between the two Members. In this model, the Invoice has been eliminated in favor of dockside scanning of incoming merchandise. Automatic payment is rendered via EDI/EFT for the goods actually received. This is the first major step in moving from the old paradigm to the new. An entire process has been eliminated.

4.   **Phase 4:**   Uses   an   EDI-based   Planning Schedule/Release Notice (X12 830) to replace the PO and PO Acknowledgment. This serves as a time-phased "build" signal to Co. C, who automatically sends material based upon agreed-upon rules stated in the Migration plan or in a separate blanket purchasing agreement. Co. G. then

uses the EDI Sales Activity Report (X12 867) to report its consumption of material back to Co. C who uses it along with the 830 as input to the production schedule, its inventory system, its sales forecasting system, and the A/R system. This results in a pull system of order management, and eliminates the old order launching system.

Co. G simultaneously issues an 820 Payment Authorization/Remittance Advice to both the bank and to Co. C, paying for the goods. Payment is either instantaneous or on a float-neutral agreement specified by the two Members. The remittance advice is used by Co. C to update and reconcile its A/R system. This is a Paid-On-Production model customized to the C-G situation. It represents the Team's view of the ideal target relationship between these two Members for purposes of compressing the Response Gap and reducing costs.

The Level Two Target Models

Each Phase of the Level One Target Model translates into a Level Two Target Model for each participating Member as shown in Figure 54 below. We will proceed with the example using only Phase 1 for Co. C, but in practice a Level Two Target Model would be developed for Phases 2, 3, and 4 as well.

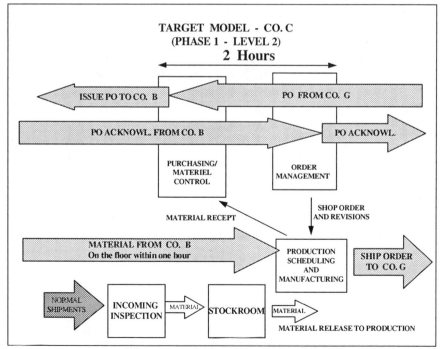

Fig. 55. Level Two Target Model For Phase 1

In the Level 2 model for Co. C, the incoming EDI PO from Co. G is received by the Order Management department. The necessary information is derived from it as it goes by. It is passed straight through to the Purchasing/Materiel Control department, where it is modified electronically for Co. B, and sent out. The PO Acknowledgment from Co. B (which will also be an EDI transaction, according to the grand strategy) conversely passes directly through the Purchasing Department to the Order Management Department, where it is electronically modified for Co. G and sent out immediately.

The goal the Team has set for Co. C is that of a 2-hour turnaround time for electronic transactions and incoming goods from Co. B on the floor in one hour. This changes the Response Gap relating to Co. C as follows:

1. <u>Demand Lag</u> down from 12 days to 6 hours: 2 hours in Co. G's Purchasing, 2 hours in Co. C's Order Management/Purchasing, instantaneous delivery of PO to Co. B, and 2 hours response from Co. B via PO Acknowledgment.

2. <u>Supply Lag</u> down from 14 days to 11 days: 10 days for material to come from Co. B, and 1 day for delivery to Co. G.

3. <u>Process Time</u> of 2 days in Co. C's Manufacturing department.

The total Response Gap for the C-G Gap is down from 26 days to a little less than 12 days (or more than 50%), just by automating the PO's and eliminating incoming inspection and stockroom activities. The lead time from Co. B, however, is still an issue that the Team needs to address with a separate Target Business Model for the A-B Gap in order to reduce Co. A's raw material lead time and therefore Co. B's 10-day contribution to the Supply Lag.

Co. C's Phase 4 Target Business Model will attempt to reduce its 2-day Process Time as much as possible within the context of a JIT implementation with Co. G. It can be seen that reducing the 2 days (even by 50%) has much less of an impact on the overall Value System than reducing the 26-day Response Gap by the same factor. By the fact of implementing Phase 1, the Members will have realized a quantum process improvement and the corresponding financial gains, even if they go no further.

In order to accomplish these goals, a Phase 1-Level Three Target Model must be developed that details each of the processes involved, and sets lower level goals to correspond with the 2-hour mandate **Figure 56** on the next page shows the steps that were taken to accomplish this (after much lively and animated discussion, no doubt).

The Level Three Target Models

In the previous Order Management function for Co. C, there were 11 separate steps before a Purchase Requisition was cut for the Purchasing Department. The newly designed Order Management function has only 4 steps as it relates to incoming PO's from Co. G. Remember, all other business is still handled the old 11-step way. Only the Co. G processes have changed at this point.

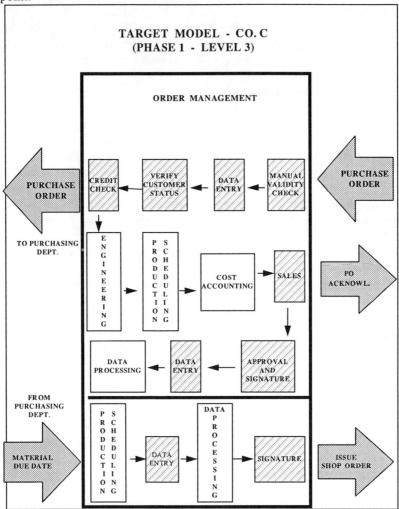

Fig. 56. Level Three Target Model For Phase 1 (Order Management)

1.   Manual Validity Check: Eliminated.   Total step time: 0 hours

2.   Data Entry: Eliminated.   The internal tracking number and salesman information are assigned electronically. Step time: 0 hours.   Total elapsed time: 0 hours.

3.   Verify Customer Status: Eliminated.   All relevant information is already on file and pre-validated.   Step time: 0 hours.   Total elapsed time: 0 hours.

4.   Credit Check: Eliminated. All relevant information is already on file and the customer is pre-approved. Step time: 0 hours. Total elapsed time: 0 hours.

5.   Engineering: The PO is reviewed electronically by the Design Engineering Department for changes in design, technical specifications, materials, etc. Changes are noted for review by cost accounting. Step time: .5 hours. Total elapsed time: .5 hours.

6.   Production Scheduling: The PO is reviewed electronically by Production Scheduling to determine possible conflicts or delays in production, as well as to review existing orders in progress for that customer. Step time .5 hours overlapping with Engineering review. Total elapsed time: 1 hour.

7.   Cost Accounting: The PO, with engineering changes if any, is reviewed electronically against the customer's existing price agreement. If there is a change in price, it must be negotiated with the customer before approving the order and committing to production. For normal orders, the computer generates a PO Acknowledgment with an estimated Material Due Date. Step time: .5 hours. Total elapsed time: 1.5 hours.

8.   Sales: Eliminated. Step time: 0 hours. Total elapsed time: 1.5 hours.

9.   Approval and Signature: Eliminated. Step time: 0 hours. Total elapsed time: 1.5 hours.

10.   Data Entry: Eliminated. Step time: 0 hours. Total elapsed time: 1.5 hours.

11.   Data Processing: Upon electronic authorization from Cost Accounting, the computer processes the PO information, posts the PO into the Purchasing Data Base, and updates the Production Schedule. Step time: 0 hours. Total elapsed time: 1.5 hours   Previous elapsed time: 16 hours (2 days).

The Purchasing Department receives Co. G's PO electronically at the same time as Order Management does, and follows a 2-step process before issuing a PO to the final Vendor. These are:

1.   Sort By Requisition #: Eliminated. Step time: 0 hours. Total elapsed time: 1.5 hours.

2.   Set Up File for PO: Eliminated. The file is already on the system. No internal tracking number is necessary. Step time: 0 hours. Elapsed time: 0 hours. Total elapsed time: 1.5 hours.

3.   Data Entry: Eliminated. Step time: 0 hours. Elapsed time: 0 hours. Total elapsed time: 1.5 hours.

4.   Retrieve Parts Master File: Eliminated. Verification of part numbers, product structure (Bill of Material), etc. Is now performed during the Engineering Validation step below. Step time: 0 hours. Elapsed time: 0 hours. Total elapsed time: 1.5 hours.

5.   Engineering Validation: The Manufacturing Engineer validates the product structures and the technical specifications, schedules equipment maintenance and setup, etc. Any differences in the parts master file

specifications and the specifications maintained at the sales office are resolved at this point. Step time: .5 hours. Elapsed time: .5 hours. Total elapsed time: 2 hours.

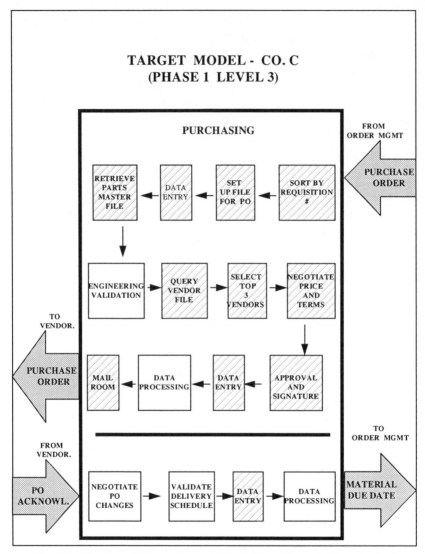

Fig. 57. The Level Three Target Model For Phase 1 (Purchasing)

      6.   Query Vendor File: Eliminated. There is only one Vendor for this product. Step time: 0 hours. Elapsed time: 0 hours. Total elapsed time: 2 hours.
      7.   Select Top 3 Vendors: Eliminated. Step time: 0 hours. Elapsed time: 0 hours. Total elapsed time: 2 hours.

8.   Negotiate Price and Terms: Eliminated.   Price and terms already part of blanket purchase agreement.   Exceptions are handled outside this process. Step time: 0 hours. Elapsed time: 0 hours. Total elapsed time: 2 hours.

9.   Approval and Signature: Eliminated.   Step time: 0 hours. Elapsed time: 0 hours. Total elapsed time: 2 hours.

10.   Data Entry: Eliminated. Any changes have been entered in as a part of the process up to this point. Step time: 0 hours. Elapsed time: 0 hours. Total elapsed time: 2 hours.

11.   Data Processing: The computer processes the information and generates an EDI Purchase Order for Co. B. The step time shown here includes all computer processing time for both Departments. Step time: .5 hours. Elapsed time: 1 hour. Total elapsed time: 3 hours.

12.   Mail Room: Eliminated. Step time: 0 hours. Elapsed time: 0 hour. Total elapsed time: **3 hours.** Previous Total elapsed time: 32 hours (4 days).

By EDI, the PO takes 0 hours to arrive at CO. B, saving 6 days. It is turned around immediately (within 2 hours) with an EDI PO Acknowledgment, which is received immediately by Co. C. The total elapsed time is now 5 hours from receipt of the original PO from Co. G. Co. C's Purchasing Department now takes the following steps:

1.   Negotiate PO Changes: The Purchasing Department's EDI Coordinator (Co. C) and Co. B's Order Management Department's EDI Coordinator discuss any changes that have taken place (if any) since the PO was issued, and verbally verify the quantities, price, terms, and delivery. When verified, the PO Acknowledgment is electronically released by Purchasing. Step time: .5 hours. Total elapsed time: 5.5 hours.

2.   Validate Delivery Schedule: The Purchasing EDI Coordinator contacts the carrier that will be delivering the material to Co. C and books the shipment. The carrier verbally confirms the booking and the system is updated with the Material Due Date. the paperwork is created off-line. Step time: .5 hour. Elapsed time: .5 hour. Total elapsed time: 6 hours.

3.   Data Entry: Eliminated. Step time: 0 hours. Elapsed time: 0 hour. Total elapsed time: 6 hours.

4.   Data Processing: The computer processes the information, updates the Purchasing and Order Management systems, and notifies the relevant managers via internal E-Mail. This information is now available on-line. Step time: 0 hours. Elapsed time: 0 hour. Total elapsed time: 6 hours Previous total elapsed time: 96 hours (12 days).

When the final Material Due Date is available to Order Management, the following 4 steps occur:

1.   Production Scheduling: Production Scheduling matches the Material Due Date up with the planned order and electronically verifies the upcoming production schedule. Step time: .5 hours. Elapsed time: .5 hours.

Total elapsed time: 6.5 hours.

  2. Data Entry: Eliminated. Step time: 0 hours. Elapsed time: 0 hours. Total elapsed time: 6.5 hours.

  3. Data Processing: The computer verifies Material Due Date and the Production Schedule and issues a PO Change to Co. G if it does not match the estimated Material Due Date on the original PO Acknowledgment sent earlier. The computer does its daily production run later in the day, and issues a paper shop order and associated production documentation. Step time: .5 hours. Elapsed time: .5 hours. Total elapsed time: 7 hours.

  4. Signature: Eliminated. Step time: 0 hours. Elapsed time: **7 hours.** Total elapsed time: 7 hours (1 day). Previous total elapsed time: 112 hours (14 days).

  This reduces the internal elapsed time from receipt of the original order to the issue of a Shop Floor order from 14 working days (including surface mail to Co. B) down to 1 working day, eliminating 13 working days. The elimination of incoming inspection and the stockroom has shaved off another 3 days, making a total savings of 16 working days, or more than 3 working weeks from the business cycle. In addition, the Team's mandate of a 2-hour door-to-door turnaround time was met, both from the C-G side and from the B-C side.

  Having saved that 16 days, Co. C is now in a position to use conventional surface transportation to get the order to Co. G and eliminate the excessive cost of the overnight courier. This will likely add 2 days to the current 1-day delivery time, making the total savings of 14 days or just under 3 working weeks. Co. C's total lead time now stands at 16 days as opposed to 30 days (1-day order processing, 10-day material lead time, 2 days manufacturing, and 3 days delivery), a reduction of almost 50%. The internal processing time has gone from 20 days down to 6 days, a 70% reduction.

  The ICBE exercise has now accomplished two main objectives for Co. C:

  1. Quantum time reduction
  2. cost reduction through reduced staff time and elimination of
     courier charges.

These should be quantified for the report to the Steering Committee. Further reductions are likely possible in future passes, and they will be actively pursued, but a quantum leap has been achieved here already. The next question likely to be asked by Co. C's CEO will be, "Well, if we can do it for them ......".

The Critical Path Revisited

  The 14-day savings at the C-G Gap alone have reduced the total cumulative lead time from 45 days to 31 days, or almost 30%. For illustration purposes, we have focused on the C-G Gap. During this time, the Team has simultaneously been working with the Member companies at the other Gaps along the Critical Path with the intent to achieve similar results. We will briefly walk through the final design that emerges for the Critical Path, assuming that each of the Members goes through the above exercise.

Phase 1:

A-B: EDI PO and PO Acknowledgment (2 hour limit) - internal process improvements - reduction from 8 days internal time to 3 days. Total lead time: 3 days to get to B.

B-C: EDI PO and PO Acknowledgment (2 hour limit) - internal process improvements - reduction from 2 days internal time to 1 day. Total lead time: 4 days to get to C.

C-G: EDI PO and PO Acknowledgment (2 hour limit) - internal process improvements - reduction from 20 days internal time to 6 days - total lead time 10 days to get to G.

G-J: EDI PO and PO Acknowledgment (2 hour limit), Internet Order Status Request and Response (1 hour limit) - internal process improvements - reduction from 10 days internal time to 3 days - total lead time 13 days to get to J.

J-Customer: Internal process improvements - reduction from 5 days internal time to 3 days - total lead time 16 days to get to the customer. That is now the shortest path, but the other two legs of the Value System are now longer, so they must be reduced as well

Phase 2:

A-B: Internet Order Status Request and Response - internal process improvements - reduction from 3 days internal time to 2 days. Total lead time: 2 days to get to B.

B-C: Internet Order Status Request and Response - no internal improvements - no reduction in internal time. Total lead time: 3 days to get to C.

C-G: Internet Order Status Request and Response - no process improvements - no reduction in internal time. Total lead time: 8 days to get to G.

G-J: EDI Ship Notice/Billing and electronic settlement - no internal process improvements - no reduction in internal time. Total lead time 10 days to get to J.

Phase 3:

A-B: EDI Ship Notice/Billing and electronic settlement - no internal process improvements. Total lead time: 3 days to get to B.

B-C: EDI Ship Notice/Billing and electronic settlement - no internal process improvements - no reduction of internal time. Total lead time: 4 days to get to C.

C-G: EDI Ship Notice/Billing and electronic settlement - no internal process improvements - no reduction of internal time. - total lead time 10 days to get to G.

G-J: EDI Planning Schedule, Consumption Record, and electronic payment (Paid On Production model) - internal process improvements - reduction from 3 days internal time to 2 days. Total lead time 12 days to get to J.

Phase 4:

A-B: EDI Planning Schedule, Consumption Record, and electronic payment - internal process improvements - reduction from 3 days internal time to 2 days. Total lead time: 2 days to get to B.

B-C: EDI Planning Schedule, Consumption Record, and electronic payment - no internal process improvements - no reduction in internal time. Total lead time: 3 days to get to C.

C-G: EDI Planning Schedule, Consumption Record, and electronic payment - internal process improvements and alternative transportation methods - reduction from 6 days internal time to 3 days - total lead time 6 days to get to G.

G-J: Shared data base for planning and consumption data - internal process improvements - reduction from 3 days internal time to 2 days - total lead time 8 days to get to J.

By the end of Phase 4, it is planned to reduce the 40-day lead time from A through J to 8 days--an 80% reduction across the entire Critical Path. Co. J is also implementing process improvements that will reduce its 5-day internal time to 2 days. If ICBE can achieve the same results along each of the other Paths, it will result in a cumulative lead time of 10 days (2 weeks) from the time the Customer placed the order. This is down from 9 weeks. It is sure to rank Co. J as a leading supplier. The Customer's other suppliers average 6 weeks. Also, now that the costs are reduced across the entire System, there is more margin to play with, and Co. J can be more competitive on that front.

Co. G, who is the first-tier supplier to Co. J, spearheads new developments during each Phase, culminating in a shared data base with Co. J, while the downstream suppliers build their capability. While this example is artificial, the concepts are valid for real life situations. Actual results may be more or less than the example, but ICBE, if properly applied, will lead to dramatic reductions in both time and costs.

The Remainder of the Level Zero Target Model

Once the original Critical Path has been shortened, then the next Critical Path emerges--that of B-F-J. The A-B Gap has already been addressed as part of the original Critical Path. The same exercise is undertaken here, with the additional complication that two of the Members have multiple Gaps to contend with and to develop Target Business Models for.

Co. B has four Gaps, and Co. F has five. We also have to revisit Co. C and Co. G now, because of their Gaps with Co. F. While this is somewhat more complex, it is only a matter of degree because the same concepts are applied in analysis and design. When that is complete, it leaves the B-D-E-G-J path to be addressed in the same manner. As in the original Critical Path implementation, Co. J's first-tier supplier is the one who spearheads the leading edge of the implementation, and is always one Phase ahead of the others.

When the first pass through the System has been completed and the Target Models have been designed for all Gaps, the Team now has its working strategy for transforming the Value System. the new System should look something like the Big Board model in **Figure 58** below:

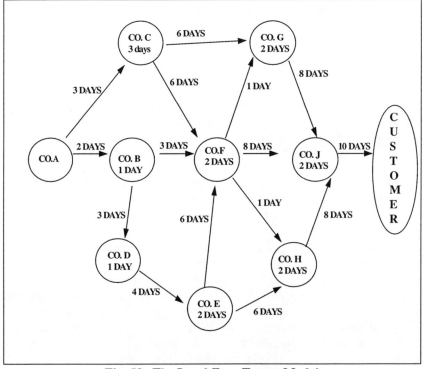

Fig. 58. The Level Zero Target Model

If we look at the new Big Board, we can see that the reductions in the original Critical Path have served as an example for all Members. Co. J, knowing that it can now have the product to the customer in 10 days (or better), naturally wants the rest of the System to conform to the improvements planned for the A-B-C-G path. This results in a System that achieves the stated time goals and synchronizes the product flows.

For example, Co. J can count on getting all of its components in 8 days; Co. F can count on getting all of its material in 6 days. Co. G and Co. H can count on getting their "basic units" in 6 days and their "add-ons" from Co. F in 7 days. This allows each of the Members to schedule production with much more certainty than before, reduce the costs of tearing down and setting up manufacturing equipment, and permit better scheduling of transportation resources.

This has been the goal of ICBE all along, to align the business processes of the Members in order to eliminate the Response Gaps, shrink the business cycle and reduce costs across the entire Value System. The design has accomplished that, and now it is time to put the theory into actual practice.

Summary

Now that the Analysis is complete and we have a basic understanding of the problem areas to be addressed, we turn to the technique of Benchmarking to provide us with Best Practices and objective performance measurements against which to develop our new Value System model. Internal benchmarking, that being the "Good Practices" and "pockets of excellence" that we have observed in other Members, may be used for short term cherry-picking to make some immediate improvements.

Long term improvements, however, can only be made by adapting the Best-In-Class (BIC) benchmarks from such companies as Fedex, American Express, Ford, Wal-Mart, and others who are recognized for excellence in a particular area. It is from these Best Practices that we develop our Target Models. We strive to develop clear superiority to the competition by implementing these models, even though some competitors may indirectly benefit from the advances made by our Members. This should not cause undue concern in any case, since our competitors are not set up to pursue excellence with the same degree of focus and vigor that we are. They will continue to "do EDI", while we develop entirely new modes of commerce and leave them far behind.

The Target Models are designed by the entire Team looking at every aspect of the Big Board operation. Since the Big Board is at Level Zero, the Target Models for each Gap (for instance between Co. C and Co. G) begin at Level One, and these Models are used to set out a phased strategy to achieve the selected Best Practices between the two Members. Each of the Phases in the Level One Model is then broken down into the lower level Target Models that will achieve that strategy. The Team sets stretch goals for the Members (such as an 80% reduction in lead time), and the Models are developed to attain those goals. This fosters true "breakthrough thinking" and can result in some dramatic changes.

When this is done for each of the Gaps, a picture begins to emerge that helps the Team refine its strategy for the Value System. The Level One Models are reworked and redesigned until they fit together in a cohesive pattern that makes a quantum improvement in the System. The Target Models are now coordinated across the entire System, resulting in savings in time and cost that could not have previously been imagined.

Now that the designs are in place and they all fit together, it is time to develop the actual Migration Plans at each Gap that will execute the design.

CHAPTER XIV

STEP 6: BUSINESS PROCESS TRANSFORMATION

Migration Plans

The development of the Target Business Models has been, so far, a purely theoretical exercise. Some of the process changes have been identified and some of the technological changes have been hinted at. However, there is nothing concrete at this point to say "Here is exactly <u>how</u> we are going to do it". We have identified the "what" to a large extent, and have determined that the changes that have been proposed are feasible, at least at first glance, but now we need to work on the "how".

The changes we have designed in the Target Models cannot be put into place all at once. We must find a practical way to get us from here to there in a smooth, coordinated manner without undue disruption to the various businesses involved. This requires a "Migration Plan" that sits behind the Level One Target Model at each Gap. This sets out the sequence of events, milestones, timetable, processes and mechanisms necessary to effect the joint implementation of the Model. Based on the Level One Migration Plan, each Member develops an internal Migration Plan. This implements its own Level Two, Three and Four Target Models in close conjunction with the other Member, cooperating where there are reciprocal or common processes and undertaking joint development where appropriate.

The Members now have the broad strategic context within which to work and a shared focus. They have established a common direction and a common timetable for their internal lower-level Migration Plans, and have the freedom to develop them internally in their own way. The Level One Migration Plans, in turn, are orchestrated and coordinated by the Team to achieve the overall Level Zero "Strategic Plan" displayed on the Big Board.

The Level One Migration Plan for each Gap consists of two parts:

1. Demand side
2. Supply side.

The two are developed in conjunction with each other and are linked together by the Level One Target Model. In fact, a significant portion of the Migration Plan has likely been developed already, through preliminary plans that were made during the development of the Target Models. These may be collected, embellished, enhanced, and improved upon during this exercise to arrive at an actual workable and executable Migration Plan.

In the Migration Plan, the overall strategy of the Level One Target Model is briefly described, and each Phase is laid out at a high level of detail Only Phase 1 is shown in the example in **Figure 60**, but in actual practice they would all be completed. This document identifies the sequence of tasks to be performed, the resources to be put in place, and the processes to be developed by each of the members involved.

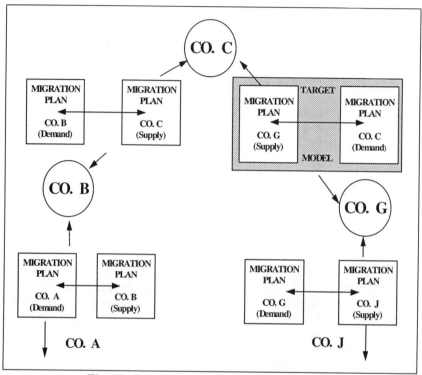

Fig. 59. Target Models and Migration Plans

To continue our C-G example, Phase 1 of the C-G Migration Plan (**Figure 60**) calls for each company to develop an EC/EDI Policy statement, appoint an EC/EDI Coordinator, and develop its own internal parallel processing methods for EC/EDI. The Policy Statement would likely be developed jointly or at least in cooperation. Filling the EC/EDI Coordinator positions could also be a joint effort. This would ensure that the two Coordinators have more or less equal qualifications, that they can work together, and that they are initiated into a true inter-corporate environment right from the beginning. As the inter-corporate environment matures, a single individual (or service provider) might hold the Coordinator position for both companies or even the entire Value System.

The "parallel paper-electronic" processes, however, are completely specific to each Member, and these could be developed independently of each other. The next step called for in the Migration Plan is for the Members to streamline their reciprocal processes. Co. C would streamline its Order Management system in conjunction with Co. G streamlining its Purchasing effort. Similarly, Co. C's A/R upgrade would match Co. G's A/P upgrade.

On the Systems and Technology side, it is planned for both companies to install EDI systems and equipment at the same time and in cooperation with each other. While the general characteristics and capabilities of this equipment should be mutually compatible, they do not have to be identical. This can be a "cooperative" activity as opposed to a "joint" activity. The application system changes would probably be an independent activity since the applications are completely specific to each company, but designing the EDI messages is definitely a joint activity.

Installation of bar-code equipment is a joint activity since it represents a reciprocal process. Co. C implements bar coding in its shipping department while Co. G implements bar coding in its receiving department, ensuring compatibility of the bar codes and equipment as well as the handling and reconciliation procedures. Integrating bar-coding into the internal applications is an independent activity of each Member company.

The measurements that each Member uses to assess the operation of the new systems and processes are different but complementary, and are designed to show the effect on the performance of the two organizations. Co. C, being the supplier, wants to measure:

1. Customer satisfaction issues (# complaints including expediting calls)
2. Whether the new System reduces the variability in the existing process (# PO Changes and Engineering Change Notices)
3. Whether it actually saves money over time. (Changes in costs).

Co. G, being the customer, wants to know if the new System results in:

1. Getting the goods faster (Lead time, % on-time deliveries)
2. Whether it reduces variability in its own processes (# expediting calls)
3. Whether it results in better quality (# rejects)
4. Whether it reduces the cost of the units purchased.

Together, these key performance indicators are deemed to provide both Co. C and Co. G with a complete picture of the success of the operation.

This picture, however, is based on the current problem set faced by the two organizations. The measurements may change as these problems are overcome and new issues arise. For instance, when PO's have been completely eliminated from the process, it is not useful to keep measuring the PO Changes. In a concurrent engineering environment, Engineering Change Notices are no longer a relevant measurement, etc.

For Phase 1, the Members agree that a simple set of external controls are sufficient to establish the correct delivery of EDI transactions between them. Each Member will produce a report that details the orders sent and the orders received by EDI. These will be reconciled on a daily basis by the EDI Coordinators, and problems resolved immediately. During actual operation of the EDI system, the Translation software at each end will return a Functional

Acknowledgment each time it receives and EDI transaction. These will also be reconciled by the EDI Coordinators, and problems will be resolved immediately.

MIGRATION PLAN - C-G
GENERAL:
      Co. C and Co. G will jointly implement an Electronic Commerce facility, using EDI transactions and Internet communications to streamline the Order Management and the Financial Settlement functions. This will be accomplished in four Phases, as follows:

        Phase 1 ....*(high level description expanding on the Business Model)*
        Phase 2 - ....
        Phase 3 - ....
        Phase 4 - ....

PHASE 1

CO. C (Supply Side)	CO. G (Demand Side)
Processes and Procedures: • Joint EDI/EC Policy statement • Appoint EDI/EC Coordinator • Design parallel paper/electronic process • Update Order Management procedures • Update A/R procedures	• Joint EDI/EC Policy statement • Appoint EDI/EC Coordinator • Design parallel paper/electronic process • Update Purchasing procedures • Update A/P procedures
Systems and Technology: • Install EDI systems & equipment • Implement application system changes • Joint EDI Message design • Install bar-code technology (shipping)	• Install EDI systems & equipment • Implement application system changes • Joint EDI Message design • Install bar-code technology (receiving)
Measurements: • # Purchase Order Changes • # Engineering Change Notices • # complaints • Change in overhead costs (G&A) • Change in delivery costs	• Lead time • # expediting calls • % on-time deliveries • # rejects • Cost per unit
Controls: • EDI Orders Received report • PO Acknowledgment • EDI Functional Acknowledgments	• EDI Orders Sent report • PO Acknowledgment • EDI Functional Acknowledgments

Figure 60. C-G Migration Plan (Partial)

The lower-level Migration Plans specify the exact means by which each Member will implement their own Target Models, and exactly how, when and where they will cooperate in joint development. If the Target Model is the high-level "architecture" of the inter-corporate system, the Migration Plans are the low-level "blueprints", consisting of the specific hardware, software, documents, forms, methods, processes, procedures, disciplines, technologies, functions and staffing that will be put in place. where there are common processes or reciprocal processes (such as Logistics, A/P and A/R, etc.), those aspects of the Migration Plans should be developed jointly to ensure alignment

This synchronizes the methods, technology and functional capabilities between the Members, and standardizes the details of their implementations. Your bar code is the same as my bar code, your EDI message is the same as my EDI message, etc. The systems work together as one. The controls also complement each other so that it is easier to trace operational problems.

An individual Member's Migration Plan is really a synthesis of the Migration Plans on each side of their Gap. For instance, Co. B's Migration Plan will consist of the "supply side" A-B Migration Plan as well as the "demand side" B-C Migration Plan. Co. C's Migration Plan will consist of the "supply side" B-C Migration Plan and the "demand side" C-G Migration Plan, and so on.

The fact that Co. G's "demand side" Migration Plan and Co. C's "supply side" Migration Plan are developed jointly by C and G ensures that they will be synchronized. The fact that Co. C's "demand side" Plan and Co. B's "supply side" Plan are developed jointly by B and C also ensures synchronization from that end, and provides Co. C with continuity of purpose and design throughout these two business relationships. It should then be a relatively straightforward exercise for Co. C to coordinate its own demand side and supply side Plans into a cohesive Migration Plan that is specific to its own situation (**See Figures 61 and 62**).

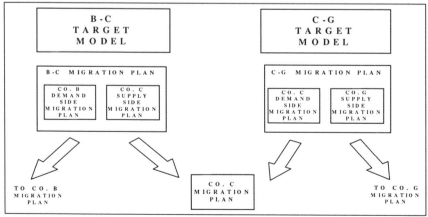

Figure 61. The Migration Plan for Co. C

Co. C 's Migration Plan is now based on actual field requirements vs. perceived or assumed requirements. There is a reasonable degree of certainty that it will meet the need, and that the effort has full support from the senior management of all participants. In addition, these Migration Plans relate to each other in such a way as to synchronize the common implementation of inter-corporate functions while permitting each Member to undertake its own internal projects according to its unique situation (see **Figure 62** below). In fact, the Migration plan can be viewed as a high-level launch pad for a series of coordinated projects.

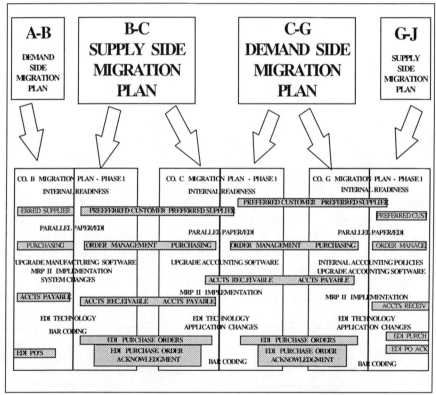

Fig. 62. The Relationships Between the Migration Plans

Migration Plan Content

In **Figure 62**, the shaded boxes that span organizational boundaries are the external projects that are shared between Members; the others are the internal projects that are company-specific. Each is a self-contained entity, with its own schedules, deliverables and a project plan (see also **Figure 61**). As we examine **Figure 62** more closely, the following sequence of projects emerges:

- **Readiness Project**: Each Team Member undertakes its own internal readiness program (see Chapter X). This is different for each of the Members, but there can and should be regular communication while this exercise is going on. Each Member has a road map of where the effort is headed, so they should develop along somewhat similar lines. However, it could be useful for each of them to have an informal review by the other Members at some point. This is the point at which the Members begin to develop their individual ECE's so that they will be able to develop a true inter-enterprise systems architecture in later Phases of the program.

- **Pilot 1 - Customer-Supplier Project**: Each Team Member puts a Preferred Customer Program in place for its upline customer, and a Preferred Supplier Program in place for its downline supplier. These Programs can include:

  1. Policy changes
  2. Sole-source agreements
  3. Volume agreements
  4. Discount schedules
  5. Performance guarantees
  6. Quality guarantees
  7. Onsite inspection
  8. The assignment of a Customer/Supplier Service Representative
  9. Special "hotline" numbers, and other mechanisms designed to foster a close business relationship.

- **Paper-EDI Project**: Each Team Member develops its own internal procedures for parallel processing of paper transactions and EDI transactions. All other business transactions except for these Members will still be handled on paper, so there needs to be a way to handle both streams without loss of integrity and control. This is where the internal audit trails and system controls are developed and implemented for the new EC system.

- **Pilot 2 - Purchasing-Order Management Project**: The Team undertakes a joint project to align their Purchasing and Order Management processes and procedures. In this example, all Members in the Critical Path are involved simultaneously. This is the result of a conscious decision on the part of the Team to do it this way so that no one is lagging behind in basic capabilities when it is time to start sending EDI transactions back and forth. This is where Co. C would implement the process changes for its Level Two and Three Target Business model in the Order Management and Purchasing Departments (**Figures 54-56**).

- **Internal Systems Project**: The Team Members once again turn their attention inward, and upgrade their accounting and manufacturing systems to cope with the plans for Phase 1. Co. G develops new internal accounting policies to accommodate the electronic commerce, and installs new accounting software.

Co. C already has adequate accounting policies and procedures in place, but must also upgrade its accounting software. Needless to say, the G and C Team members communicate during the implementation to ensure that there are no surprises when the systems eventually have to do business with each other.

Co. B decides to modernize its manufacturing system as it relates to this Value System, upgrades its manufacturing software, implements MRP II for those products provided to Co. C (later for Co. F and Co. D, and then for all of its other customers), and makes other system changes as necessary. This creates a time delay, but it is an important step, so the Team approves the action and delays its next joint project.

- **Pilot 3 - A/P-A/R Project**: The Team begins a joint project to align C and G's A/P and A/R systems, both procedurally and technologically. In this particular case, they decide to use the services of a VAB (Value-Added Bank) to outsource their joint A/P and A/R. All other business except for that between C and G are handled the old way with the old processes. This is done for two reasons:

1. It provides proof-of-process for the new way of handling settlements, and paves the way for future migration of other business for both C and G.

2. It sets up the system for the later implementation of electronic settlements through the bank.

When it is time, everything will be in place and ready to go at the flip of a switch. When this is completed successfully, the Team then implements the same system with G and J, and C and B. Co. B implements a more manual A/P A/R alignment with Co. A.

While this is going on and being validated, C and G implement a limited MRP II system to handle the products that flow through this Value System. This ensures that the manufacturing data is accurate, that there is a formal scheduling process, and that there is a foundation for coordinated production of goods across the Critical Path. Co. J's plan is not shown, but they are doing the same thing.

- **EDI Infrastructure Project**: Each Member then installs the appropriate EDI technology, such as PC's EDI Translators, VAN's, Internet access, etc. Application changes are made as necessary to integrate EC/EDI into the legacy environment.

- **Pilot 4 - EDI PO Project**: The Team begins the first EDI System Pilot. EDI Purchase Orders and PO acknowledgments are sent between C and G, and G and J. More about the System Pilot later.

- **Bar-code Project**: While this is going on, the Team installs bar-coding equipment at Co. B as a mini-pilot project. This works out all of the bugs, establishes a common configuration for the rest of the Membership, and gives the Team some experience.

• **Pilot 4 - Continued**: The Team then begins the second EDI Pilot between B and C, for PO's and Acknowledgments, and between A and B for PO's. Since the Team has already done this once, there is the benefit of experience. As with the bar-coding pilot, the bugs have been worked out, and this Pilot should go much more smoothly than the first one. When it comes time for the System Pilot, everyone will know what to do and how to do it (more on this later as well).

• **Bar-Code Project - Continued**: The bar-coding system is now implemented in Co. C, B, and J (not shown). Since G and J are only two blocks away from each other, the bar-coding can be used to send EDI Ship Notices that are physically attached to the shipment, as opposed to sending them through the VAN, thereby making the information available instantaneously. This not only speeds up data collection throughout the system, but it also prepares for the future Evaluated Receipts Settlement project planned for Phase 3.

In actual practice, the Migration Plans would have other information associated with each of the activities in sufficient detail to provide direction for the external projects between the Members, and for the various internal projects within each Member. Where possible, Members should try to leverage any economies of scale that could be gained by joint implementation, such as cost savings through joint acquisition of technology, systems and equipment, and inter-corporate sharing of resources and expertise.

Controlling The Implementation:

Now the deliberations are over. The Operations Team (OT) and the Technology Team (TT) have designed the Target Models and the associated Migration Plans for each of the Members, and the Project Management Team (PMT) is now ready to implement the projects specified in those Migration Plans. As has been stated several times in this book, this requires a large measure of coordination and control. No longer is each Member an independent individual company. There are others in the mix now as well. The above scenario was developed in such a manner as to demand a central coordination and control, while still allowing each Member to control its own destiny insofar as purely internal considerations are concerned.

The controlling entity is the PMT (Torchbearer-level senior management from each Member), assisted by: the Planning and Facilitation Team (PFT), who does all of the planning, organizing, scheduling, reporting, motivating, expediting, and day-to-day interface between the Members; and the Audit and Commissioning Team (ACT) who keeps everyone honest, establishes the audit trails and controls, and independently measures the success of the effort (see **Figure 35**). The PMT reports results periodically to the Alpha Team (Steering Committee), and receives direction from them

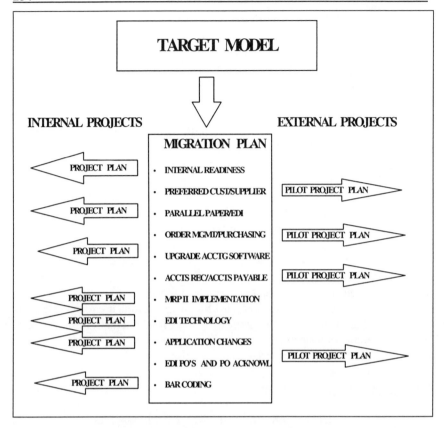

Fig. 63. Internal and External Projects

By way of review, the lower level ICBE Implementation Teams (OT, TT, and others as required) consist of senior individuals from each of the Members, who develop solutions and make decisions jointly. They take back these decisions and solutions to their own company, where they serve as the project managers, backed internally by their own Torchbearer from the PMT. This maintains management commitment all the way through.

The PMT , in the above example, has decided that the entire A-B-C-G-J Critical Path should be re-engineered at the same time. To accomplish this, the individual Migration Plans must be in place and operational before the entire System can be tested. The PMT aligns the Migration Plans as in **Figure 61**, sets the milestones and timetables, and proceeds with the sequence as described therein by coordinating the internal and external projects. This can be considered as a "Level Zero" Migration Plan, because it implements the Level Zero Target Model as developed on the "Big Board" (see **Figure 57**).

While the PMT does not directly control the internal projects of the Members, it nonetheless holds them to a timetable for implementation as established by the Level Zero Migration Plan, and provides assistance from other members as required to move them past any difficult situations that may occur during implementation. The external projects (those between Members, such as EDI PO's) are directly controlled by the PMT and the ICBE Teams through Pilot projects as described below.

STEP 7: SYSTEM PILOTS AND OPERATIONAL ADJUSTMENTS:

The external interfaces dictated by the Level One Migration Plans are implemented through a series of controlled Pilot projects (**Figure 62**). In our example, Pilot 1 will implement Preferred Customer/Preferred Supplier status between C-G, A-B, B-C, and G-J concurrently. Pilot 2 will implement the Order Management and Purchasing process changes across the Membership. Pilot 3 (Accounts Receivable/Accounts Payable) will be implemented first by C-G, and later by A-B, B-C, and G-J. Pilot 4 will implement EDI PO's and PO Acknowledgments between C-G first, followed by the others as above.

Treating these as joint Pilot Projects is not intended to slow the effort down or to institute an artificial bureaucracy, but to facilitate a common business environment among the Members. Upon conclusion of Pilot 4, Phase 1 can be "Commissioned" (more on this later) and rolled out to the other Critical Paths as required, while this Team can start on Phase 2. The lessons learned during the Pilots may be carried forward into the following Phases. They can also benefit the other Members as they implement the same or similar facilities between them in their own Critical Path implementations.

There are really two levels of Pilot: the Level One Pilot discussed above that implements, tests and adjusts each Phase of the Level One Migration Plans, and the Level Zero Pilot, that verifies that the big Board concepts are working. There may be several Level One Pilots for each Phase, but only one Level Zero Pilot. The Level One Pilots concentrate on the success of the individual inter-corporate processes and information flows, while the Level Zero Pilot concentrates on the success of the implementation from end-to-end. Level One Pilots deal with lower levels of detail, and Level Zero deals with Big Board issues.

For instance, the Team may decide to hold a formal Level Zero test at the end of Phases 1, 3 and 4 of the Tactical Plan for the Critical Path Members, to ensure full end-to-end functionality. In our example, the PMT decided that Phase 2 did not need full formal testing at Level Zero since it involved human-to-human status communication over the Internet and thus did not pass legally or financially operative business transactions. Since the format of the human-to-human communications could vary over time according to the needs of the individuals involved, it was not deemed necessary to subject Phase 2 to the same degree of rigor that would be applied to PO's or invoices.

Whether it is a Level One Pilot or a Level Zero Pilot, the essential elements are the same. Only the level of detail and the level of visibility are different. **Figure 64** illustrates these elements, and shows the Pilot process itself.

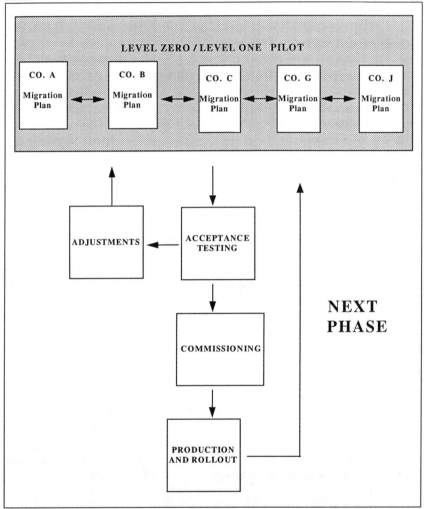

Fig. 64. The Elements of an ICBE Pilot Project

The Project Plans

Project Plans should be under the control of the individual Members as much as possible. It is not to anyone's advantage to impose unfamiliar methodologies on another company. Each Member must be free to manage its internal projects with conventional project teams operating under its own company-specific project planning mechanisms. This book will not attempt to lay out the details of how the Members should construct their project plans, since that topic is dealt with in detail in several other books that are readily available. The Members should use whatever project planning technique they are comfortable with, that provides visibility into the development process, and that fixes accountability.

The key to tying it all together at the inter-corporate level is the Pilot Project Plan, which sets broad objectives, monitors key indicators and co-ordinates all Team members at the highest level via the PMT. A (modified) real-life example of a successful Pilot Project Plan is included in **Appendix A.** Names and specific references have been deleted or changed to protect the confidentiality of the Members involved   This is the Project Plan that is reviewed at the PMT meetings, and against which reports are made to the Alpha Team. Whether it is a Level One Pilot or a Level Zero Pilot, the principles are the same, only the activities and focus will vary.

This example does not show real ICBE Teaming, since the Members were separated by inter-continental distances and were economically and logistically unable to work as physical Teams. However, it illustrates many of the other principles and structures we have discussed in this book. This Project not only involved different countries, but also different governments, regulatory bodies, languages and cultures. If such a degree of co-operation can be accomplished in that environment, it can be accomplished just about anywhere.

Under normal circumstances, however, the Members would form work teams during the Pilots. They would develop joint methods, processes, systems and procedures while working physically together as much as possible and sharing as many common resources as possible. The Members should gain a sense of community, even though they are from different companies.

Progress-to-Plan is monitored regularly by the PMT, assisted by the PFT (Planning and Facilitation Team). Where necessary, assistance may be rendered by other Members to ensure that the objectives are met on time and that all the members' interests are maintained. While each of the individual Project Managers is responsible for progress reporting to the PMT according to the requirements of the Pilot Project Plan, such reporting should be kept to an absolute minimum and not impose an unnecessary burden. Reporting should be used only for purposes of highlighting exceptions or problems rather than showing strengths or weaknesses of individual Members.

Acceptance and Commissioning

The success of the Pilots cannot be ascertained until there has been a formal Acceptance Test that verifies compliance to the original design and establishes the operational validity and robustness of the system from end to end. When undertaking a multi-corporate endeavour such as this, the stakes are high. Not only is one company at risk, all Members are. This is particularly true wherever there are legally or financially operative transactions that are being exchanged electronically (such as PO's and Invoices). Care must

be taken to minimise the risk of false or "runaway" transactions. The system must
be shown to be immune to tampering or compromise from either inside or outside.

Mistakes and oversights will have a much farther-reaching impact when there are external projects. With internal projects, mistakes can be glossed over, covered up, shrugged off and rationalised as being an "experiment". No one else has to know. With external projects, this is not so. There can be serious consequences for any errors or mis-steps. It is therefore imperative to subject the Pilots to such a degree of rigor that there can be no question, now or ever, that due process was followed, that all reasonable eventualities were tested for, and that the parties are duly authorised and qualified to conduct business in this manner.

The Standard Acceptance Test (SAT)

There must be objective evidence, maintained by a trusted party, to demonstrate that:
1.   The systems operate according to specification.
2.   There are mechanisms in place to ensure the prevention, detection and correction of errors.
3.   There are consistent and reliable testing and diagnostic procedures.
4.   There is a mechanism to ensure proper change control.
5.   The system being tested has in fact gone through these tests and has produced the expected results.
6.   The test results are acceptable to the parties involved as well as to the responsible authority.

This evidence is provided by the Standard Acceptance Test (SAT) Plan, duly completed, signed and registered (example included in **Appendix B**).

The SAT Plan consists of a standard set of "known" data and testing procedures that is followed consistently for each and every implementation of a joint project. It is essential that the SAT process remain intact and unchanging throughout, to ensure that the same mechanisms and procedures are followed **each and every time that a new condition is introduced to the system**. Adherence to this principle allows for a much quicker rollout to new participants, with the attendant benefits of scale. In some instances, Members may wish to develop the SAT Plan first, then use it as high-level specifications for their systems development. This ensures that the focus is on results, not on technology.

There are many variations of the Acceptance Testing process. Some well-known Hubs such as Wal-Mart and Home Depot have introduced their own for the very reasons stated above. Home Depot has a four-stage process for Acceptance Testing of Purchase Orders, and a six-stage process for Acceptance Testing of Invoices. These may be used as models, or a company-specific SAT may be developed to conform to individual requirements.

The model in **Appendix B** shows a three-stage process for the Acceptance Testing of EDI messages. These messages were not legally or financially operative transactions in the manner of Purchase Orders and Invoices, so the SAT concentrated only on verifying the mechanics of exchange and the "external" performance of the individual participants' computer systems. The next stage would normally be that of verifying the "internal" performance of the systems at each end in terms of the correctness of Purchase Order information and the handling of the Purchase Order by all of the related application systems.

The ACT (Audit and Commissioning Team), in conjunction with the PMT, determines the content of the SAT and administers it throughout the Testing process. The SAT in **Appendix B** is not complete, but there is sufficient detail to convey the concept of how an SAT is constructed, the type of testing that is done, and the Acceptance Testing process itself.

Pilot Operation

When all planning and organisational exercises are complete and the SAT has been prepared and approved, the Pilot may begin. The Pilot, as stated above, usually consists of a known set of predefined transactions sent between the Members, or a predefined process that is performed by the Members (Preferred Vendor, etc.) for a specified period of time (for instance 3 months or to the end of the fiscal year, etc.). Its purpose is not "proof of concept", but "proof of process".

During the operation of the Pilot, the lower levels of the SAT are exercised thoroughly, and all of the obvious problems should be worked out from the technical, procedural and business standpoints. The standard SAT documentation is created and maintained, problems are dealt with via the NCR mechanism (**Appendix B**), and the Members literally do a series of "dry runs" of the SAT over and over again until they are satisfied, and their documentation shows success. From this, the partners should be able to gain valuable experience and insight from their observations as well as a degree of comfort with proceeding.

This activity must be subject to rigorous discipline and constant management attention. This is the wrong time to become complacent and let things slide. This is where you change things, the point where the new system becomes the system of choice, the default, the "way things are done". This is where the rubber meets the blue sky. It takes constant reinforcement and training.

Training

Training must be an ongoing exercise, not a one-shot activity done at the beginning or the end of the project. As the Pilot progresses, things are going to go wrong. People are not going to do what they're supposed to. Beautifully crafted policies and procedures are not going to work, and a host of other people-related problems will arise. An integrated training program will ensure that, by the time the Pilot is complete, the new system has become ingrained into the daily operation to the extent that people can't imagine why they used to do it the old way.

Real training is not just sitting in a classroom and reading books, not just educating individual people, not just developing policy and procedure manuals and handing them out. Real training is re-focusing and re-directing the entire organisation to change the way it does things. Real training requires both the Project Manager and the Torchbearer to do hands-on, shirtsleeves daily "grunt work" side by side with the people who are doing the job, and to help them use their knowledge and experience to implement the internal processes that make it all work. Real training inculcates, internalises, and institutionalises the new way of doing business at all levels of the company.

This is where the real ICBE takes place; down in the trenches during the operation of the Pilot. The "boardroom engineering" exercises are put to the acid test here. The people learn and internalise the new way of doing things, and the system is refined again and again until it works.

Adjustment of Operations

It is not unusual for a Pilot to result in some major procedural changes for one or more Members during the period of operation. These adjustments are brought before the PMT and are factored back into the overall design as appropriate, perhaps even changing the SAT to compensate for the new circumstances or conditions. The post-pilot evaluation will also highlight these and provide suggestions as to their resolution. During the operation of the pilot, each Member will make necessary adjustments as they come to light. The Non-Compliance Reports (NCR's) will be the vehicle for managing these changes (**Appendix B**).

Performing the SAT

When the Members are satisfied that the Pilot is operating properly and can substantiate it through their own SAT's, a date can now be set for conducting a Final SAT. This is the "white-tie-and-tails" formality that authenticates the process and verifies the content of the business transactions to the PMT itself. Upon successful completion, both parties sign the acceptance document and the system is ready for full production use (see **Appendix B**). This may be as formal as a scheduled event and detailed checklists as per **Appendix B**, or as informal as an automated set of sign-on and validation procedures like those you see when you sign on to CompuServe.

In our example ICBE implementation, a formal SAT will likely be performed several times:

1. Once when the two Members at a given Gap have executed the Level One Migration Plan and are ready to commence production operations with each other.

2. Once when all Gaps in the Critical Path have completed the SAT.

3. Once again when all Critical Paths have completed the SAT. At that point, the PMT would schedule a System SAT, and operate it as above. In this case, the PMT would be verifying that the entire Value System operates as specified by the Level Zero Target Model.

As above, the corrective action mechanism of the SAT is the Non-Compliance Report (NCR). This is issued to the offending Members each time there is a problem encountered in the execution of the SAT. It specifies the nature of the problem, the suggested corrective action, and the date for re-test. When a given level of the SAT has been conducted satisfactorily, the ACT will issue a Certificate of Compliance (COC) for that level and the Member may proceed to the next level of SAT. When all levels have been completed, the ACT recommends to the PMT that the Members begin Pilot operation (**Appendix B**).

The Post-Pilot Audit

The ACT or a third party conducts a formal evaluation and audit with each Trading Partner, concentrating on identifying areas for improvement or adjustment in the processes, and identifying non-conformance issues to be resolved (**Appendix B**).

Once again, this is an activity that must not be compromised in any way. With the flush of victory, it is very easy to become careless and to gloss over or ignore problems or inadequacies in the system. This is the time for a sober evaluation of exactly what went right and how to repeat it, and what went wrong and how to correct it. Any problems must be brought to light at this time in order that corrective action may be taken before the system becomes ingrained.

When the Post-Pilot Audit is complete and all NCR's have been resolved, the ACT sends the Completion Audit Report (CAR) to the PMT, certifying that the parties comply in all respects to the letter and intent of the SAT. At a special PMT meeting, the recommendation is ratified and the

License To Trade, including any restrictions or exclusions, is signed by the PMT members and issued to each of the Members. The License To Trade is the "permit" so to speak, and authorises that Trading Partner to proceed with full production operation of the new system.

STEP 8: PRODUCTION AND CONTINUOUS IMPROVEMENT

Production

Full production operation may begin at this point. The SAT's are completed, and the Members have been issued with a License To Trade. Production may occur as a four-stage process:

1. Production operation between two individual Members following implementation of each Phase of the Migration Plan at their Gap.
2. Production operation that includes Members of the Gaps on either side of them as they in turn are issued with their Licenses To Trade. This serves as a "ripple effect" integration mechanism.
3. Production operation that includes the Critical Path as a whole.
4. Production operation of the entire Value System.

At each of these stages, Members will have to re-qualify under the SAT rules that apply to that level of testing. When in production mode, the Members will maintain close watch until a solid comfort level has been achieved, but by that time the system should more or less run itself with little intervention. This is the point at which the Alpha Team may begin to consider extending the envelope.

Now that the Value System is operating more or less as envisioned, the Alpha Team may want to proceed to the next stage of its vision of excellence. The same process must be followed as before, but it should now be much easier because of prior experience and hopefully it has saved enough money to fund the new venture.

Publicising Success

It is extremely important for the Alpha Team to publicly promote the ICBE effort and to celebrate its successes. This may be accomplished through such mechanisms as:

1. In-house ICBE newsletters. Either as part of each Member's existing in-house publication, or as a separate entity held in common by all Members (or both). In the internal publications, the Torchbearer and the Project Manager can give regular progress reports, lay out planned activities, and hold public forum regarding ICBE and internal process re-engineering. The ICBE effort is given an objective existence and becomes an entity unto

itself. The newsletters may be sent out via E-Mail, or the company may create a newsgroup on the Internet.

2.   Regular internal presentations, workshops and seminars. These can take the form of auditorium-style presentations, CEO videos, progress reports, workgroup-style seminars designed for brainstorming and breakthrough thinking, special interest groups tasked with a particular problem, or "Town Hall Meetings" where a widely dispersed organisation meets regularly through video-conferencing to discuss issues of importance to the staff regarding ICBE and process re-engineering (there will be a great deal of fear, uncertainty and doubt unless it is dispelled properly) .

3.   ICBE Membership conferences may be conducted in much the same manner as above, but this is the chance for each of the Members to share its own success stories with the others in a public forum. This gives the working individuals in each of the Member companies a chance to meet and form their own special interest groups and participate in focused breakout sessions.

4.   ICBE social events following each Phase. This is the chance to get all Members together at an off-site party or other social event and celebrate their success. This builds Team spirit and a sense of commitment like little else can. It is important for the people involved to have a sense of closure, and the closer together these minor closures are, the easier it is to maintain the individual energy level.

5.   Public awards to Members and individuals within the Member companies. Personal and Team recognition is critical to maintaining the energy level and sense of contribution to the effort. Awards (cash and/or physical items such as pen sets, mugs, etc.) can be given for such things as :

- • "Tiger Team" jackets and crests, etc.
- • Most Valuable/Creative Idea
- • Greatest Reduction in Non-Value-Added Activity
- • Process Engineer of the Year

These are only a few of the many possibilities, and the Members will undoubtedly come up with their own ideas. Awards can be given at the social events, special ceremonies, published in newsletters, trade journals, professional magazines, etc. They will soon become much sought after.

6.   Special articles and regular columns in trade journals. As the Team builds experience in an area that most companies have not even though about, key Members may wish to share their story. Trade journals (such as the ones quoted in this book) are usually willing to publish real-life success stories. This is a way to widely publicise the effort at no cost except the time it takes to write the material. As more people read these articles, the Members will be sought out for information.

7.   Signs on the Members' premises (as some companies do that have achieved ISO 9000 certification or the Baldridge Award). This shows pride in the initiative and a firm commitment to making it happen. This is

evidence that is visible to the public at large, not just other companies, and can be a powerful advertising tool if properly managed.

8.   Press releases.   At a major point of closure, such as the completion of Phase 1 for the Critical Path Members, it may be useful to issue a press release. Depending on the importance of the initiative, it may warrant televised coverage or professional video services.   This vehicle should be carefully chosen. It should not be used every time there is an event, only when there is a newsworthy event such as accomplishing something no other company or group of companies has accomplished before. It should be a truly leading-edge event to warrant this type of coverage.

9.   A formal signing ceremony where a symbolic agreement (or a real Trading Partner Agreement) is signed by the top executives of the Membership, and speeches are delivered about what a leading-edge event has just taken place. This is closely related to the press release, and should be done under the same conditions. Dignitaries, such as political figures, the president of the appropriate trade association, the Chamber of Commerce, the president of the EDI Council, etc. should be invited to speak and to publicly support the effort.

10.   The media may be present, so a formal setting and prepared speeches are a must. Get a professional speechwriter and media specialists to assist with the staging and presentation, if at all possible.   A professional appearance is a great asset and lends credibility to the exercise. At the very least, there should be professional video tapes of the ceremony for presentation to the Members' staff.

What this accomplishes is to secure the visible commitment of the highest levels of all companies involved and to announce their joint venture to the business world. The power of this is enormous as a motivating tool within the companies and as a public expression of progressiveness.

System Rollout

In addition to the joint publicity effort, each Member may now use the same techniques to publicise its new-found capabilities to its other customers and suppliers that were not involved in this effort, and to recruit them for its own ICBE initiative. Now that the capability is present, and the Member has experience in implementing ICBE, there is every reason to confidently expand the initiative out into other lines of business.

Each Member is now in the position to become its own ICBE Champion as it relates to these separate lines of business or separate Value Systems. Since it has already gone through the ICBE process once, it may skip Steps One and Two, go directly to Step 3 (Inter-Corporate Team Building), and start all over again with a new set of Members and a new Alpha Team.

It may also wish to start trading other business transactions or conducting electronic commercial relationships with the original Gap Members that are not directly related to the original ICBE vision or to its core business, such as:

- Inter-corporate E-Mail
- Common Web pages on the Internet
- Joint membership in CommerceNet or other Internet commercial enterprises
- Price catalogues/Item Master file updates
- Enterprise information/Credit reports
- Engineering drawings/technical specifications
- Promotional announcements/price changes
- Electronic Coupons or credit notices
- Warranty claims/Returns/Exchanges
- Shipping and brokerage information/instructions/documentation
- Testing results
- Regulatory compliance material (Customs Declaration, Hazardous Material Advice, Sales Tax Exemption Certificate, etc.)
- Financial transactions (Debit/Credit Advice, multiple payment, etc.)

All of the infrastructure is in place now on both sides for this to happen. The corporate experience is in place, and the Members have developed a trusting working relationship. These rollout facilities will serve to enhance this business relationship, and should be able to be put in place very quickly with a high degree of certainty of success.

The Audit and Review Plan

The Audit and Review Plan is constructed and administered by the ACT. It details the procedures and schedules for conducting ongoing verification of the system following the initial commissioning. This is extremely important from the standpoint of catching live errors before they do too much damage, and of preventing them from happening again.

Once the system has been implemented, the audit and review plan monitors its effectiveness on an ongoing basis and sets the schedule and specific audit objectives for each review. This allows flexibility in the audit process, while maintaining full coverage. A well-constructed and administered audit and review plan will have the additional benefit of providing the objective evidence that may be required in a legal dispute, or of actually avoiding legal disputes.

Continuous Improvement

Once the System is in place and operating, the Alpha Team does not get to rest on its laurels. It now has to go to work to ensure that the processes that have just been re-engineered are placed into a Continuous Improvement (CI) program in each of the Member companies, overseen by the original ICBE Team that looks at the entire Value System.

The initial ICBE go-round has only made gross changes in the processes, even though they have achieved quantum improvements through those gross changes. Those changes must now be constantly refined and reworked by the people who do the job on a daily basis, the Continuous Improvement Teams. The CI Teams have a different focus, a different character, and a different composition than the Teams that implemented ICBE. The CI Team members, rather than focusing on radical change, will focus on incremental change. They will obsessively pursue the elimination of non-value-added activities and the reduction of internal cycle time until it is equal to process time. Then they will reduce the process time itself until nothing remains but the absolute essentials. These are the ones who make it work over the long haul.

It is important to maintain the overall ICBE Team structure as this goes on, so that the internal teams may share the results of their efforts and leverage each other's expertise. In the meantime, the original Teams proceed with the next Phase of the overall ICBE effort. By the time that is implemented, there will be a new challenge to hand over to the CI teams.

Summary

The principles and practices outlined in this book have covered:
1.   The various corporate disciplines such as MRP II, JIT, TQM, and BPE and their interrelationships.
2.   The concept of expanding the "Corporate Self" outward to include partners in the business cycle.
3.   The concept of the Value System and the relationships of the Member companies.
4.   The recent advances in Electronic Commerce for inter-corporate business and the basics of the Electronic Commerce toolset available to companies wishing to undertake inter-corporate commerce.
5.   The process of achieving management commitment to proceed with a strategic approach to conducting business electronically.
6   The internal EC-Readiness program and the ECE (Electronic Commerce Environment).
7.   The process of recruiting ICBE Members and gaining commitment from their top management to participate in a joint ICBE implementation.
8.   Analysing the Value System and producing Current Process Maps to aid in the design of the Target Models that will drive commerce within the Value System.

9. Using Best Practices, workshops, and BPE tools to transform the Current Process Maps into the Target Models.
10. Developing Migration Plans to implement the Target Models.
11. Conducting controlled Pilot projects to provide proof-of-process for the new system.
12. Acceptance Testing (The SAT) and Commissioning the System (License To Trade) to ensure that the system operates as specified, that all eventualities have been tested for, and that the Members are duly qualified and authorised to conduct business together in this manner.
13. Production Operation, Rollout, Publicity, and ongoing Audit and Review of the System
14. Continuous Improvement of the redesigned processes to eliminate Non-Value-Added activities and further reduce internal cycle time.

ICBE is not a trivial exercise. Certainly it is not as easy as reading this book would make it seem. It's tough to accomplish. It takes a lot of hard work from everyone, a lot of commitment and staying power from the top executives of several previously adversarial companies, a lot of money, and a lot of time from people whose workload is already too much to handle. It introduces problems unlike any the company has ever dealt with before. It shakes the very foundations of what you have done for years. Those readers who have already been involved in an MRP II or TQM implementation will have direct experience as to the difficulty of implementing such a program even within the walls of a single company. A multi-corporate implementation adds yet another dimension of difficulty.

Why do it? In practice, you will likely do it because you have proved to upper management that it will provide a substantial return in terms of accelerated business flows, reduced inventory, reduced staff time, reduced overall costs, reduced time to market, higher market share, and other financially measurable goals over the short term. This is because the current corporate thinking in North America is oriented toward "this-quarter" results. If that is what it takes to gain the commitment, that's fine, because the rest will hopefully come later.

The real reason, however, should be that it is the right thing to do over the long term. The rationale for ICBE should be that the Members realise that a co-operative endeavour such as this is the only way to ensure survival in the coming century. Those companies that cooperate and devise ways to reduce the business cycle and respond more quickly to actual marketplace demand are those companies that are going to survive. They may not survive in the same form that the are now, but they will be successful where the more traditional companies will not.

The concept of companies co-operating in a commercial enterprise is not new. This book gives several examples of just that. There are pioneers and road-builders such as JC Penney, Sears, Wal-Mart, Ford, and many others who have shown us how companies can profit by working together and can save time and money through conducting commerce electronically. The work done by these companies is invaluable as a "proof-of-concept" for electronic commerce, and as a lesson in how to proceed to the next stage, the stage of full Inter-Corporate Business Engineering.

It is through ICBE that the business community can prepare itself for competition in the global marketplace. The ability to achieve internal efficiency of operation, to form specialised inter-corporate relationships quickly, to work together profitably, to respond nimbly to changes in the marketplace, and to take the bold new steps necessary for success will be some of the determining factors in ensuring survival in the world economy of the future. You need to be ready, willing and able to play the game when it gets here.

Good Luck.

APPENDIX A:

THE PROJECT PLAN

INTEGRATED TRANSPORT INFORMATION MANAGEMENT

KEY OBJECTIVE: Integrated Transport Information Management
Commentary:
This was the fourth of seven Key Objectives from the Strategic Plan (not shown). The Group decided, after much deliberation, to phrase all Key Objectives in terms of the desired result. The verbs "to achieve", "to gain", etc. were felt to be redundant. In this way, the Key Objective became the Project name and was constantly visible to the participants, providing an ongoing reality check against the direction of the Project.

PURPOSE: To improve control of the exchange of goods between participants by providing a facility for the electronic exchange of transport-related information at the item, receptacle, shipment and despatch level between:

a)	Participants	b)	Distribution Centers
c)	Offices of Transit	d)	The HUB
e)	Third Party Carriers	f)	Customs
g)	Other external parties		

Commentary:
The HUB in this case was a specialized distribution center jointly supported by the members, who would send goods to the HUB for overnight sortation and distribution to other members. Shipment pre-advice was sent to the HUB via FAX, which was then entered into the HUB computer system for scheduling purposes (employees, dock space and other resources). This was unreliable, inefficient and costly, and did not address any accounting issues between members. Receipt confirmations were nonexistent, and errors in shipments were discovered too late for easy resolution. These problems gave rise to this Key Objective in the Strategic Plan.
Commentary:
In the original Level Zero Plan, a diagram was inserted depicting the elements in the transport chain that were to be addressed by this Project. This proved to be a useful tool for the Steering Committee to understand the overall scope of the Project in terms of the other Key Objectives. Using this diagram, it was easier to segment the Project into five logical Phases, and to determine how each Phase would address a specific portion of the chain. In turn, this set the level of expectation for the magnitude of the Project up front.

PROJECT PHASES:

PHASE 1:	Transport Document Management
PHASE 2:	Despatch Document Management
PHASE 3:	Carrier Interface
PHASE 4:	Container and Item Tracking
PHASE 5:	Customs Interface

INTEGRATED TRANSPORT INFORMATION MANAGEMENT

PHASE 1: TRANSPORT DOCUMENT MANAGEMENT

OBJECTIVE: To exchange transport-related information electronically
between all partners in the transport chain.

PURPOSE:

1.   Improvement in the quality and timeliness of data transfer   Pilot 1
2.   Control over the Transport chain   Pilot 2

PILOT 1:

OBJECTIVE: To exchange XXXX EDI messages between Point of Origin,
HUB, and Point of Destination.

PURPOSE: To improve the quality and timeliness of data transfer in
order to provide the HUB with more accurate information
regarding incoming freight volumes and greater lead time for
scheduling of operations.

PARTICIPANTS:

Trading Partner # 1   Trading Partner # 2
Trading Partner # 3   HUB
Trading Partner # 4   Trading Partner # 5
Trading Partner # 6

SUCCESS CRITERIA:

1. Cost Savings:

Requirement: Savings must exceed the current cost of operations
by 25 %

Measurement: a)   Data Entry savings - each participant measures
reduction in staff hours andcomputes internal cost savings.
The sum of these is the total Data Entry cost savings.
b)   Operating savings - computed by:
Additional communications services LESS Fax & telephone
savings LESS Reductions in staff costs

**Note: These are operating cost savings and do not include capital
equipment and fixed costs.**

2.   Accuracy Improvement:

Requirement: Elimination of transcription errors at the HUB

Measurement: Monthly average of the number of items on the
XXXX form due to transcription errors versus current level

3.   Reduce HUB processing time

Requirement: 100 % Increase in planning lead time at the HUB
due to faster availability of information.

Measurement: Average difference between time of availability on
HUB computer system and time of arrival of the despatch

versus current lead time

Commentary:

   These measurements are critical. They will be used during the Completion Audit to establish whether or not the Project has attained its objectives.

TASK/ACTIVITY LIST

TASK/ACTIVITY	RESP.	PLAN	START	COMP.
1. Complete Pilot definition & Scope	PFT	Mar 93	Mar 4	Mar 31
2. Complete EDI message requirements	PMT	Mar 93	Mar 10	Apr 6
3. Create message definitions	MDT	May 93	Apr 10	May 27
4. Approve message definitions	PMT	May 93	May 30	May 30
5. Obtain VAN contract and user account	PFT	June 93	Jun 4	Jun 15
6. Complete HUB software development	HUB	June 93	Apr 10	Jul 15
7. Complete internal application changes	ALL	July 93	Apr 10	Sep 15
8. Submit preliminary EDI messages - Stage 1 Acceptance Test	ALL	Aug 93	Sep 18	Sep 30
9. Review & approve preliminary messages	ACT	Aug 93	Sep 30	Oct 10
10. Begin electronic transmission of messages- Stage 2 Acceptance Test	ALL	Aug 93	Oct 15	Oct 15
11. Complete Acceptance Testing	ACT	Sep 93	Oct 15	Oct 31
12. Issue Certificate of Compliance	ACT	Sep 93	Oct 31	Oct 31
13. Completion Audit	ACT	Oct 93	Nov 2	Nov 30
14. Adjustments	ALL	Nov 93	Nov 2	Dec 5
15. Issue License To Trade	PMT	Dec 93	Dec 10	Dec 15
16. Pilot 1 Production	ALL	Dec 93	Dec 10	Dec 30

INTEGRATED TRANSPORT INFORMATION MANAGEMENT
PILOT 2:

OBJECTIVE: To exchange XXXX, YYYY, and ZZZZ EDI messages between Point of Origination, HUB, and Point of Destination.

PURPOSE: To achieve control over the operation of the transport chain and to expedite corrective action.

PARTICIPANTS:

Trading Partner # 1	Trading Partner # 2
Trading Partner # 3	HUB Trading Partner # 4
Trading Partner # 5	Trading Partner # 6

SUCCESS CRITERIA:

1. Improvement in ability to identify and exercise corrective action:

Requirement: Reduce time in locating containers in the transport chain from X days to Y days

Measurement: Average time between despatch and receipt of EDI "lost container" message vs average time between despatch and receipt of current "lost container notification" form.

2. Diagnostic statistics to improve end to end service

Requirement: Point-to-point delivery information along the transport chain delivered in a timely manner.

Measurement: Reduction in time required to find missing containers or despatches.

PILOT 2: TASK/ACTIVITY LIST

TASK/ACTIVITY	RESP.	PLAN	START	COMP
1. Complete Pilot definition & Scope	PFT			
2. Comp. EDI message requirements	PMT			
3. Create message definitions	MDT			
4. Approve message definitions	PMT			
5. Implement container scanning sys.	ALL			
6. Develop central routing and tracking system	HUB			
7. Comp. internal application changes	ALL			
8. Submit preliminary EDI messages Stage 1 Acceptance Test	ALL			
9. Review & approve preliminary messages	ACT			
10. Begin electronic transmission of messages Stage 2 Acceptance Test	ALL			
11. Complete Acceptance Testing	ACT			
12. Issue Certificates of Compliance	ACT			
13. Completion Audit	ACT			
14. Adjustments	ALL			
15. Issue License To Trade	PMT			
16. Pilot 2 Production	ALL			

INTEGRATED TRANSPORT INFORMATION MANAGEMENT

PHASE 2: DESPATCH DOCUMENT MANAGEMENT

OBJECTIVE: To exchange despatch information between participants electronically

PURPOSE:

1. Preplanning of inbound operations for all participants
2. Receipt Confirmation back to Point of Origination
3. Quality of Service information
4. Accounting information

PARTICIPANTS:

Trading Partner # 1
Trading Partner # 2
Trading Partner # 3
HUB
Trading Partner # 4
Trading Partner # 5
Trading Partner # 6

SUCCESS CRITERIA:

1. Control of the movement of despatches between Point of Origin and Point of Destination

    Requirement: Visibility into the integrity of despatches between participants

    Measurement: Correspondence between XXXX/YYYY messages and the physical despatch allowing automatic reconciliation

2. Ability to measure Quality of Service at the despatch level

    Requirement: Visibility of the transit time of a despatch between participants

    Measurement: Automated measurement in time between the closing of a dispatch at Point of Origination and the opening of the despatch at the Point of Destination.

3. Basis for identification of weak points in the transport chain for the purposes of corrective action

    Requirement: Visibility into the transport chain to measure individual carrier performance

    Measurement: Automated measurement of time between :

    a)   Arrival at the Point of Transfer (XXXX message)

    b)   Departure from the Point of Transfer (YYYY message)

           c)   Arrival at the next Point of Transfer, the HUB, or the Point of Destination (XXXX message)

4.   Provision of electronic weight and volume information for accounting purposes between participants

      Requirement: Reduce the invoicing process from X days to Y days and provide a basis for future electronic invoicing

      Measurement: Reduction in cycle time between closing of a despatch and the sending of the invoice

5.   Establish a basis for rationalization of transportation resources based on pre-advice of freight volumes

      Requirement: a)   Improve delivery service by 20 %

                       b)   Reduce delivery cost by 40 %

      Measurement: a)   Average time from arrival of inbound shipment to delivery to consignee or customer

                       b)   Average cost of delivery based on invoices submitted by third-party carriers, corporate carriers, and courier companies.

Commentary:

The Task List for this Phase and all other Phases follows the models outlined in Phase 1. In the interests of brevity, they will not be repeated here.

The Level Zero Project Plan model described here applies to the joint ventures of the participants only. Each individual participant will return to his/her company and work with the internal project management systems in force there.

Prior to the PMT meetings, each participant will prepare and submit a simple Project Report as outlined on the following pages. This is the linkage mechanism that the PMT and the PFT will use to track progress-to-plan, while allowing the participants the greatest degree of autonomy and flexibility possible.

PHASE 1: TRANSPORT DOCUMENT MANAGEMENT
PROJECT REPORT

PARTICIPANT: PERIOD ENDING:

1.   PROGRESS TO PLAN:

TASK	PLANNED	ACTUAL
1. Complete internal EDI-readiness preparations		
2. Begin application development		
3. Submit message for Stage 1 Acceptance Test		
4. Begin electronic test transmission		
5. Complete Stage 2 Acceptance Test		
6. Begin Pilot operations		
7. Complete adjustments		
8. Begin Production operations		

2.   ISSUES IMPACTING PROGRESS

3.   RED FLAG ITEMS

4.   NEXT PERIOD PLAN

APPENDIX B:

ACCEPTANCE AND COMMISSIONING

STANDARD ACCEPTANCE TEST (SAT) PLAN

STANDARD ACCEPTANCE TEST (SAT)
COMMISSIONING PROCEDURES

A: PURPOSE: These commissioning procedures are intended to provide:
a)   A formal mechanism for ensuring successful baseline implementation of EDI transactions, and for providing objective evidence of compliance with the terms of Trading Partner Agreement.
b)   A consistent means of ensuring and certifying the EDI-readiness of prospective EDI Trading Partners.
c)   Specific authorization for both parties to conduct limited business using a defined set of EDI transactions.
d)   A means to ensure that all parties have adequate audits and controls in place in support of electronic commerce.
e)   A consistent method for diagnosing problems with the EDI system of either party or the EDI network.

B: ADMINISTRATION: Responsibility and authority for EDI system commissioning rests with the Audit and Commissioning Team, (ACT) which consists of at least one member from each of the Trading Partners, headed by the Commissioner who is either a neutral third party or is one of the Team members. The Audit and Commissioning Team is independent of all outside influences; its sole purpose is to:
a)   Develop and conduct the SAT (Standard Acceptance Test) in an unbiased manner.
b)   Highlight problems and errors encountered during the SAT process.
c)   Record and issue appropriate test reports and other documentation at each stage of the SAT process.
d)   Recommend commissioning/licensing upon successful completion of the final stage of the SAT.
e)   Conduct post-implementation audits and reviews as required under the Trading Partner Agreement.

C: METHODOLOGY: The SAT is the mechanism for regression testing of the EDI system. It is developed by the ACT at the beginning of the project, and reflects the terms and conditions of the Trading Partner Agreement as well as the output of the EDI Message definition exercise.
The ACT schedules a formal Acceptance Test with each Trading Partner as specified in the Project Schedule. The Commissioning Team member for that Trading Partner represents his company in the SAT process, and serves as liaison between the ACT and the Trading Partner for purposes of corrective action. The Commissioning Team operates out of the HUB location for that project. The SAT consists of 3 stages:

1.   Stage 1 verifies that the participants are capable of producing the correct message outputs. Stage 1 requires each partner to produce the EDI transaction on its own computer system and to send it in both printed form and on diskette to the ACT. The ACT reviews each member's submission in detail and reports non-conformance issues for corrective action. A re-test date is set at that time.

At the re-test, the SAT is restarted from the beginning to ensure that changes do not impact previously tested areas of the system. This process is repeated until the entire Stage 1 Acceptance Test is complete and signed by the Commissioner and the partner.

Upon satisfactory completion of Stage 1, i.e. the message complied to the Trading Partner Agreement and EDI standard requirements, the partner is authorized to proceed to Stage 2 Testing.

2.   Stage 2 requires each partner to generate a standard "Test Document Packet", consisting of known transactions, and to transmit it through the network to the ACT. The ACT reviews each submission for completeness and passes it through the Translator at the "Hub" end of the EDI system. The ACT generates a standard "Response Packet" from the "Hub" and sends it back to the partner, who passes it through his Translator and reports the results to the ACT. As with Stage 1, failure of the SAT at any point during the process results in a Non-Conformance Report and a re-test from the beginning of Stage 2.

Upon compliance, the partner is authorized to proceed to Stage 3 Testing. Stage 2 verifies that the partners were able to produce multiple documents and to use the network.

3.   Stage 3 uses actual production data, and verifies that application systems are responding correctly. This stage typically requires the most time and attention.

D: DOCUMENTATION:

1.   The Standard Acceptance Test (SAT). This is filled out by the ACT each time a Test is conducted. A copy is filed with the ACT, the participant, and the PMT is notified of the results through a Non-compliance Report (NCR) or a Certificate of Compliance (COC). The results recorded in the SAT are used to complete either an NCR or a COC.

2.   The Non-Compliance Report (NCR). This is filled out as a result of failure of a Test at any point. It is assigned a control number and tracked by the ACT until resolved.

3.   The Certificate of Compliance (COC). This is filled out as the result of successful completion of a Test, and permits the participant to proceed to the next stage of the SAT. When all Stages have been passed successfully, the COC's are passed to the PMT along with a recommendation for approval to begin Pilot Operation.

4.   The Completion Audit Report (CAR). This is the result of the Completion Audit which is undertaken at the end of the Pilot period (set by the PMT). The results of this Report will determine the degree of adjustment to be undertaken by individual participants, and/or whether all participants are in compliance with the objectives and intent of the Project. The CAR will provide an initial assessment of the attainment of the measurement objectives, and will make recommendations for improvement. The Completion Audit may result in additional NCR's, which must be resolved before the ACT issues a recommendation for a License To Trade.

5.   License To Trade. This is the final authorization to trade a specific transaction or set of related transactions between specified Trading Partners. This is issued by the PMT when all conditions have been met and the CAR has been returned with verification.

NON-COMPLIANCE REPORT
NCR # XXXXX

ISSUED TO: DATE: xx/xx/xx
PROJECT: TEST #:   RE-TEST: xx/xx/xx

Standard Acceptance Testing Procedures were conducted between xx/xx/xx and xx/xx/xx under the auspices of the Audit and Commissioning Team as designated under (Schedule #) of the Agreement Respecting Electronic Data Interchange, signed between the parties on xx/xx/xx. The test identified the following issues of non-compliance:

CORRECTIVE ACTION #   PROBLEM DESCRIPTION:
        1.
        2.
        3.
        4.

The issues of non-compliance identified above must be resolved by the date specified for Re-Test, at which time another Standard Acceptance Test will be conducted.

Signed this xx day of xxxxxxxxx, xxxx   at

(Signature)

(Title)

CERTIFICATE OF COMPLIANCE

ISSUED TO: DATE: xx/xx/xx

Subject: Acceptance of   Stage X Acceptance Testing for the xxxxxxxxx Project between (Company) and (Trading Partner).

The Audit and Commissioning Team, in its capacity as coordinator of the Acceptance Testing process, hereby certifies that (Trading Partner) has successfully completed Stage X of the required Standard Acceptance Test Procedure of (Pilot #) of (Project).

RECOMMENDED ACTION:
1.   Proceed to Stage X Acceptance Testing
                    OR
2.   Issuance of approval to begin Pilot operations.
                    OR
3.   Issuance of License To Trade

RESTRICTIONS OR SPECIAL CONDITIONS:
1.
2.
3.

The Standard Acceptance Testing Procedures were completed between xx/xx/xx and xx/xx/xx under the auspices of the Commissioning Team as designated under (Schedule #) of the Agreement.

This Certificate remains valid until such time as a change is made to one or more of the Schedules of the Agreement, to the structure or content of the XXXXX message, or to the underlying business transaction(s) supported by this EDI message, such that the message in question is obsolete or otherwise rendered invalid. At such time this Certificate becomes null and void, and must be re-issued according to Standard Acceptance Testing Procedures.

CERTIFICATE OF COMPLIANCE

Signed this xx day of xxxxxxxxx, xxxx   at

_____

(Signature)

_____

(Title)

COMPLETION AUDIT REPORT
XXXX PROJECT

DATE:
GENERAL FINDINGS SECTION:
COMPLIANCE:

OVERALL ATTAINMENT OF OBJECTIVES:

        1.   FINANCIAL

        2.   PERFORMANCE

        3.   OPERATIONAL

        4.   INFORMATIONAL

        5.   OTHER

ISSUES:

RECOMMENDATIONS:

_____   _____ _____
     (Signature)   (Title)   (Date)

LICENSE TO TRADE

ISSUED TO: DATE: xx/xx/xx

Subject: Authority to conduct business electronically using the
                  XXXXX message between (Company) and (Trading Partner).

      The Project Management Team, (PMT), in its capacity as coordinator of the EDI Community as designated in (Schedule xx) of the Agreement Respecting Electronic Data Interchange dated xx/xx/xx, hereby certifies that (Trading Partner) has successfully completed the required Standard Acceptance Test Procedure of (Pilot #) of (Project) and has completed the required period of live operation and is therefore authorized to transmit the XXXXX message to (Company) as specified in (Schedule #) with the following restrictions and/or conditions:

    1.

    2.

    3.

    4.

      This License remains valid until such time as a change is made to one or more of the Schedules of the Agreement, to the structure or content of the X12 850 message, or to the underlying business transaction(s) supported by this EDI message, such that the message in question is obsolete or otherwise rendered invalid. At such time this License becomes null and void, and must be re-issued according to Standard Acceptance Testing Procedures.

Signed this xx day of xxxxxxxxx, xxxx   at

_____

    (Signature)

_____

    (Title)

STANDARD ACCEPTANCE TEST:

PARTICIPANT   STAGE 1

STEP	ACTION	EXPECTED
1	Submit sample printed forms to ACT	
2	Submit printed versions and machine readable version (diskette)	
3	Review printed version of EDI message	Conformity with printed paper form. Compliance with Public Standard (X-12 or EDIFACT). Compliance with message structure. Data content as per message definition.
4	Translate EDI message from diskette. Print and review electronic version of message	Conformity with printed paper form. Compliance with X-12 or EDIFACT standard. Compliance with message definition structure.. Data content as per message definition.

COMMISSIONER_____

SIGNATURE_____

XXXX PROJECT

TEST #

ACTUAL	COMMENTS	RESPONSE	INIT
		Company Trading Partner	
		ACT	

PARTICIPANT_____DATE_____

SIGNATURE_____

STANDARD ACCEPTANCE TEST:

PARTICIPANT   STAGE 2

STEP	ACTION	EXPECTED
1	From the participant's Test Document Packet (TDP), generate an XXX, YYY & ZZZ transaction in X-12 or EDIFACT format, using the participant's translator	Valid XXX, YYY, and ZZZ transactions in full compliance with the known content of the TDP
2	Transmit the XXX, YYY, and ZZZ messages to the ACT over the Network.	Participant's system creates log of EDI transaction. Interchange received intact. Network info accurate 1. Sender ID 2. Receiver ID 3. Interchange time 3. Stamp All documents present. Documents comply with X-12, EDIFACT syntax. Documents comply with the message definitions
3	ACT sends 'control' TDP with the EDI translator & prints the messages for return to the ACT.	ACT system creates log of EDI transactions. Participant receives interchange intact.
4	Participant translates TDP with the EDI translator and prints the messages for return to the ACT's.	All documents present. Documents comply to X-12 or EDIFACT syntax
5	Return printed messages to ACT with verification.	All documents and verification received for filing.

COMMISIONER_____

SIGNATURE_____

XXXX PROJECT

TEST #

ACTUAL	COMMENTS	RESPONSE	INIT
		Company Trading Partner	
		ACT	

PARTICIPANT_____DATE_____

SIGNATURE_____

STANDARD ACCEPTANCE PROJECT

PARTICIPANT   **STAGE 3**

STEP	ACTION	EXPECTED
1	Participant 1 sends message to Participant 2	Sent intact with audit trail. Complies with proper syntax and content. Both systems log through all applications.
2	Participant 2 sends message to Participant 1.	Received intact with audit trail. Complies with proper syntax and content. Both systems log through all applications. Response is correct according to Trading Partner Agreement and to business practice.
3	Participant 2 sends message to Participant 1	Received intact with audit trail. Complies with proper syntax and content. Both systems log through all applications. Response is correct according to Trading Partner Agreement and to business practice
4	Sent intact with audit trail. Complies with proper syntax and content. Both systems log through all applications. Response is correct according to Trading Partner Agreement and to business practice.	

COMMISSIONER_____

SIGNATURE_____

XXXX PROJECT

TEST #

ACTUAL	COMMENTS	RESPONSE	INIT
		Company Trading Partner	
		ACT	

PARTICIPANT_____DATE_____

SIGNATURE_____

BIBLIOGRAPHY

Albin, Hohn T. (1992, January), *Competing In a Global Market*. Performance Advantage, 29-32.

Amochaez, Tania (1994, June), *Supply Chain Management: a Quick Response Evolution*. EDI World, 4.

Anderson, Donald E. (1992, September), *Bar Coding and EDI: A Strategic Partnership*. EDI World, 4.

Anderson, Ron (1993, November), *Maximize Re-engineering Success: Manage Performance*. Performance Advantage, 33-36.

Automatic Identification Manufacturers (1993), Quick Response conference proceedings. Atlanta: AIM USA Publication Sales.

Barber, Norman F. (1989). The Organizational Aspects of EDI: a Project Manager's Guide. Alexandria, VA: Electronic Data Interchange Association.

_____ (1992, July), *World Transition and EDI*. EDI World, 10.

_____ (1992, August), *Simultaneous Process Re-engineering (SPR)*. EDI World, 5-9.

_____ (1993, April), *EDI II: The Next Generation*. EDI World, 18-19.

_____ (1993), *Electronic Commerce: Toward the Virtual Corporation*. EDI Forum Vol. 6 No. 3, 18-21.

_____ (1994, February), *EDI and The National Information Infrastructure*. EDI World, 8.

_____ (1994, May), *EDI II and Re-engineering: A Design Approach*. EDI World, 20-22.

Barr, Robert E. (1992, August), *EDI and EFT: The Future of Tax Collection*. EDI World, 32-34.

_____ (1992, September) *EDI and EFT: The Future of Tax Collection--Part 2*. EDI World, 19-22.

Barrett, Lee (1994, June), *EDI & Healthcare: The Time for Integration Is Now*. EDI World, 32-37.

Benesko, Gary G.   (1994)   Strategic Positioning For Electronic Commerce: Introducing EDI Into The Organization. Toronto: EDI Council of Canada.

Bishop, Willard R. Jr. (1993, September), *The ECR Train Has Already Left The Station*. EDI World, 14.

Berry, Thomas H.   (1991),   Managing the Total Quality Transformation. Milwaukee: ASQC Quality Press.

Blackburn, J.   (1991, July),   *Time Based Competition: JIT As a Weapon*. Performance Advantage, 30-34.

Bocard, Ronald R.   (1991, December), *A Paperless Manufacturing Environment Is Possible*. Performance Advantage, 34-37.

Bowman, Jerry (1992, October), *Just-in-time and MRP II: A Winning Combination*. Performance Advantage, 49-50.

Browning, Daniel (1993), *Closing the EDI Loop At Baxter*. EDI Forum Vol. 6 No. 2, 42-46.

Brunell, Thomas and DeFusco, Robert (1994), *Case Study: Reengineering Procurement at Bull Electronics*. EDI Forum Vol. 7 No. 2, 48-51.

Buffkin, Ralph (1991) *EDI At Ciba-Geigy Corporation: A Catalyst for Change and Improvement*. EDI Forum Vol. 4 No. 1, 80-83.

Burgan, John W. (1993, November), *JIT & MRP II Could Make Beautiful Music Together*. Performance Advantage, 25-29.

Byles, Torrey   (1993, November), *Electronic Commerce and Business Efficiency*. EDI World, 24-28.

_____ (1993), *Electronic Commerce: The New Foundation For Trade*. EDI Forum Vol. 6 No. 2, 12-17.

_____ (1995), *The Commercial Use of the Internet*. EDI Forum Vol. 7 No. 4, 72-77.

Cadaret, Roger J. (1992, December), EDI Or Electronic Commerce?. EDI World, 36-40.

Camp, Robert C. (1989), Benchmarking: The Search for Industry Best Practices That Lead to Superior Performance. Milwaukee: ASQC Quality Press

____ (1995), Business Process Benchmarking. Milwaukee: ASQC Quality Press.

Capron, Bill (1992, September), *MRP II's Changing Face.* Performance Advantage, 33-36.

Cerf, Vinton G. (1995 Special Issue Vol. 6 No. 1), Networks.   Scientific American, 46

Cerrito, Toni and Halpern, Don (1993, August), *A Paperless Warehouse? It Could Happen With Real-time Connectivity.* Performance Advantage, 47-49.

Chatterjee, Subir (1993, October), *Transportation EDI--The Real Benefits.* EDI World, 20-21.

Cingari, John (1992, February), *What Is The Role of Quality In MRP II?.* Performance Advantage, 24-25.

Cronin, Mary J. (1994, Doing Business on the Internet: How the Electronic Highway is Transforming American Companies. New York: Van Nostrand Reinhold.

Crosby, Philip B. (1979), Quality Is Free. Milwaukee: ASQC Quality Press.

____ (1984), Quality Without Tears. Milwaukee: ASQC Quality Press.

Crowley, R.T. (1993, EDI: Charting a Course to the Future. Raleigh, NC: Research Triangle Consultants, Inc.

Dailey, Lance (1994, May), *Re-engineering: Cliche or Concept?.* EDI World, 6.

Dailey, L. and Douglas, T. (1990) EDI At Sears, Past, Present and Future. EDI Forum Vol. 3, 81-89.

DeJean and DeJean (1991), Lotus Notes At Work. New York: Brady Division of Simon & Schuster.

DISA (1994, August 8) EDIFACT Standards List. Alexandria: EDI Council of Canada.

____ (1994, August 8) X12 Standards List. Alexandria: EDI Council of Canada.

Drummond, Richard (1993 April), *Why Will EDI Need X.400?* EDI World, 10-11.

_____ (1993, May), *Will EDI and E-Mail Become Integrated in the Marketplace?.* EDI World, 12-13.

_____ (1993, July), *Should EDI Personnel Be Negative On the Use of X.400.* EDI World, 6.

_____ (1993, October), *X.500--Scratching The Surface.* EDI World, 18-19.

_____ (1993, November), *E-Mail Enabled EDI.* EDI World, 16-17.

_____ (1993, December), *Times Are Changing.* EDI World, 16.

Echols, David (1992, July), *Extending The Enterprise Electronically.* Performance Advantage, 27-31.

Eckstein, Michael G. (1993, December), *EDI Tactics To Implement Clinton's Healthcare Reform Strategy.* EDI World, 45-49.

EDI World (1994), 1994 EDI Software Directory.

EDS (1990, April?), Presentation To Government EDI User's Group, Ottawa.

Ehinger, Robert W. (1992, August), *U.S. Customs Service and EDI.* EDI World, 27-28.

Emmelhainz and Emmelhainz, (1992), *EDI and TQM: Mutual Means To Superior Performance.* EDI Forum No.1, 22-26.

Engel, Wilson F. (1994, December), *Re-engineering Healthcare For The New World Order--Part 1.* EDI World, 33-37.

Ericsson, Eric (1992), *Procuring Office Supplies On The Fly: EDI At Digital Equipment Corporation.* EDI Forum No. 1, 36-41.

Farmer, James R. (1993, March), *Re-engineering The Factory: Achieving Productivity Success.* Performance Advantage, 38-42.

Ferreira, John A. (1993, November), *Re-engineer The Materials & Procurement Function.* Performance Advantage, 30-32.

Fincher, Judith A. (1993, September). *The Role of EDI In The Clinton Administration's National Information Infrastructure.* EDI World, 32-34.

Foerster, Rachel (1991), *A History of ASAP at Baxter Healthcare: The Journey From Proprietary To X12 Standards* EDI Forum Vol. 4 No. 1, 96-100.

_____ (1994, May), *Faxination Vaccination.* EDI World, 8.

Foster, David F. (1993, April), *EDI, E-Mail, and Workflow Automation.* EDI World, 34-37.

_____ (1994, June), *Electronic Commerce: A Business Perspective.* EDI World, 28-31.

Fox, Mary Lou (1992, December), *The Role of Transportation Planning In Supply Chain Integration.* Performance Advantage, 44-45.

_____ (1993, April), *Re-engineer Your Supply Chain Planning.* Performance Advantage, 53-54.

_____ (1993, July), *A Vision Of Quick Response.* Performance Advantage, 57-58.

Garity, Robert P. and Pravetz, Christopher (1993, February), *Change Management.* Performance Advantage, 40-41.

Garwood, D. (1988), Bills of Material: Structured for Excellence. Marietta, GA: Dogwood Publishing.

Gerson, Gordon M. Sr. (1989), Data Mapping: The Integration of EDI Into the Corporate Information Structure. Alexandria, VA: The Electronic Data Interchange Association.

Gilmore, Dan (1995, February), *Increasing Retailer's Efficiency With Bar Coding and EDI.* EDI World, 18-21.

Gillen, Robert J. (1992, December), *Logistics and EDI: Lessons Learned.* EDI World. 18-20

Goddard, Walter E. (1986), Just-In-Time: Surviving by Breaking Tradition. Vermont: Oliver Wight Publications.

Golden, Charles E. (1990*), Making America and GM More Competitive Through EDI and EFT.* EDI Forum Vol. 3, 24-30.

Goll, Edmund O.   (1992, December),   *Let's Debunk The Myths and Misconceptions About Re-engineering.* Performance Advantage, 29-32.

Graham, McDowell (1992, July),   *EDI and E-Mail--A Look To The Future.* EDI World, 24-27.

____   (1992),   Global Reach: *The Emergence Of E-mail Standards In International Communications (and What It Means To EDI).* EDI Forum No. 1, 57-61.

Green, Richard H.   (1992, October),   *JIT II: An Inside Story.* Performance Advantage, 20-23.

Hammel, Todd R. and Kopczak, Laura (1993, 2nd Quarter),   *Tightening The Supply Chain.* Production and Inventory Management Journal, 63-69.

Hammer, Michael and Champy, James   (1993),   Reengineering The Corporation: A Manifesto for Business Revolution.   New York: Harper Business.

Harrold, Robert E.   (1994, February),   *X.435 Bringing EDI and E-Mail Together.* EDI World, 30-34.

Hayes, Kevin M. (1994, December), *Real-time EDI Gets McJunkin Ready For the Future.* EDI World, 18-22.

Heflin, Ray (1992, April), *Changes To Business Practices Created By Quick Response, EDI and Bar Coding.* EDI World, 16-17.

____ (1993, March), *EDI: A Major Business Function?.* EDI World, 9.

Hemley, Eugene A.   (1991, May),   *Negotiable Electronic Bills Of Lading.* Global Trade. Philadelphia: North American Publishing.

Himes, Paul R.   (1994),   *Profits, Improved Productivity, and Reengineering.* EDI Forum Vol. 7 No. 2, 13-18.

Hurd, Robert C.   (1993, December),   *Beyond International EDI--The Next Step?.* EDI World, 4.

Hyduk, S .J.   (1992, November),   *System Integration Provides The Answer For Multiple Systems Operation.* Performance Advantage, 27-30.

Hymas, Kimberly (1991, August), *A Partnership In Success*. Performance Advantage, 30-34.

Jalinous, Mady (et al.) (1994, June), "IBEX International Business Exchange." presentation delivered to the US Chamber of Commerce.

Jenkins, Gordon and Lancanshire, Ray (1991), The Canadian Electronic Data Interchange Handbook. Toronto: EDI Council of Canada.

Johansson, Henry J. (et al.) (1993), Business Process Reengineering: Breakpoint Strategies For Market Dominance. Chichester: John Wiley & Sons.

Juran, J.M. (1992), Quality By Design: The New Steps for Planning Quality Into Goods and Services. Milwaukee: ASQC Quality Press.

Kane, Michael E. (1992, March), *Companies Must Integrate Global Measurements*. Performance Advantage, 32-34.

Keane, Patrick T. and King, James P. (1990), Failing in the Factory. Wilton, CT: Brown House Communications.

Khanna, Raman (1994), Distributed Computing: Implementation and Management Strategies. New York: PTR Prentice Hall.

Kilmer, Carleton (1992), *The Competitive Weapons of the '90s: Concurrent Engineering & Integrated Product Development*. Performance Advantage, 55-56.

Kropp, Jerome D. (1993, September), *Business Process Redesign In MRP II Implementations: A Critical But Neglected Requirement*. Performance Advantage, 37-39.

Lavery, Hank (1993, April), *The Third Party Logistics Services*. EDI World, 16-17.

_____ (1993, December), *The Top Ten Issues In EDI For Transportation*. EDI World, 9.

_____ (1994, November), *Just-In-Time Manufacturing and Transportation*. EDI World, 8.

Loucks, Vernon (1995, February), *Electronic Commerce Helps Bridge The Communication Gap At Baxter International*. EDI World, 22-27.

Low, James T. (1992, December), *Strategic Linkages Between Purchasing and Production Management*. Performance Advantage, 33-34.

Martin, Andre J. (1990), DRP: Distribution Resource Planning. Vermont: Oliver Wight Publications.

Maskell, Brian H. (1993, September), *MRP II Has Not Created World Class Manufacturing: Where Do We Go From Here?*. Performance Advantage, 33-36.

Matthews, John (1993, May), *Healthcare, EDI, The Clinton Administration and WEDI*. EDI World, 9-15.

_____ (1994, February), *The WEDI Report: Can EDI Reduce Healthcare Fraud?*. EDI World, 16-17.

McFarland, Terry (1993, December), *Truly Global Trade Requires "Open" EDI*. EDI World, 23-25.

McNair, C.J. and Liebfried, K. (1992), Benchmarking: A Tool for Continuous Improvement. Vermont: Oliver Wight Publications

Meyer, Christopher (1993), Fast Cycle Time: How to Align Purpose, Strategy, and Structure for Speed. New York: The Free Press.

Mickelwright, Michael J. (1993, June), *Competitive Benchmarking: Large Gains For Small Companies*. Quality Progress, 67-68.

Middlebrook, William (1994, May), *Re-engineering The Procurement Process*. EDI World, 46-48.

Millar, Victor E. (1985 July-August). *How Information Gives You Competitive Advantage*. Harvard Business Review.

Miller, Shawn (1993, August), MRP II At Eastman Kodak: *It's Not Just A Job--It's An Adventure*. Performance Advantage, 55-57.

Mitchell, George F. (1994, June) *EDI & Community Health Information Networks*. EDI World, 38-41.

Northey, Patrick and Southway, Nigel (1993), Cycle Time Management: The Fast Track to Time-Based Quality Improvement. Milwaukee: ASQC Quality Press.

Ohmae, Kenichi (1991), The Borderless World: Power and Strategy in the Interlinked Economy. New York: HarperPerennial.

Olson, Paul (1993), *EDI and Electronic Commerce: Evolution, Not Revolution.* EDI Forum Vol.6 No.2, 69-72.

_____ (1992), *Megashifts and Future Trends In EDI.* EDI Forum No. 1, 12-16.

_____ (1994), Growth and Partnership: *The Future of Financial EDI.* EDI Forum Vol. 7 No. 2, 37-41.

O'Mahony, Donald and Welden, Neil (1993), X.500 Directory Services For Electronic Data Interchange (EDI). Dublin: Computer Science Department, Trinity College.

O'Roark, Frank (1993), *In The Trenches: Blue Cross and Blue Shield Labors On Behalf of Healthcare EDI.* EDI Forum Vol. 6 No. 2, 28-32.

Paine-Lilly, Elaine and Wallace, Sharon (1994), *Financial EDI at IBM Canada: A Reengineering Case Study.* EDI Forum Vol. 7 No. 2, 32-36.

Paulson, Jeff (1993, 2nd Quarter), *EDI--An Implementation Review.* Production and Inventory Management Journal, 77-81.

Payne, Terry 91993, 2nd Quarter), *ACME Manufacturing: A Case Study In JIT Implementation.* Production and Inventory Management Journal, 82-86.

Porter, Michael E. (1985, May-June), *From Competitive Advantage To Corporate Strategy.* Harvard Business Review.

Picrauz, Tim (1993, July), *Image Processing As A Quality Tool.* Quality Progress, 113-115.

Pitts, James M. (1992, September), *EDI Reduces Manufacturing Costs.* EDI World, 6.

_____ (1993, April). *EDI and Integration.* EDI World, 9.

Plossl, George W. (1983), Production and Inventory Control: Principles and Techniques. New Jersey: Prentice Hall.

Profant, Marie (1994, June), *Just-In-Time Shampoo.* EDI World, 20-24.

Ragsdale, Cliff and Gilbert, James (1990), *Is EDI Needed For JIT? A Survey of U.S. Firms Using JIT*. EDI Forum, 13-16.

Rhodes, Philip (1992, August), *Activity-Based Costing: What Will It Do For You?*. Performance Advantage, 29-31.

Ritter, Jeffrey B. (1992, April), *Electronic Purchase Orders and The Law*. EDI World, 20-23.

Roll, Ralph (1993, December), *Efficient Consumer Response (ECR) Implementation*. EDI World, 6.

Ross, David F. (1993, March), *DRP II: The Answer To Connecting The Distribution Enterprise*. Performance Advantage, 59-62.

Roth, David (1993, November), *Do You Understand Supply Chain Management?*. Performance Advantage, 45-46.

Salmon, Kurt and Associates (1993), Efficient Consumer Response: Enhancing Consumer Value in the Grocery Industry. Washington, DC: Food Marketing Institute.

Samni (et al.) 1993), International Marketing: Planning and Practice. New York: Macmillan.

Sample, Thomas A. (1994, June), *Haggar Apparel Works The Wrinkles Out of EDI*. EDI World, 22-23.

Sanderson, Gerald A. (1991, August), *Scheduling Logistics*. Performance Advantage, 48-50.

Sauer, Paul (et al.) (1991), *The Impact of EDI On Marketing Channels*. EDI Forum No.2, 14-23.

Schaap, Alexander (1991), *Paid On Production In The Automotive Industry*. Oak Park, IL: EDI Forum Vol. 4 No. 1, 72-76.

Schaic, Robert L. (1993, December), *Healthcare Reform--Costs and Benefits*. EDI World, 50-52.

Schonberger, Richard J. (1986), World Class Manufacturing: The Lessons of Simplicity Applied. New York: The Free Press.

____ (1987), <u>World Class Manufacturing Casebook: Implementing JIT and TQC</u>. New York: The Free Press.

Schramm, Nancy (1991), *Real-time EDI: The Next Step*. <u>EDI Forum</u> No.2, 104-107.

Sharma, Ken (1993, August), *What's Wrong With JIT/Kanban?*. <u>Performance Advantage</u>, 35-38.

Shaw, Jack (1993), <u>EDI & Electronic Reengineering</u>. Marietta, GA: EDI Strategies.

____ (1991), *Integrating E-mail and Expert Systems: New Applications of EDI*. <u>EDI Forum</u> No. 2, 25-30.

Shaw, Jack and Cadaret, Roger (1993, November 8). "Re-Engineering: realizing the true benefits of EDI." Presentation delivered to the "Broadening Horizons" EDI conference, Orlando, FL.

Souchik, David (1993, September), *Closed Loop Value Chain*. <u>Performance Advantage</u>, 54-56.

Snee, Ronald D. (1993, February), *Creating Robust Work Processes*. <u>Quality Progress</u>, 37-41.

Stelzer, John (1992, August), *EDI Roulette: Do You Know The Odds?*. <u>EDI World</u>, 23-26.

Stevens, Samuel (1993, March), *EDI In a Custom-Order Environment*. <u>EDI World</u>, 30-37.

Stites, Katy (1994, June), *Evaluated Receipts Settlement*. <u>EDI World</u>, 20-21.

Stockton, Thomas H. (1994, May), *Real Re-engineering Begins With Re-vitalization*, <u>EDI World</u>, 28-32.

Stronstadt, Bruce (1992, February), *Lessons Learned: A JIT Implementation Case Study*. <u>Performance Advantage</u>, 29-32.

Sullivan-Trainor, Michael (1994), <u>Detour: the Truth About the Information Superhighway</u>. San Mateo, CA: IDG Books Worldwide.

Suri, Ashu (1992, July), *Master Production Schedule: The Driver of Planning and Control Systems*. <u>Performance Advantage</u>, 34-36.

Suri, Rajan (1995, June) *Slaying the Beast.* Performance Advantage, 28-32.

Symbol Technologies (1990), Quick Response: A Better Way. New York: Symbol Technologies (monograph 3).

Tapscott, Don and Caston, Art (1993), Paradigm Shift: The New Promise of Information Technology. New York: McGraw Hill.

Tatham, Michael (1987), CPI Boot Camp: Continuous Process Improvement. Toronto: Tatham Process Engineering.

Taylor, David L. (1991), *From EDI To Inter-enterprise Systems: A Scenario For The 1990's.* EDI Forum, "Principles of EDI" special edition, 19-23.

Toscano, Diane (1992, October), *Manage the Supply Chain.* Performance Advantage, 34-36.

Toscano, Samuel Jr. (1994, December), *Transforming the Wholesale Pharmaceutical Industry.* EDI World, 30-32.

Ventucci, Robert (1992, 4th Quarter), *Benchmarking: A Reality Check For Strategy and Performance Objectives.* Production and Inventory Management Journal, 32-36.

Walton, Steve (1994), *Process Reengineering: Is EDI Part Of The Solution Or Part Of The Problem?.* EDI Forum Vol. 7 No. 2, 9-12.

Walker, Rand (1993, March, EDI and X.400: *Leveraging the Technology.* EDI World, 38-40.

WEDI (Workgroup For Electronic Data Interchange) (1992, July), Report.

_____ (1993, October), Report.

Weiser, Mark (1995), *The Computer In the 21st Century*, Scientific American Vol 6 No. 1, 78

Whitcomb, Gail B. (1994, December), *Department of Defense: A Breakthrough Approach To EDI.* EDI World, 21-22.

White, Richard E. (1993, Quarter 2), *An Empirical Assessment of JIT in U.S. Manufacturers.* Production and Inventory Management Journal, 38-42.

Wight, Oliver W. (1984), <u>Manufacturing Resource Planning: MRP II Unlocking America's Productivity Potential</u>. Vermont: Oliver Wight Publications.

Wood, Nigel: VP Technology, EDI Council of Canada (1994, July), telephone interview

Wright, Benjamin (1989), <u>EDI and American Law: A Practical Guide</u>. Alexandria, VA: Electronic Data Interchange Association.

_____ (1991), <u>The Law of Electronic Commerce: EDI, Fax, and E-Mail: Technology, Proof, and Liability</u>. Boston: Little, Brown and Company

_____ (1994), *Do We Need Trading Partner Agreements?*. <u>EDI Forum</u> Vol. 7 No. 1, 46-50.

Yakhou, Mehenna and Rahali, B. (1992, December), *Integration of Business Functions: The Roles of Cross-Functional Information Systems.* <u>Performance Advantage</u>, 35-37.

Yates, John G. (1994, November), *Paperless Purchasing Improves Bottom-line*. <u>EDI World</u>, 27-28.